LUXURY HOME PLANS

Library of Congress No.: 95-81706/ISBN: 0-938708-65-1
Cover Photography By Donna & Rob Kolb of Exposures Unlimited.
The Cover Photo is the Rear of the Home.
Cover & Interior Layouts by Paula Mennone.

TABLE OF CONTENTS

— *Publisher James D. McNair III* —

Submit all Canadian plan orders to:
The Garlinghouse Company
20 Cedar Street North
Kitchener, Ontario N2H 2WB

Canadians Order only: 1-800-561-4169
Fax#: 1-519-743-1282
Customer Service#: 1-519-743-4169

DESIGN 24650

Interesting Accents

This beautiful home has a stucco and stone facade, accented by detailing around the multi-panned windows, and a stone arched covered entrance. The two-story foyer is the visitor's introduction to the spacious open layout of this home's first floor. The formal living room is directly to the right of the foyer. A bumped-out window provides a focal point and a view of the front yard. Entertaining is made easy by the open lay out between the formal dining room and the formal living room. The sleeping quarters are located on the second floor. A luxurious master suite awaits the owner with a pampering, private bath and two walk-in closets. Three additional bedrooms share a full, double vanity, hall bath. No materials list available for this plan.

Second Floor

An EXCLUSIVE DESIGN
By Plan One Homes, Inc.

PLAN INFO:

First Flr.	1,435 sq. ft.
Second Flr.	1,462 sq. ft.
Bonus Rm.	347 sq. ft.
Sq. Footage	2,897 sq. ft.
Foundation	B, S, C
Bedrooms	Basement
Baths	(2)Full, (1)Half

REFER TO PRICE CODE E

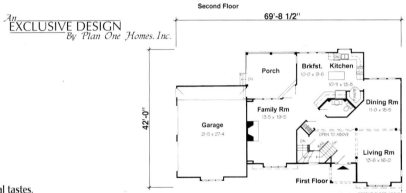

First Floor

The photographed home was modified to suit individual tastes.

PHOTOGRAPHY BY JOHN EHRENCLOU

Exquisite Interior Highlights Brick Masterpiece

WIDTH 79'-0"
DEPTH 55'-0"

SUNROOM
12'-0" x13'-0"

EATING AREA
17'-0" x 8'-0"

KITCHEN
15'-0" x 14'-0"

FAMILY ROOM
20'-0" x 15'-0"

MASTER BEDROOM
15'-0" x 14'-0"

4 CAR GARAGE
31'-0" x 38'-0"

SITTING AREA
10'-0" x 8'-0"

DINING ROOM
15'-0" x 13'-0"

STUDY
12'-0" x 12'-0"

FOYER

MAIN FLOOR

An
EXCLUSIVE DESIGN
By Ahmann Design Inc.

No. 93118

OPEN TO
FAMILY RM.

BEDROOM #2
17'-0" x 11'-0"

BEDROOM #4
13'-0" x 13'-0"

OPEN TO
FOYER

BEDROOM #3
17'-0" x12'-0"

SECOND FLOOR

The photographed home was modified to suit individual tastes.

▲ This luxurious Master Bath is sure to please with its step-up tub and attractive columns.

◄ The delightful Eating Area, abundantly windowed and conveniently located next to the Kitchen, is a wonderful spot for informal meals or curling up with your favorite book. The formal Dining Room can be saved for special gatherings.

Photography supplied by Ahmann Design

DESIGN 93118

▲ Enjoy the cozy Family Room with its two-story window wall and wood-burning fireplace guaranteed to warm up the coldest nights. One can gaze down upon this room from the second floor balcony which adjoins the three secondary bedrooms.

This plan is not to be built within a 25 mile radius of Cedar Rapids, IA.

T his-two story brick home features the old-fashioned look of turn-of-the-century homes mixed with a Contemporary floor plan. The bright two-story foyer is framed by an elegant dining room to the left and a study, for after hours work, on the right. The generous, island kitchen opens into a breakfast area surrounded by glass and perfect for reading the morning paper. The master suite features a sitting area that makes for the perfect get-away. Upstairs you'll enjoy a dramatic view of both the foyer and the family room below as you cross the bridge to any of the three additional bedrooms, all with walk-in closets and one with a private bath. No materials list is available for this plan.

PLAN INFO:

First Flr.	2,385 sq. ft.
Second Flr.	1,012 sq. ft.
Basement	2,385 sq. ft.
Garage	846 sq. ft.
Sq. Footage	3,397 sq. ft.
Foundation	Basement
Bedrooms	Four
Baths	(3)Full, (1)Half

REFER TO PRICE CODE F

Contemporary Touches Throughout
This European Classic

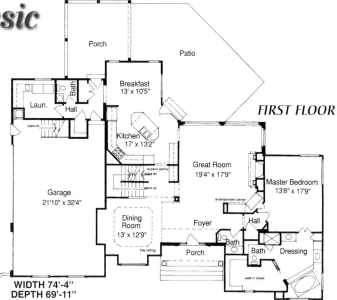

FIRST FLOOR

Porch

Patio

Breakfast
13' x 10'5"

Bath

Laun.

Hall

Kitchen
17' x 13'2"

butler's pantry

stairs dn

stairs dn

stairs up

Great Room
19'4" x 17'9"

Master Bedroom
13'8" x 17'9"

entertainment center

Garage
21'10" x 32'4"

Dining Room
13' x 12'9"

tray ceiling

Foyer

Hall

Bath

Porch

Bath

Dressing

walk-in closet

WIDTH 74'-4"
DEPTH 69'-11"

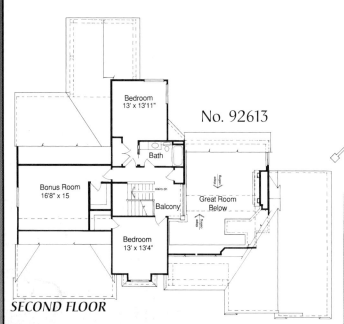

No. 92613

Bedroom
13' x 13'11"

Bath

Bonus Room
16'8" x 15

Balcony

stairs dn

slope

Great Room Below

steps

Bedroom
13' x 13'4"

SECOND FLOOR

Photography by Donna & Rob Kolb of Exposures Unlimited

▲ Step up into the tub of this deluxe Master Suite and watch the sun set after a long day at the office.

◀ Cut out spaces and the unique architectural structural of this Great Room will spark your creative decorating skills and make for a room you'll love for many years.

DESIGN 92613

*M*ultiple gables, a box window and easy maintenance combine to create a dramatic appearance to this two-story European classic home. Excitement abounds in the Great room beginning with a wall of windows across the rear, a sloped ceiling, and an entertainment center nestled in the corner set to one side of the columned fireplace. The kitchen offers an island with a sink that looks directly through French doors onto the patio and into the oversized breakfast room. The dining room ceiling has a raised center section with molding and a furniture alcove is added for extra roominess around the table. The luxury and convenience of the first floor master bedroom suite is highlighted by his-n-her vanities, a shower and whirlpool tub. The second floor provides a private retreat for a guest suite or for a family with teenagers The rear of this home is stepped for privacy and uses windows for an infusion of light. No materials list is available for this plan.

PLAN INFO:

First Flr.	2,192 sq. ft.
Second Flr.	654 sq. ft.
Bonus Room	325 sq. ft.
Sq. Footage	2,846 sq. ft.
Foundation	Basement
Bedrooms	Three
Baths	(2)Full, (2)Half

REFER TO PRICE CODE E

▲ This great Kitchen, with an abundance of cabinets, easily accommodates two or more cooks when meal preparation is to be shared. Serving takes place in either the Formal Dining Room or the Breakfast area, both conveniently located.

The photographed home was modified to suit individual tastes.

Distinctive Two-Story Colonial Design

FIRST FLOOR

WIDTH 61'-0''
DEPTH 37'-6''

Deck

Sunken Family Room
18 x 15-4

Breakfast
9-10 x 13-3

Kitchen
8-10 x 11-11

Two-car Garage
22-4 x 22

stairs up

stairs dn

Laun.

Bath

Hall

Living Room
14-8 x 12-7

Foyer

Dining Room
14-8 x 12-7

Porch

No. 92623

SECOND FLOOR

Bath

Bedroom
12-5 x 10-11

Bedroom
10-10 x 10-11

walk-in closet

walk-in closet

shelves

stairs dn

Bath

sky-light

laun. chute

Balcony

Master Bedroom
14-8 x 16-2

Foyer Below

Bedroom
12-3 x 12-7

plant shelf

▲ Formal entertaining is easy in this well-lit Dining Room with a classic decorative ceiling.

◄ Not in the mood for a formal sitdown dinner? Dine in the sunny Breakfast area adjacent to the center island Kitchen and sunken, fireplaced Family Room.

Photography by Donna & Rob Kolb of Exposures Unlimited

DESIGN 92623

The classic good looks of this Colonial two-story home are accentuated by an arch topped window over the entrance and the use of brick trim and dental molding across the front. The tray ceiling in the formal living room and dining room and the corner columns pull these two rooms into a unit to create a large and charming area for entertaining. For family convenience the stairs are located with access directly into the kitchen. Windows located on either side of the corner sink flood the counter with natural light. The sunken family room with fireplace brings a warm feeling to this area of the house. A luxurious bedroom suite with double walk-in closets and a sloped ceiling is the highlight of this four bedroom second floor. A balcony overlooking the foyer, a plant shelf, arched window, skylight, and a laundry chute are extra features that help to make this a home unsurpassed in style and value. No materials list is available for this plan.

▲ Enjoy the good looks of this Master Bedroom complete with a decorative ceiling and just steps away from two walk-in closets and a luxurious bathroom guaranteed to pamper your every need.

PLAN INFO:

First Flr.	1,365 sq. ft.
Second Flr.	1,288 sq. ft.
Sq. Footage	2,653 sq. ft.
Foundation	Basement
Bedrooms	Four
Baths	(2)Full, (1)Half

REFER TO PRICE CODE E

The photographed home was modified to suit individual tastes.

Intricate Angles & Abundant Windows Help Set This Design Apart

SECOND FLOOR

No. 10666

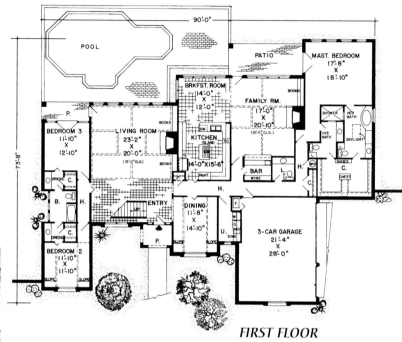

FIRST FLOOR

▲ His-n-her separate bath areas are guaranteed to ease the morning rush while two-and-a-half other baths take care of the rest of the household.

Look down upon the two-story Living Room, containing a fireplace and a window wall, from the second floor bridge that leads to a small library alcove with two skylights. ▶

PHOTOGRAPHY BY JOHN EHRENCLOU

DESIGN 10666

Gracious living is the rule in this brick masterpiece designed with an eye toward elegant entertaining. Window walls and French doors link the in-ground pool and surrounding brick patio with interior living spaces. The wetbar with wine storage provides a convenient space for a large buffet in the family room. Built-in bookcases in the living room, family room, and skylit second-floor library can house even the largest collection. Separated from living areas by halls or a bridge, every bedroom is a quiet retreat, with its own dressing room and adjoining bath.

PLAN INFO:

First Flr.	3,625 sq. ft.
Second Flr.	937 sq. ft.
Garage	636 sq. ft.
Sq. Footage	4,562 sq. ft.
Foundation	Basement
Bedrooms	Five
Baths	(4)Full, (1)Half

REFER TO PRICE CODE F

▲ Upon entering the foyer of this lovely brick home, with enticing angles and intricate detailing, you will notice all the elegant touches and amenities throughout the interior layout that make for luxurious living.

The photographed home was modified to suit individual tastes.

The Perfect Two-Story Home

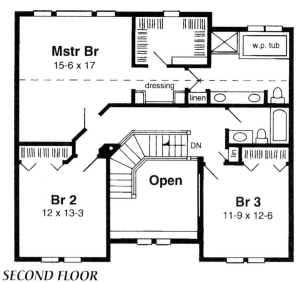

Mstr Br
15-6 x 17

w.p. tub

dressing

linen

DN

Open

Br 2
12 x 13-3

Br 3
11-9 x 12-6

lin

SECOND FLOOR

An
EXCLUSIVE DESIGN
By Britt J. Willis

No. 24567

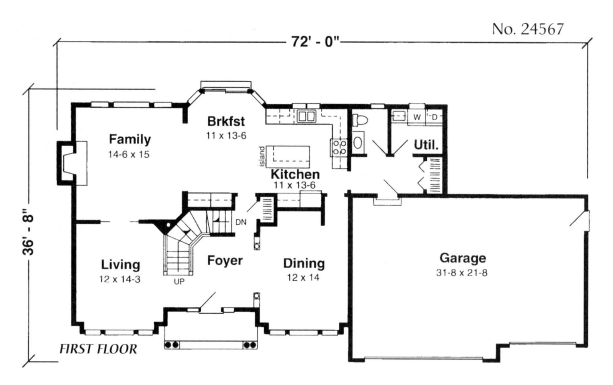

—— 72' - 0" ——

Family
14-6 x 15

Brkfst
11 x 13-6

island

Kitchen
11 x 13-6

W D

Util.

36' - 8"

Living
12 x 14-3

UP

Foyer

DN

Dining
12 x 14

Garage
31-8 x 21-8

FIRST FLOOR

Photography by Susan Gilmore

- 1 0 -

DESIGN 24?

An attractive columned shelter shelters the entrance of this stylish home. The formal, two-story, central foyer gives access to the living room, dining room and the informal living area at the rear of the home. The island kitchen will be sure to please the gourmet of the family. The highly windowed breakfast area adjoins the kitchen in an open layout. This gives the living space a more spacious appearance. A cozy fireplace enhances the family room, which has direct access to both the breakfast area and the living room. Pocket doors give privacy to the living room. The sleeping quarters are located on the second floor. The spacious master suite includes a walk-in closet and a compartmented, double vanity bath. No materials list available.

PLAN INFO:

First Flr.	1,332 sq. ft.
Second Flr.	1,100 sq. ft.
Sq. Footage	2,432 sq. ft.
Foundation	Basement, Slab, Crawl space
Bedrooms	Three
Baths	(2)Full, (1)Half

REFER TO PRICE CODE F

▲ Mealtime is a pleasure in this cozy Breakfast area. Conveniently located next to the Kitchen, serving is easy & informal for fun family gatherings. When guests are expected, use the formal Dining room.

The photographed home was modified to suit individual tastes.

Georgian Drama At Its Best In This Sprawling Beauty

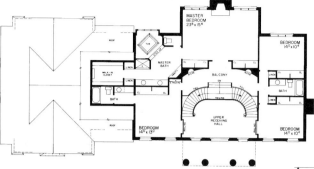

SECOND FLOOR

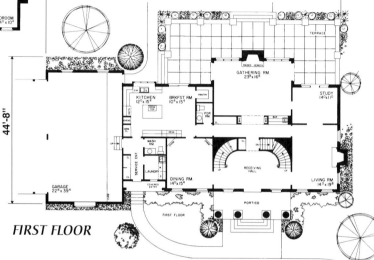

No. 90299

90'-4"

44'-8"

FIRST FLOOR

The photographed home was modified to suit individual tastes.

▲ Windows grace both sides of the fireplace in the Formal Living Room, and make for an eye-catching layout.

Turn your Basement into a deluxe ▶ Gameroom/Entertainment area like these Garlinghouse homeowners did. This home has everything and much, much more!

Photography by John Ehrenclou

DESIGN 90299

*I*magine living in the graceful elegance of this sprawling, Georgian beauty. From the impressive columned facade to the two-story drama of the receiving hall, this home has style! Flanked by the formal living and dining rooms, the receiving hall leads straight back to a sun-filled, fireplaced gathering room surrounded by an outdoor terrace. The open kitchen and breakfast room combination features a cooktop island and extra-large storage pantry. Walk up the curving staircases of the receiving hall to four spacious bedrooms, each adjoining a bath. The master suite enjoys the toasty warmth of a fireplace, a garden tub, a built-in vanity and double sinks.

PLAN INFO:

First Flr.	2,529 sq. ft.
Second Flr.	1,872 sq. ft.
Sq. Footage	4,401 sq. ft.
Foundation	Basement
Bedrooms	Four
Baths	(3)Full, (2)Half

REFER TO PRICE CODE F

▲ A two-story Receiving Hall with a double curved staircase will definitely make a lasting first impression. To the right is the Formal Living Room with a fireplace, and to the left is the formal Dining Room that is just steps away from the Kitchen.

DESIGN 10492

Appealing Rear & Front Elevations

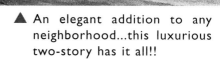

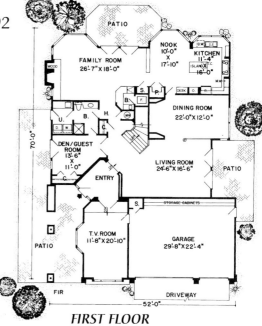

With a special television room plus a family room and an upstairs sitting room, there's plenty of opportunity for everyone in the family to enjoy personal activities and pursuits. The well-designed kitchen adjoins the formal dining room and also has its own dining nook with lots of windows for sunny family breakfasts and lunches. Both the living room and family room open onto patios for indoor/outdoor entertaining. The second floor sitting room, complete with a fireplace and warm hearth, adjoins the spacious master suite with its six-piece bath complete with Roman tub and oversized, walk-in closet. Two smaller bedrooms flank a walk-through bath to complete the second floor of this roomy, family home.

▲ An elegant addition to any neighborhood...this luxurious two-story has it all!!

The photographed home was modified to suit individual tastes.

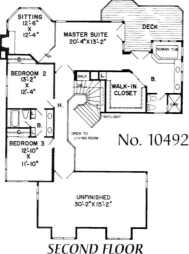

No. 10492

SECOND FLOOR

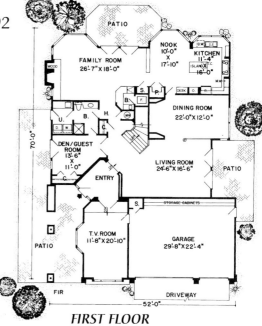

FIRST FLOOR

PLAN INFO:

First Flr.	2,409 sq. ft.
Second Flr.	2,032 sq. ft.
Garage	690 sq. ft.
Sq. Footage	4,441 sq. ft.
Foundation	Slab
Bedrooms	Three (Opt. Fourth)
Baths	Three

REFER TO PRICE CODE F

Energy Efficient Tudor Design

SECOND FLOOR

BEDROOM 3
14'-0" x 11'-4"

SUNROOM BELOW

BATH C.

OPEN TO LIVING ROOM BELOW

BEDROOM 4
14'-0" x 15'-6"

DRESSING AREA

C.
LIN.
B.
C.

DRESSING AREA

RAILING

BALCONY

LIBRARY BELOW

RAILING

OPEN TO FOYER BELOW

BEDROOM 2
14'-0" x 11'-4"

SHELF

DN

LEDGE

▲ A step-up whirlpool tub is sure to please, but that's only the beginning of the amenities that you'll find in this Tudor-style gem.

*T*ake advantage of Southern exposure and save on energy costs in this beautiful family Tudor. Heat is stored in the floor of the sun room, adjoining the living and breakfast rooms. When the sun goes down, close the French doors and light a fire in the massive fireplace. State-of-the-art energy saving is not the only modern convenience in this house. You'll love the balcony overlooking the soaring two-story foyer and living room. In addition to providing great views, the balcony links the upstairs bedrooms. You're sure to enjoy the island kitchen, centrally located between formal and informal dining rooms. And, you'll never want to leave the luxurious master suite, with its double vanities and step-up whirlpool.

No. 20071

67'-0"

WOOD DECK

SUN ROOM
SLOPED CLG.
SKYLIGHTS
15'-0" x 11'-6"

BREAKFAST ROOM
13'-10" x 13'-6"

STOR CLO

PR.

HALL

LAUNDRY
10'-0" x 7'-0"

DESK

WHIRL POOL
STEP
BATH
DRESSING AREA
C.
LIN.

LIVING ROOM
15'-0" x 20'-0"
2-STORY CEILING

KITCHEN
13'-10" x 15'-8"
ISLAND

DW
W
STEP
OVEN
PAN

3-CAR GARAGE
21'-8" x 31'-6"

DRIVEWAY

54'-6"

MASTER BEDROOM
14'-0" x 15'-8"

BALCONY ABOVE

DINING ROOM
13'-10" x 13'-4"

BOOKCASE

LIBRARY
12'-8" x 15'-4"

FOYER
2-STORY CEILING

C.
UP

SLOPE | LEVEL CEILING | SLOPE

PORCH

STEP

FIRST FLOOR

The photographed home was modified to suit individual tastes.

REFER TO PRICE CODE E

PLAN INFO:

First Flr.	2,186 sq. ft.
Second Flr.	983 sq. ft.
Basement	2,186 sq. ft.
Garage	704 sq. ft.
Sq. Footage	3,169 sq. ft.
Foundation	Basement
Bedrooms	Four
Baths	(3)Full, (1)Half

An EXCLUSIVE DESIGN
By Karl Kreeger

Splendid Stucco Design

A home designed for today's lifestyle. Formal areas are located to either side of the foyer. A decor ceiling accents the elegant dining room. Bay windows allow for natural illumination and further enhance the living and dining rooms. An open layout between the kitchen and the breakfast area provides an open, airy atmosphere to this spacious family living area. Amenities abound in the kitchen. A center work island/snack bar, a walk-in pantry and ample storage and workspace have been included. The family room includes a cozy fireplace and flows easily from the breakfast room. The sleeping quarters are located on the second floor. The grand master suite is crowned by a vaulted ceiling and includes a compartmented, luxurious bath. Two additional bedrooms and an office share the full, double vanity bath in the hall. No materials list available.

PLAN INFO:

First Flr.	1,377 sq. ft.
Second Flr.	1,264 sq. ft.
Basement	1,316 sq. ft.
Sq. Footage	2,641 sq. ft.
Foundation	Basement
Bedrooms	Three
Baths	(2)Full, (1)Half

REFER TO PRICE CODE E

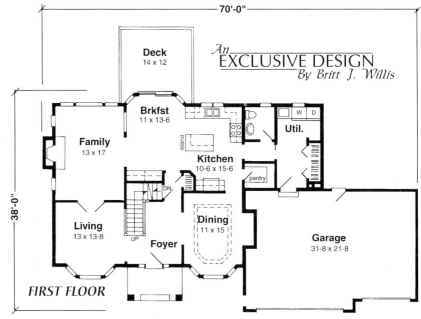

SECOND FLOOR

No. 24566

An EXCLUSIVE DESIGN
By Britt J. Willis

FIRST FLOOR

The photographed home was modified to suit individual tastes.

Updated Saltbox Design

- Flower boxes and an old-fashioned front porch add friendly charm to this updated Saltbox

- Formal Dining Room and Parlor located on each side of the Foyer offer a classic arrangement with a Contemporary approach

- Spacious family living guaranteed by the Kitchen, Breakfast area, and Family Room joined together in an expansive open space accented by a window wall overlooking the rear deck

- Guest Suite features a full Bath with handicapped access

- Private Deck, a large walk-in closet and a luxurious Bath highlight the Master Bedroom Suite

No. 20404

66'-6"

Deck

Deck

Guest Suite or Quarters 18 x 14-8

Brkfst 14 x 12

Family Rm 16-6 x 16

slope

MBr 1 15-4 x 17

slope

entertainment center

Ldry

D
W

Kitchen 12-8 x 14

desk

UP   DN

ramp

ov   pan

open above

bar

ramp

Garage 23 x 25

Dining Rm 11-8 x 15

Foyer

Parlour 11-8 x 12

50'-6"

FIRST FLOOR

open to below

DN

lin.

Br 2 11-8 x 12-8

open to entry

Opt. Br 4 11-8 x 12

ledge

Br 3 11-8 x 15-6

SECOND FLOOR

PLAN INFO:

First Flr.	2,285 sq. ft.
Second Flr.	660 sq. ft.
Garage	565 sq. ft.
Sq. Footage	2,945 sq. ft.
Foundation	Basement
Bedrooms	Five
Baths	Three

REFER TO PRICE CODE E

This Beauty Has A Uniquely Shaped Kitchen

PLAN INFO:

First Flr.	2,800 sq. ft.
Second Flr.	1,113 sq. ft.
Basement	2,800 sq. ft.
Garage	598 sq. ft.
Sq. Footage	3,913 sq. ft.
Foundation	Basement
Bedrooms	Five
Baths	4(Full), 1(Half)

REFER TO PRICE CODE F

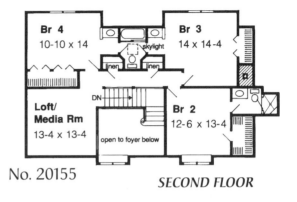

No. 20155

SECOND FLOOR

Br 4
10-10 x 14

Br 3
14 x 14-4

skylight

linen   linen

DN

Loft/
Media Rm
13-4 x 13-4

Br 2
12-6 x 13-4

open to foyer below

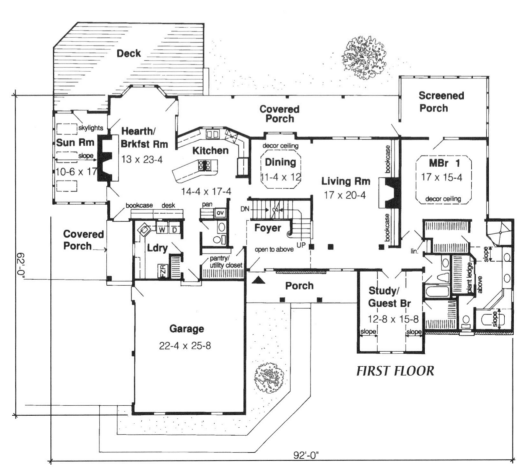

Deck

Covered Porch

Screened Porch

skylights

Hearth/
Brkfst Rm
13 x 23-4

Kitchen

decor ceiling

Dining
11-4 x 12

bookcase

Sun Rm

slope

10-6 x 17

MBr 1
17 x 15-4

decor ceiling

14-4 x 17-4

Living Rm
17 x 20-4

bookcase   desk

pan

ov

DN

Foyer

W D

Covered Porch

Ldry

pantry/
utility closet

open to above

UP

lin.

plant ledge above

slope

Porch

Study/
Guest Br
12-8 x 15-8

Garage
22-4 x 25-8

slope   slope

62'-0"

92'-0"

FIRST FLOOR

An
EXCLUSIVE DESIGN
By Karl Kreeger

- *Sprawling family home has an attractive fieldstone clapboard facade*

- *The open Foyer has an L-shaped Living and Dining Room arrangement wrapping around it*

- *An elegant Bath, walk-in closet and private access to a Screened Porch highlight the Master Suite*

- *Three additional bedrooms with private access to a full Bath are on the second floor*

- *Separating the informal Hearth/Breakfast Room and the skylit Sun Room is a fireplace with wood storage*

- *A gourmet Kitchen with a built-in pantry, planning desk and bookshelves and a fantastic cook top island and eating bar will thrill the cook in your family*

$\mathcal{P}$assive Solar $\mathcal{D}$esign $\mathcal{F}$or Six-Sided $\mathcal{H}$ome

PLAN INFO:

First Flr.	2,199 sq. ft.
Loft	336 sq. ft.
Basement	2,199 sq. ft.
Garage	611 sq. ft.
Sq. Footage	2,535 sq. ft.
Foundation	Basement
Bedrooms	Three
Baths	2(Full), 1(Half)

REFER TO PRICE CODE D

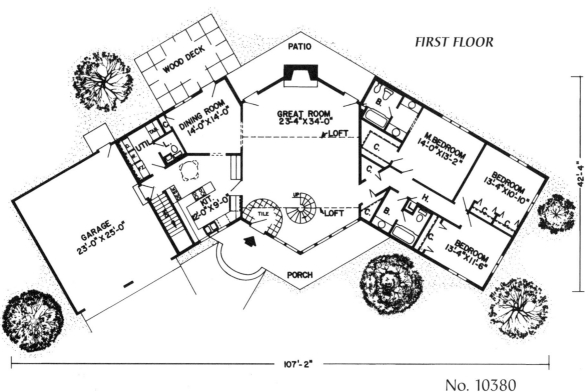

FIRST FLOOR

No. 10380

- Unique Great Room features, tiled entrance, two walls of glass, rugged beamed ceiling, central fireplace flanked by atrium doors to Patio

- A spiral staircase to spacious Loft presenting many options

- Private Master Bedroom suite offers a walk-in closet, twin vanities separate from Master Bath

- U-shaped Kitchen with peninsula cooktop, built-in desk and eating area adjacent to Dining Room, Utilities and Garage

- Two additional bedrooms with ample closet space share a full bath

- Dining Room opens onto Wood Deck for expanded living

*S*pacious *Stucco Has*
Everything You Need & More

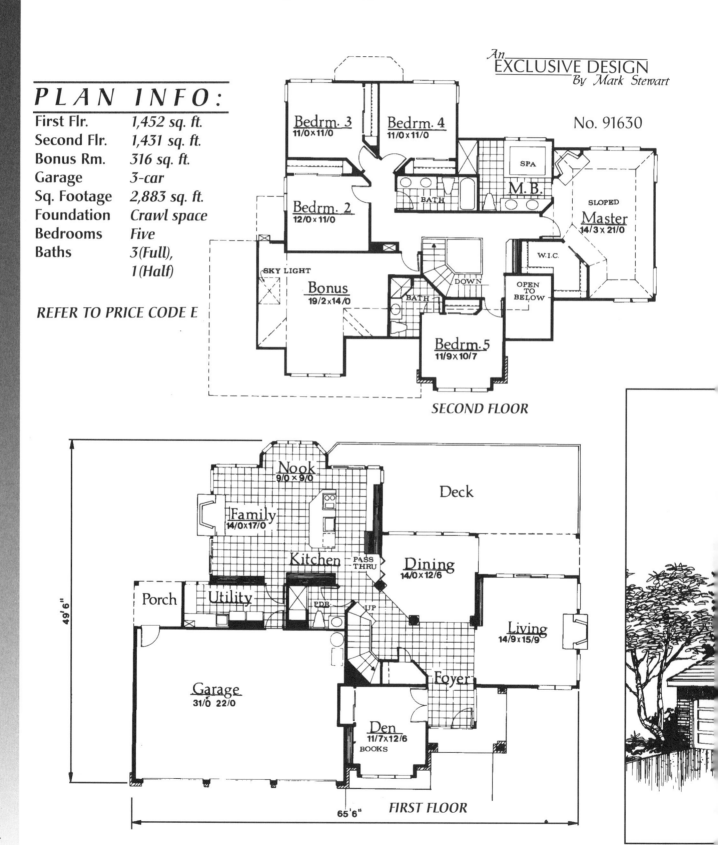

An
EXCLUSIVE DESIGN
By Mark Stewart

No. 91630

PLAN INFO:

First Flr.	1,452 sq. ft.
Second Flr.	1,431 sq. ft.
Bonus Rm.	316 sq. ft.
Garage	3-car
Sq. Footage	2,883 sq. ft.
Foundation	Crawl space
Bedrooms	Five
Baths	3(Full),
	1(Half)

REFER TO PRICE CODE E

SECOND FLOOR

Bedrm. 3
11/0 × 11/0

Bedrm. 4
11/0 × 11/0

SPA

Bedrm. 2
12/0 × 11/0

BATH

M. B.

SLOPED

Master
14/3 × 21/0

SKY LIGHT

Bonus
19/2 × 14/0

DOWN

W.I.C.

OPEN TO BELOW

BATH

Bedrm. 5
11/9 × 10/7

FIRST FLOOR

Nook
9/0 × 9/0

Deck

Family
14/0 × 17/0

Kitchen

PASS THRU

Dining
14/0 × 12/6

Porch

Utility

PDR.

UP

Living
14/9 × 15/9

Garage
31/0 22/0

Foyer

Den
11/7 × 12/6
BOOKS

49'6"

65'6"

- *Open Foyer gives sunny, airy atmosphere and leads straight through to rear of home*

- *Fireplaced Living Room off Foyer is studded with windows on three sides and has sliders to the deck*

- *Four other bedrooms are all good-sized with extra closet space and are effectively located near two equally beautiful baths*

- *Powder room with shower makes the book-lined Den ideal guest room*

- *Plush Master Bedroom shows sloped ceilings, large walk-in closet and private Bath*

- *Magnificent Family Room has efficiency of a fireplace, added light from desirable sliding glass doors and plenty of windows, and adds outdoor feeling to wide-open Nook and Kitchen*

Charming Front Porch Adds Victorian Detail

PLAN INFO:

First Flr.	1,450 sq. ft.
Second Flr.	1,341 sq. ft.
Basement	1,450 sq. ft.
Garage	629 sq. ft.
Sq. Footage	2,791 sq. ft.
Foundation	Basement
Bedrooms	Four
Baths	2(Full), 1(Half)

REFER TO PRICE CODE E

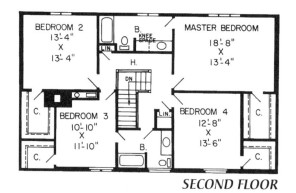

SECOND FLOOR

An
EXCLUSIVE DESIGN
By Karl Kreeger

No. 10593

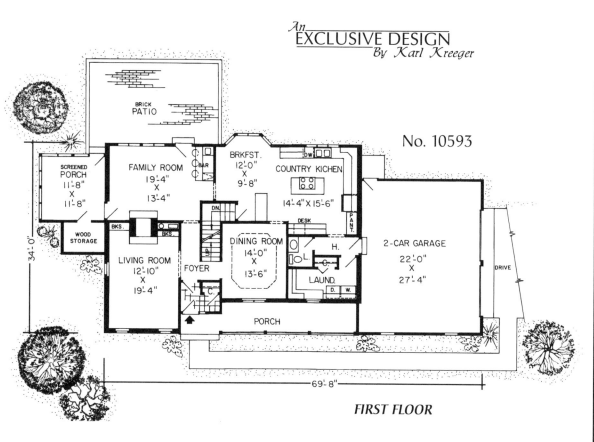

FIRST FLOOR

- Covered Porch shelters tiled entrance into Foyer with graceful landing staircase, flanked by formal Living and Dining Rooms

- Gracious Dining Room topped by recessed ceiling easily served by Country Kitchen

- Double fireplace provides warm accent for Living and Family Rooms

- Comfortable living and entertaining in Family Room with access to Patio, Screened Porch, snack bar and Kitchen

- Ultimate Country Kitchen with island cooktop, serving bar and glassed Breakfast alcove, convenient to Laundry and Garage

- Comfortable Master Bedroom suite features large walk-in closet, triple window and private bath with dressing table

- Three additional bedrooms with walk-in closets share full bath

Master Suite Crowns Outstanding Plan

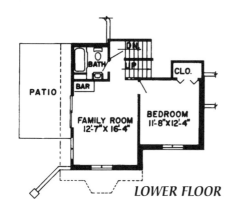

LOWER FLOOR

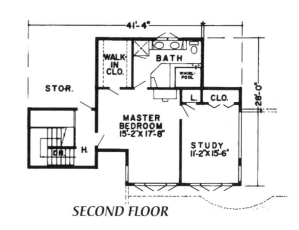

SECOND FLOOR

PLAN INFO:

First Flr.	1,742 sq. ft.
Second Flr.	809 sq. ft.
Lower Flr.	443 sq. ft.
Basement	1,270 sq. ft.
Garage	558 sq. ft.
Sq. Footage	2,994 sq. ft.
Foundation	Basement
Bedrooms	Four
Baths	3(Full), 1(Half)

REFER TO PRICE CODE E

No. 10334

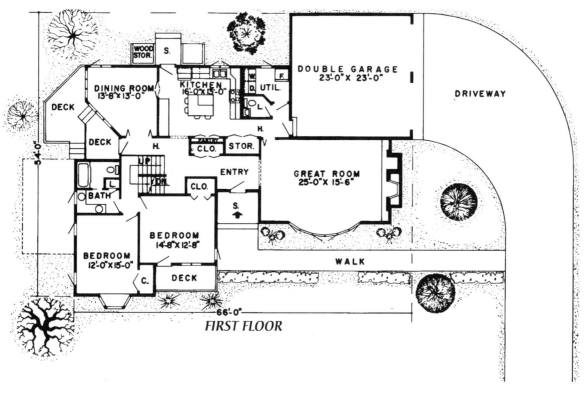

FIRST FLOOR

- *Luxurious Master Suite includes private Study and walk-in closet*
- *Master Bath sports double vanities, shower and whirlpool for total relaxation in privacy*
- *Two additional bedrooms situated away from living areas provide ample space for children*
- *Fourth Bedroom adjoins the Family Room on lower level*
- *Spacious Kitchen boasts pantry and snack island*

- *Family Room joins backyard patio via sliding glass doors*
- *25-foot oak floors and bow window in Great Room portray magnificent appreciation of finer things in life*
- *Slate floors add elegance to formal Dining area*
- *Plan features numerous decks for added enjoyment of outdoor living*
- *Extra storage space provided on second floor*

*L*ots Of Windows *A*nd Covered *P*atio

PLAN INFO:

First Flr.	*2,277 sq. ft.*
Second Flr.	*851 sq. ft.*
Basement	*2, sq. ft.*
Garage	*493 sq. ft.*
Sq. Footage	*3,128 sq. ft.*
Foundation	*Slab*
Bedrooms	*Four*
Baths	*3(Full), 1(Half)*

REFER TO PRICE CODE E

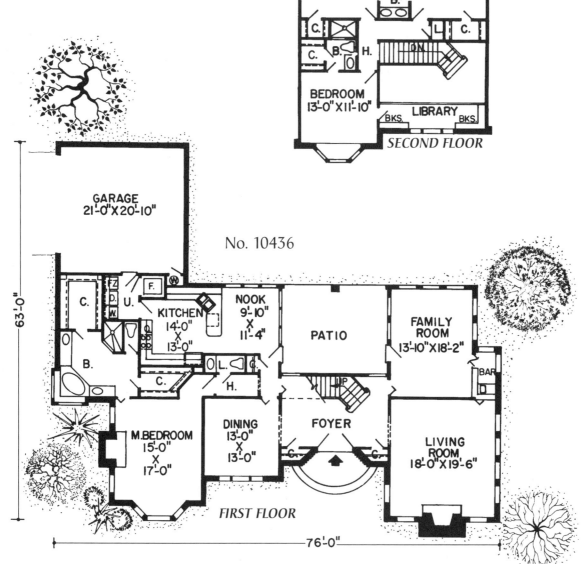

No. 10436

SECOND FLOOR

BEDROOM 12'-10"X11'-0"
BEDROOM 12'-10"X11'-0"
BEDROOM 13'-0"X11'-10"
LIBRARY
B.
C.
H.

GARAGE 21'-0"X20'-10"

63'-0"

KITCHEN 14'-0" X 13'-0"
NOOK 9'-10" X 11'-4"
PATIO
FAMILY ROOM 13'-10"X18'-2"
BAR
M.BEDROOM 15'-0" X 17'-0"
DINING 13'-0" X 13'-0"
FOYER
LIVING ROOM 18'-0"X19'-6"
B.
C.
H.

FIRST FLOOR

76'-0"

- ■ *Impressive double door entry with recessed arch leads into room-sized Foyer with graceful staircase*

- ■ *Windows surround massive fireplace in formal Living Room and accent formal Dining Room*

- ■ *Bright Family Room shares wet bar with Living Room and accesses covered Patio for outdoor relaxing*

- ■ *Efficient Kitchen adjacent to Utilities*

and Garage easily serves glass Nook, Patio and Dining Room

- ■ *Luxurious Master Bedroom suite offers another fireplace, decorative bay window and a plush dressing area with huge walk-in closet, two vanities and corner garden tub.*

- ■ *Three additional bedrooms on second floor have decorative windows share two full baths and a Library*

*T*hree *F*ireplaces *A*dd *E*legant *W*armth

PLAN INFO:

First Flr.	2,962 sq. ft.
Second Flr.	1,883 sq. ft.
Lower	
(not shown)	1,888 sq. ft.
Basement	2,962 sq. ft.
Garage	890 sq. ft.
Sq. Footage	6,733 sq. ft.
Foundation	Basement
Bedrooms	Four
Baths	3(Full), 1(Half)

REFER TO PRICE CODE F

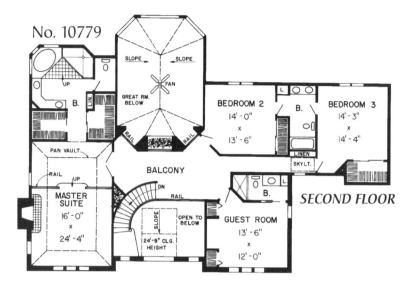

No. 10779

SECOND FLOOR

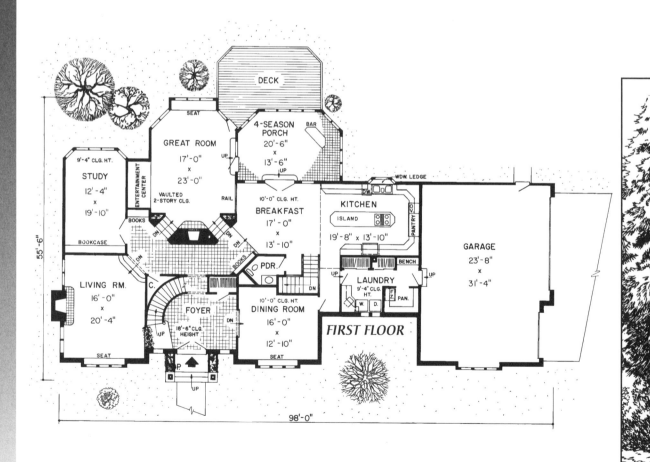

FIRST FLOOR

- *Enjoy sweeping view of the vaulted Great Room and two-story Foyer from the second floor Balcony*

- *Bi-level Master Suite features unique ceiling lines, personal fireplace, and two walk-in closets*

- *Relax in billions of bubbles designed to tantalize the senses in your raised tub in the Master Bath*

- *Each remaining Bedroom off the skylit hall adjoins a full Bath and possesses plenty of individual closet space*

- *Country Kitchen features cooktop island and greenhouse window ledge ideal for growing herbs*

- *Four-season Porch adjoins Breakfast Room and Great Room, and exits onto deck in backyard*

- *Impressive Great Room features built-in seats, fireplace, entertainment center, and vaulted two-story ceiling*

- *Retreat to the book-lined Study next to the Living Room for a quiet spot to get away from it all*

Mixture Of Stucco & Stone Create An Elegant Facade

No. 92505

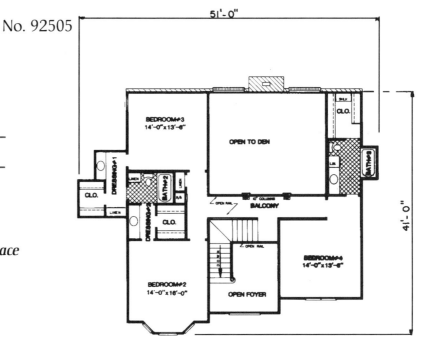

PLAN INFO:

First Flr.	2,442 sq. ft.
Second Flr.	1,062 sq. ft.
Garage	565 sq. ft.
Sq. Footage	3,504 sq. ft.
Foundation	Slab, Crawl space
Bedrooms	Four
Baths	3(Full), 1(Half)

REFER TO PRICE CODE F

SECOND FLOOR

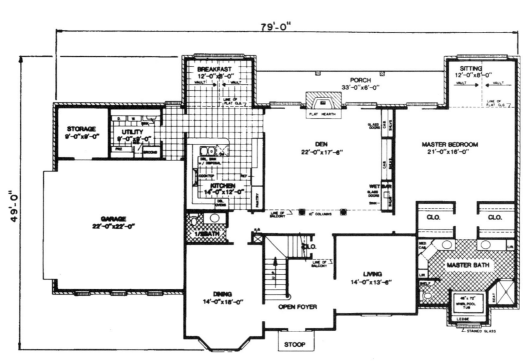

FIRST FLOOR

- *Arched top windows, copper roof over the two-story bay, and a detailed mixture of stucco and stone create a unique and elegant home*

- *Grand Foyer shows off a wide and open staircase, two-story ceiling and a magnificent balcony*

- *Large two-story columns frame the entrance to the magnificent Den featuring built-in cabinets and shelves, a wetbar and a full two-story fireplace framed by glass door leading to the outdoor porch*

- *A vaulted ceiling adds to the spacious feel of the gourmet Kitchen that includes a breakfast bar and built-in pantry*

- *Cozy, private Sitting Area with a vaulted ceiling provides quite moments in the Master Suite*

- *Master Bath features his-n-her walk-in closets, separate vanities and linen closets, and a whirlpool garden tub*

- *Three large additional bedrooms, each with walk-in closets and adjacent baths, are located on the second floor*

Comfortable Living Is Easy With This Design

PLAN INFO:

First Flr.	2,267 sq. ft.
Second Flr.	705 sq. ft.
Basement	2,267 sq. ft.
Garage	793 sq. ft.
Sq. Footage	2,972 sq. ft.
Foundation	Basement
Bedrooms	Three
Baths	Three

REFER TO PRICE CODE E

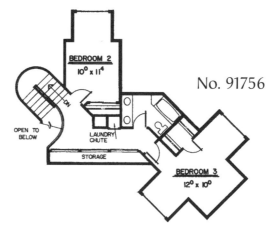

No. 91756

SECOND FLOOR

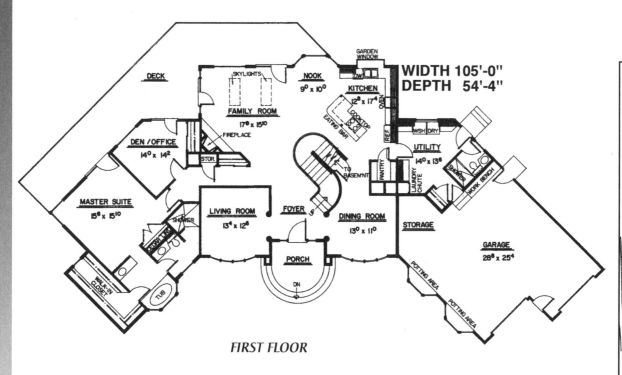

WIDTH 105'-0"
DEPTH 54'-4"

FIRST FLOOR

- *Exterior Tudor and Queen Anne styling hides a comfortable, Contemporary interior*

- *Stately, formal two-story Foyer leads smoothly into all living areas*

- *Formal Dining Room and Living Room are traditionally placed at the front of the home*

- *Gourmet Kitchen with garden window includes double sinks, a L-shaped cook top island/eating bar and a walk-in pantry*

- *Expansive Family Room is equipped with a corner fireplace and two skylights naturally illuminating the room*

- *First floor Master Suite, adjacent to Den/Office, has a enormous walk-in closet, an oversized tub tucked into its own nook with a bay window, and private access to the outdoor deck*

- *Two additional bedrooms on the second floor share a full hall Bath and enjoy the added convenience of a laundry chute*

Bedrooms Secluded On The Second Level

No. 10761

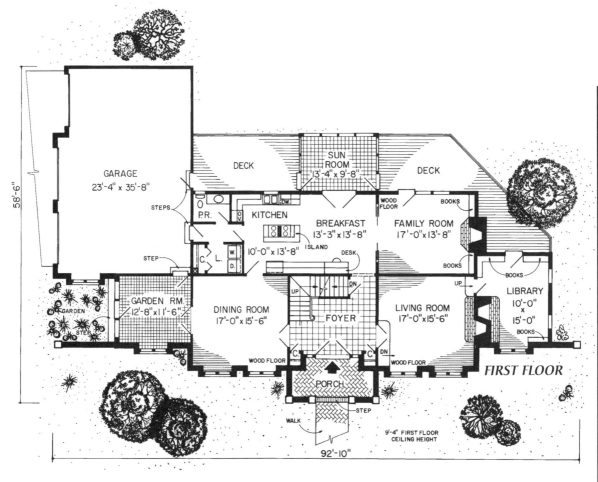

PLAN INFO:

First Flr.	1,926 sq. ft.
Second Flr.	1,606 sq. ft.
Basement	1,926 sq. ft.
Garage	840 sq. ft.
Sq. Footage	3,532 sq. ft.
Foundation	Basement
Bedrooms	Four
Baths	3(Full), 1(Half)

REFER TO PRICE CODE F

SECOND FLOOR

BEDROOM 13'-6"x13'-10"

BEDROOM 11'-2"x11'-2"

B.

C.

C.

RAIL HALL

DN

LIN.

C.

C.

MASTER BEDROOM 17'-0"x18'-4"

BEDROOM 17'-0"x11'-4"

VANITY TABLE

B.

SITTING AREA

GARAGE 23'-4" x 35'-8"

DECK

SUN ROOM 13'-4" x 9'-8"

DECK

STEPS

P.R.

KITCHEN

WOOD FLOOR

BOOKS

BREAKFAST 13'-3" x 13'-8"

FAMILY ROOM 17'-0"x13'-8"

STEP

C.

L.

W.

D.

10'-0"x13'-8"

ISLAND

DESK

BOOKS

GARDEN

GARDEN RM. 12'-8"x11'-6"

STEP

DINING ROOM 17'-0" x 15'-6"

UP

DN

FOYER

UP

LIVING ROOM 17'-0"x15'-6"

DN

LIBRARY 10'-0" x 15'-0"

BOOKS

WOOD FLOOR

C.

C.

WOOD FLOOR

FIRST FLOOR

PORCH

WALK

STEP

9'-4" FIRST FLOOR CEILING HEIGHT

58'-6"

92'-10"

- Double doors open to a huge Foyer from the fireplaced, sunken Living Room

- Cozy elegance of a book-lined Library allows needed solitude for concentration

- Convenient Kitchen with rangetop island adjacent to formal Dining Room opens to the sunny Breakfast Room

- Informal areas overlooking your backyard unite into one wide-open space

- Four bedrooms share private second floor location

- Enter from the 3-car Garage into a conveniently situated Laundry room and half-Bath

- Fireplaced Master Bedroom features his-n-her walk-in closets and double vanities

- All bedrooms include ample closet space for individual storage

- Scintillating odors filtrate house from plants and flowers in Garden Room

PLAN INFO:

First Flr.	*1,375 sq. ft.*
Second Flr.	*1,206 sq. ft.*
Basement	*1,375 sq. ft.*
Garage	*528 sq. ft.*
Sq. Footage	*2,581 sq. ft.*
Foundation	*Basement*
Bedrooms	*Three*
Baths	*2(Full), 1(Half)*

REFER TO PRICE CODE D

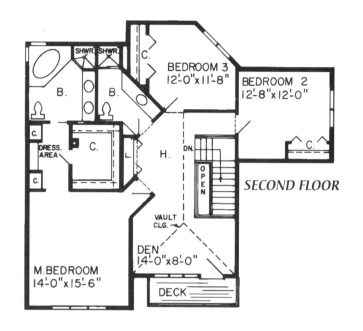

SECOND FLOOR

No. 10678

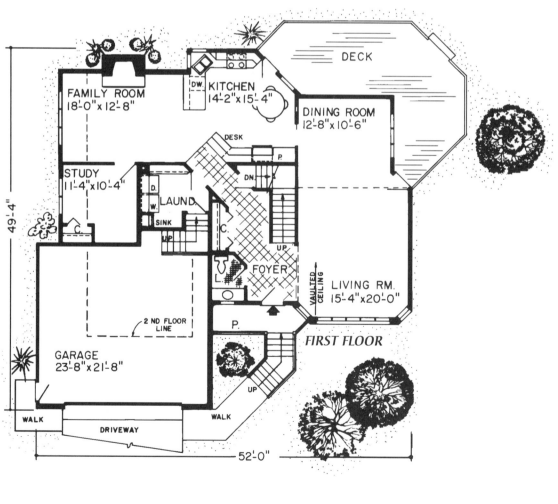

FIRST FLOOR

- *Covered Porch leads into tiled Foyer and Living Room with unusual corner window topped by vaulted ceiling*

- *Dining Room open to Living Room and Deck adjacent to Kitchen with pocket door*

- *Bright, efficient Kitchen with peninsula counter serves Deck, Family and Dining Rooms*

- *Quiet Study adjacent to open Family Room with warm, hearth fireplace*

- *Lavish Master Bedroom suite features separate Dressing area and private bath with double vanity and corner window, garden tub*

- *Two additional bedrooms with ample closets share full bath and upstairs Den with balcony*

Decorative Ceiling Treatments

PLAN INFO:

First Flr.	2,282 sq. ft.
Second Flr.	660 sq. ft.
Basement	2,282 sq. ft.
Garage	772 sq. ft.
Sq. Footage	2,942 sq. ft.
Foundation	Basement
Bedrooms	Three
Baths	2(Full), 1(Half)

*No materials list available

REFER TO PRICE CODE E

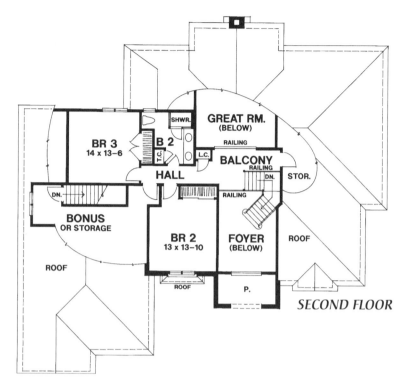

SECOND FLOOR

An
EXCLUSIVE DESIGN
By Patrick Morabito, A.I.A. Architect

No. 93325

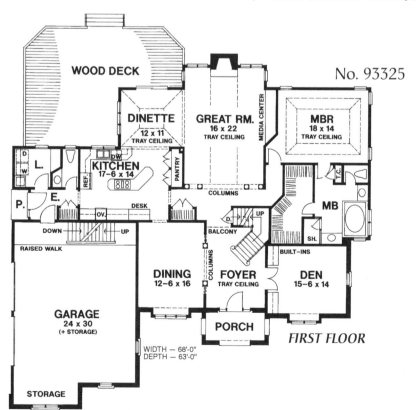

WIDTH — 68'-0"
DEPTH — 63'-0"

FIRST FLOOR

- *Distinctive entrance created by a covered Porch, windows surrounding the front door, a tray ceiling in the Foyer with an open staircase and balcony, columns framing entrance to the formal Dining Room and French doors leading into the Den*

- *Elegant formal Dining Room also has a decorative bumped out window*

- *More columns create a dramatic entrance into the Great Room equipped with a Media center, a huge fireplace surrounded by windows and topped with a tray ceiling*

- *Oversized Kitchen is a dream come true with a cooktop island/snack bar, built-in pantry and adjacent Dinette with tray ceiling and sliding glass doors to an outdoor deck*

- *Large Master Bedroom Suite with yet another tray ceiling offers luxurious privacy with an over-sized walk-in closet, raised corner window tub and two vanities*

- *Two second floor bedrooms share a full hall Bath, loads of storage and access to front and back stairways*

Balcony Offers Sweeping Views

No. 10778

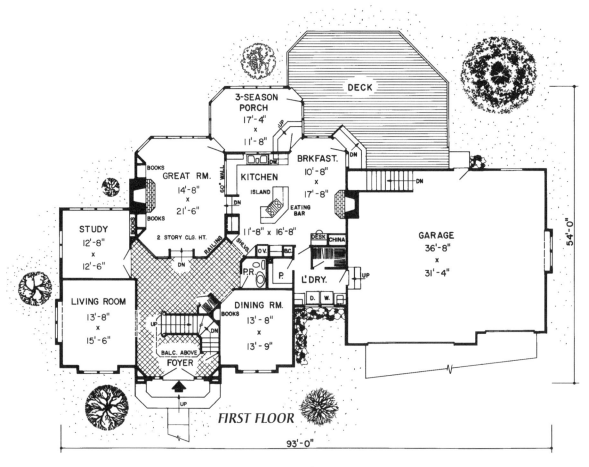

PLAN INFO:

First Flr.	1,978 sq. ft.
Second Flr.	1,768 sq. ft.
Basement	1,978 sq. ft.
Garage	3-car
Sq. Footage	3,746 sq. ft.
Foundation	Basement
Bedrooms	Four
Baths	3(Full), 1(Half)

REFER TO PRICE CODE F

SECOND FLOOR

DECK

SITTING
10'-6"
x
14'-6"

MASTER SUITE
22'-6"
x
18'-0"

BATH

OPEN TO BELOW

PAN VAULT CLG.

DESK

BR. 2
12'-8"
x
12'-0"

B.

BALCONY

BR. 3
13'-8"
x
12'-3"
SEAT

RAILING

OPEN TO BELOW

SLOPE   SLOPE

LIN.

BOOKS

B.

UP

VAN.

SPA

GUEST RM.
11'-3"
x
12'-6"
SEAT

FIRST FLOOR

DECK

3-SEASON PORCH
17'-4"
x
11'-8"

KITCHEN
ISLAND

BRKFAST.
10'-8"
x
17'-8"

DN

GREAT RM.
14'-8"
x
21'-6"
2 STORY CLG. HT.

BOOKS

BOOKS

60" WALL

EATING BAR
11'-8" x 16'-8"

DESK CHINA

GARAGE
36'-8"
x
31'-4"

STUDY
12'-8"
x
12'-6"

RAILING

SHLVS.

DN

O.V.

B.C.

P.R.

P.

L'DRY.

D. W.

UP

LIVING ROOM
13'-8"
x
15'-6"

UP

BOOKS

DN

BALC. ABOVE
FOYER

DINING RM.
13'-8"
x
13'-9"

UP

54'-0"

93'-0"

- Greet arriving guests in the impressive Foyer enhanced by a two-story ceiling and attractive staircase

- Large Living Room adjacent to Foyer offers ample accommodations for entertaining many guests

- Step out from the Three-Season Porch to enjoy a breath of fresh air on the deck in backyard

- Master Suite on second floor provides ideal retreat with raised spa, walk-in closet, sunny Sitting Room, and private deck

- Overlook beauty of Great Room from Balcony connecting three additional Bedrooms

- Each bedroom features built-in window seats or deck and loads of closet space

- Kitchen opening to Breakfast Room features stove-top island, built-in shelving, eating bar, and much more!

With All The Amenities You Need

An
EXCLUSIVE DESIGN
By Patrick Morabito, A.I.A. Architect

No. 93329

PLAN INFO:

First Flr.	*1,823 sq. ft.*
Second Flr.	*1,492 sq. ft.*
Basement	*1,823 sq. ft.*
Garage	*832 sq. ft.*
Sq. Footage	*3,315 sq. ft.*
Foundation	*Basement*
Bedrooms	*Four*
Baths	*2(Full), 1(Half)*

*No materials list available

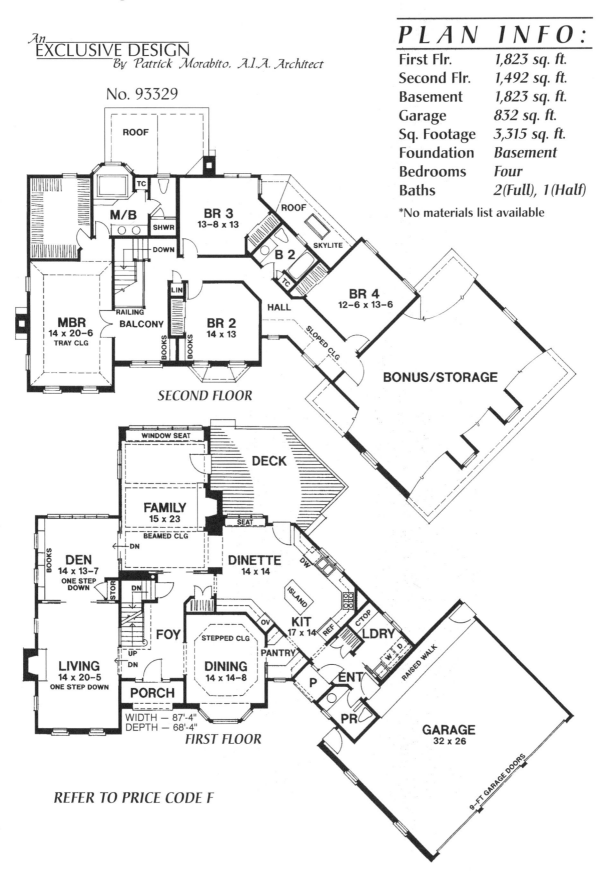

ROOF

TC

M/B

SHWR

DOWN

BR 3
13-8 x 13

ROOF

SKYLITE

B 2

TC

BR 4
12-6 x 13-6

LIN

MBR
14 x 20-6
TRAY CLG

RAILING
BALCONY

BOOKS   BOOKS

BR 2
14 x 13

HALL

SLOPED CLG

BONUS/STORAGE

SECOND FLOOR

WINDOW SEAT

DECK

FAMILY
15 x 23
BEAMED CLG

SEAT

DEN
14 x 13-7
ONE STEP DOWN

DN

STOR

DN

DINETTE
14 x 14

DW

ISLAND

KIT
17 x 14

REF

C-TOP

LDRY

W D

RAISED WALK

FOY

OV

STEPPED CLG

PANTRY

UP
DN

LIVING
14 x 20-5
ONE STEP DOWN

PORCH

DINING
14 x 14-8

P

ENT

PR

BOOKS

WIDTH — 87'-4"
DEPTH — 68'-4"

FIRST FLOOR

GARAGE
32 x 26

9-FT GARAGE DOORS

REFER TO PRICE CODE F

- *Arched, covered front entrance with sidelights and a fan transom window greets one and all into the Foyer and formal living areas*

- *Step down into the Formal Living Room with lots of windows and a hearth fireplace, easily expanded by opening pocket doors into the adjoining Den*

- *Bay window and stepped ceiling add elegance to the formal Dining Room*

- *Comfortable Family Room with another fireplace, beamed ceiling, a wall of glass above a long window seat, and direct access to the outdoor deck*

- *Large but efficient, gourmet Kitchen features a work island, walk-through pantry, loads of counter and cabinet space, a Dinette area with another window seat, and easy access to the Laundry area, Garage, and yards*

- *Scrumptious Master Bedroom Suite, topped with a tray ceiling, has windows on three sides, a walk-in closet large enough to be another room, and a segmented Bath with double vanity and a raised atrium tub*

- *Three additional large bedrooms have ample closet space and share a full hall Bath*

*S*tucco Opulence

No. 93270

SECOND FLOOR

PLAN INFO:

First Flr.	*2,329 sq. ft.*
Second Flr.	*1,259 sq. ft.*
Lower(Stairs)	*68 sq. ft.*
Basement	*1,806 sq. ft.*
Garage	*528 sq. ft.*
Sq. Footage	*3,656 sq. ft.*
Foundation	*Basement*
Bedrooms	*Four*
Baths	*3(Full), 2(Half)*

*No materials list available

REFER TO PRICE CODE F

An
EXCLUSIVE DESIGN
By Jannis Vann & Associates, Inc.

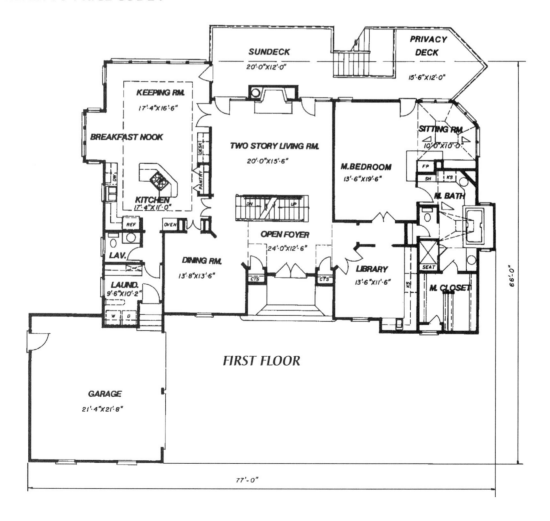

FIRST FLOOR

- *Impressive double door entrance with a two-story glass Foyer leads graciously into an open Foyer centered by an elegant staircase*

- *Fantastic two-story Living Room includes a cozy fireplace framed by windows and doors with direct access to an outdoor Sundeck*

- *Expansive Kitchen is equipped with a cooktop island/snack bar, built-in pantry and desk, as well as a Breakfast Nook and Keeping Room, topped with a decorative ceiling*

- *Scrumptious, three-sided glass Sitting Room with direct access to a private*

- *outdoor Deck, an unusual corner fireplace, luxurious Bath with an atrium tub, and a double walk-in closet add to the appeal of the Master Bedroom Suite*

- *Double door entry to the Library, directly off the Foyer and across from the Master Suite, offers a quiet corner, loads of built-in shelves and a possible home office*

- *Three additional bedrooms on the second floor have walk-in closets and easy access to full baths and a separate Children's Den*

Uncommon Brickwork Enhances Facade

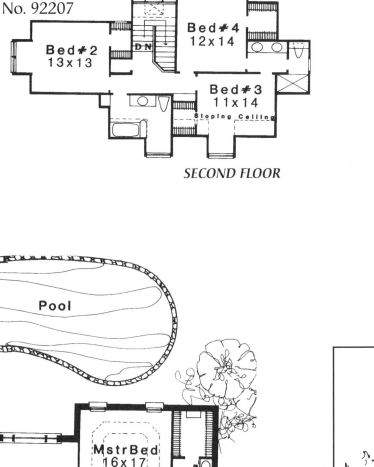

No. 92207

SECOND FLOOR

Bed #2
13 x 13

DN

Bed #4
12 x 14

Bed #3
11 x 14

Sloping Ceiling

PLAN INFO:

First Flr.	*2,304 sq. ft.*
Second Flr.	*852 sq. ft.*
Garage	*3-car*
Sq. Footage	*3,156 sq. ft.*
Foundation	*Slab*
Bedrooms	*Four*
Baths	*3(Full), 1(Half)*

*No materials list available

REFER TO PRICE CODE E

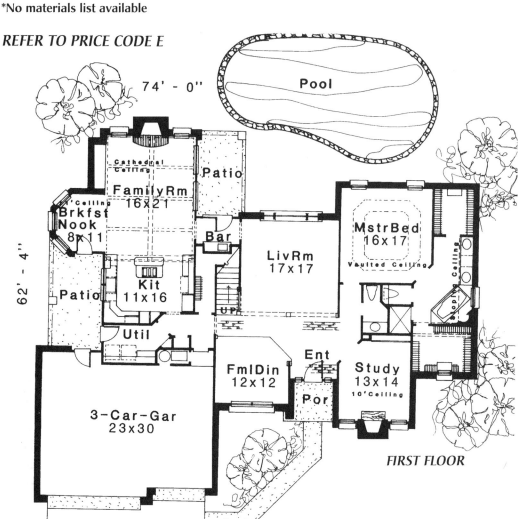

74' - 0''

Pool

62' - 4''

Cathedral Ceiling

Patio

FamilyRm
16 x 21

'Ceiling

Brkfst
Nook
8 x 11

Bar

LivRm
17 x 17

MstrBed
16 x 17

Vaulted Ceiling

Sloping Ceiling

Kit
11 x 16

UP

Patio

Util

3-Car-Gar
23 x 30

FmlDin
12 x 12

Ent

Por

Study
13 x 14
10'Ceiling

FIRST FLOOR

- ■ *Study adjacent to main Entry located in Master Suite wing to insure quiet solitude*

- ■ *Vaulted Master Suite sports individual his-n-her walk-in closets and twin basin vanity*

- ■ *Provocative raised tub with window overlooking side yard and sloping ceiling is focal feature of Master Bath*

- ■ *Placement of wetbar just off formal Living Room conducive to simplified servicing of guests*

- ■ *Living Room with sliding glass doors overlooks poolside vistas*

- ■ *Spacious Kitchen with food preparation island flows directly into Family Room with exposed beams on the cathedral ceiling*

- ■ *Breakfast Nook with lots of windows provides eating area for informal family meals*

- ■ *Three additional bedrooms and two full baths on second floor supply plenty of room for remainder of family*

$\mathcal{D}$istinctive Keystone Arches, Turret Library

PLAN INFO:

First Flr.	*2,294 sq. ft.*
Second Flr.	*1,029 sq. ft.*
Basement	*2,274 sq. ft.*
Garage	*820 sq. ft.*
Sq. Footage	*3,323 sq. ft.*
Foundation	*Bsmt, Slab, Crawl space*
Bedrooms	*Four*
Baths	*3(Full), 1(Half)*

*No materials list available

REFER TO PRICE CODE F

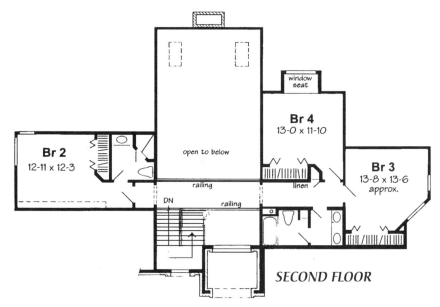

No. 24613

SECOND FLOOR

Br 2
12-11 x 12-3

open to below

railing

DN

railing

window seat

Br 4
13-0 x 11-10

linen

Br 3
13-8 x 13-6
approx.

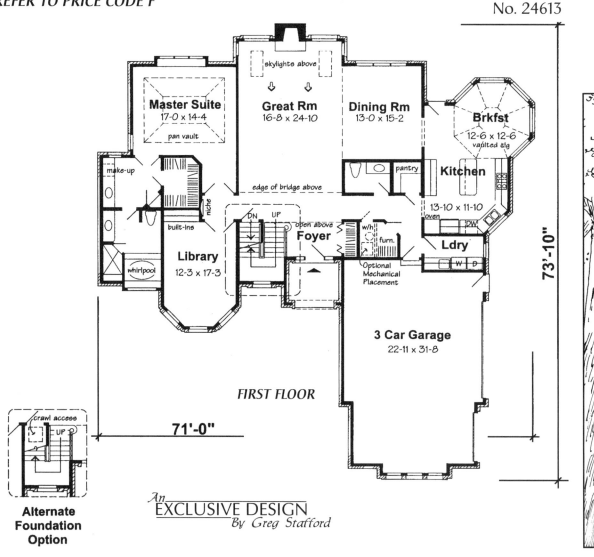

FIRST FLOOR

Master Suite
17-0 x 14-4
pan vault

make-up

niche

built-ins

whirlpool

Library
12-3 x 17-3

skylights above

Great Rm
16-8 x 24-10

edge of bridge above

DN   UP

Foyer

open above

Optional Mechanical Placement

Dining Rm
13-0 x 15-2

pantry

Brkfst
12-6 x 12-6
vaulted clg

Kitchen

13-10 x 11-10
oven

w/h   furn.

Ldry

DW

W D

3 Car Garage
22-11 x 31-8

73'-10"

71'-0"

Alternate Foundation Option

crawl access

UP

An EXCLUSIVE DESIGN
By Greg Stafford

-50-

- *Impressive two-story entrance with lots of glass and brick detail leads into Foyer, Great Room and Dining Room*

- *Formal Dining Room with windows overlooking the rear yard offers easy entertaining between Kitchen and Great Room*

- *Luxurious Master Suite, adjacent to quiet Library, highlighted by recessed window, huge walk-in closet, dressing area and whirlpool tub*

- *Unique Kitchen with an octagon Breakfast area features a built-in pantry, a work island/snackbar and access to the outdoors, the Laundry and the Garage*

- *Cozy fireplace set in wall of windows below skylights accents Great Room*

- *Three additional bedrooms, one with private bath, have over-sized closets and decorative windows*

Upper Deck Affords Roadside View

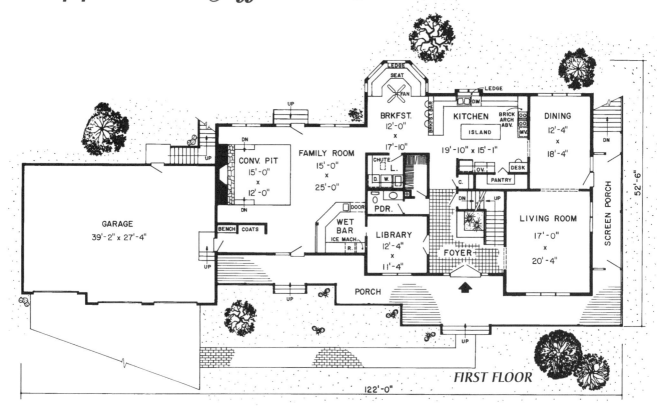

FIRST FLOOR

122'-0"

52'-6"

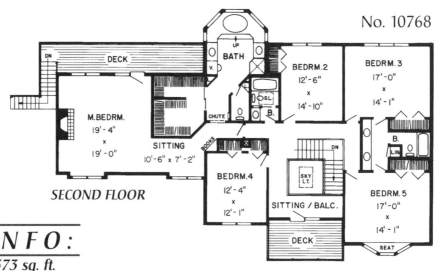

No. 10768

SECOND FLOOR

REFER TO PRICE CODE F

PLAN INFO:

First Flr.	*2,573 sq. ft.*
Second Flr.	*2,390 sq. ft.*
Basement	*1,844 sq. ft.*
Crawl Space	*793 sq. ft.*
Garage	*1,080 sq. ft.*
Sq. Footage	*4,963 sq. ft.*
Foundation	*Basement*
Bedrooms	*Five*
Baths	*3 (Full), 1 (Half)*

- Dominating staircase in Foyer wraps around planter basking in light from skylight far above

- Flanked by the Library and Living Room, the Foyer leads back to the island Kitchen with extra amenities

- Kitchen centrally located to serve the formal Dining Area and Breakfast Room

- Warm up informal gatherings at the fireplace in the Family Room containing large wetbar

- Master Suite on upper floor presents formidable escape spot from remainder of home

- Private deck, oversized double walk-in closet, double vanities and special tub setting render Master Suite truly luxurious

- Three additional Bedrooms on second floor provide ample room for children

- Overlook staircase and planter in Foyer from Sitting Area/Balcony or enjoy roadside view from deck

$\mathcal{S}$olarium Accents Active Living Area

PLAN INFO:

First Flr.	*2,466 sq. ft.*
Garage	*482 sq. ft.*
Sq. Footage	*2,466 sq. ft.*
Foundation	*Slab*
Bedrooms	*Three*
Baths	*2(Full), 1(Half)*

REFER TO PRICE CODE D

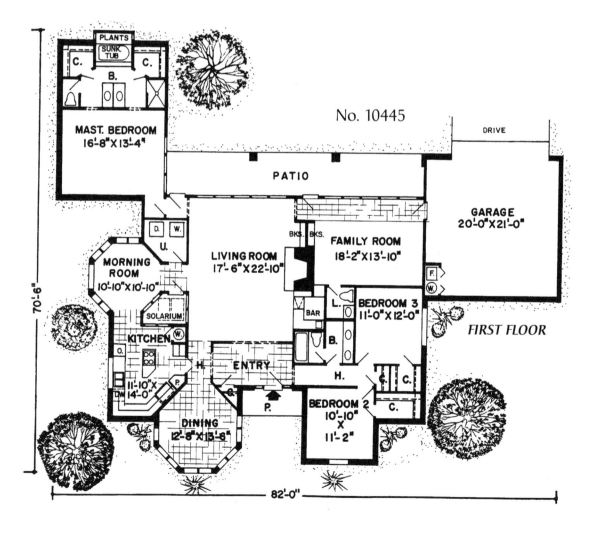

No. 10445

PLANTS
SUNK. TUB
C.   C.
B.
MAST. BEDROOM
16'-8" X 13'-4"

DRIVE

PATIO

GARAGE
20'-0" X 21'-0"

LIVING ROOM
17'-6" X 22'-10"

BKS. BKS.

FAMILY ROOM
18'-2" X 13'-10"

MORNING ROOM
10'-10" X 10'-10"

SOLARIUM

KITCHEN
11'-10" X 14'-0"

BAR

L.

F.
W.

BEDROOM 3
11'-0" X 12'-0"

B.

FIRST FLOOR

70'-6"

H.   ENTRY

H.

C.   C.

DINING
12'-8" X 13'-6"

P.

BEDROOM 2
10'-10" X 11'-2"

C.

82'-0"

■ *Gracious arched glass Entry with easy care tile leading into expansive Living Room accented by huge fireplace, Solarium and wall of windows overlooking covered Patio*

■ *Secluded Master Bedroom with easy access to Patio offers two walk-in closets and vanities, and sunken garden tub*

■ *Two additional bedrooms with walk-in closets share double vanity bath*

■ *Octagon shaped Dining and Morning Rooms provides both elegant morning and evening meals*

■ *Efficient Kitchen with cooktop/work island enjoys a Solarium, a Morning Room, a Dining Room and a Utilities Room nearby*

$\mathcal{A}$ngled Garage Draws Eyes Toward This Home

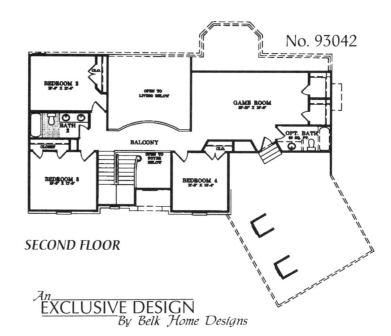

No. 93042

SECOND FLOOR

PLAN INFO:

First Flr.	*1,832 sq. ft.*
Second Flr.	*1,163 sq. ft.*
Garage	*591 sq. ft.*
Sq. Footage	*2,995 sq. ft.*
Foundation	*Slab, Crawl space*
Bedrooms	*Four*
Baths	*2(Full), 1(Half)*

*No materials list available

REFER TO PRICE CODE E

An
EXCLUSIVE DESIGN
By Belk Home Designs

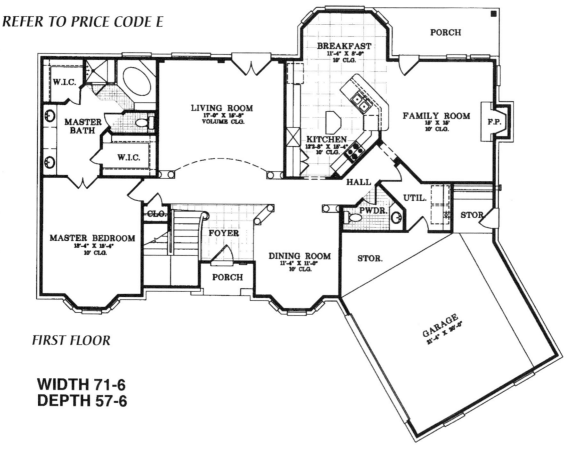

FIRST FLOOR

WIDTH 71-6
DEPTH 57-6

- Elegance accented by twin bay windows and an angled Garage

- Tiled Foyer opens to a breath-taking two-story Living Room framed by columns and featuring French doors

- Elegant formal Dining Room also features a column entrance and one of the lovely bay windows

- Island dream Kitchen, with a peninsula counter and eating bar, connects with the Breakfast Room that flows easily into the Family Room

- Spacious Family Room that includes a cozy fireplace and access to an outdoor porch

- Pampering Master Suite features the other bay window, his-n-her walk-in closets and a segmented Master Bath

- Three bedrooms share a full double vanity hall Bath

You Deserve This Spacious Design

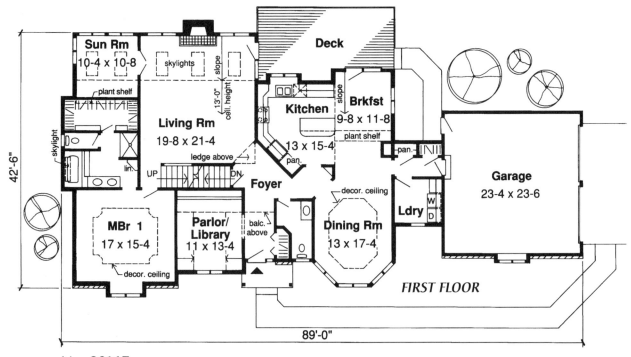

No. 20167

FIRST FLOOR

Sun Rm
10-4 x 10-8

skylights

slope

Deck

Living Rm
19-8 x 21-4

13'-0"
ceil. height

plant shelf

skylight

lin.

UP

ledge above

DN

Foyer

Kitchen
13 x 15-4

Brkfst
9-8 x 11-8

plant shelf

pan.

pan.

Garage
23-4 x 23-6

MBr 1
17 x 15-4

decor. ceiling

Parlor/
Library
11 x 13-4

balc.
above

decor. ceiling

Dining Rm
13 x 17-4

Ldry

W
D

42'-6"

89'-0"

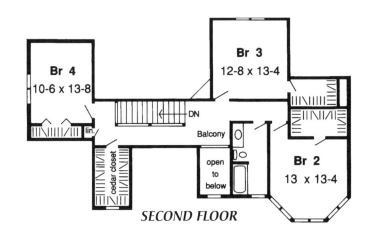

SECOND FLOOR

Br 4
10-6 x 13-8

lin.

DN

Br 3
12-8 x 13-4

Balcony

open
to
below

Br 2
13 x 13-4

cedar closet

PLAN INFO:

First Flr.	*2,216 sq. ft.*
Second Flr.	*916 sq. ft.*
Basement	*2,089 sq. ft.*
Garage	*576 sq. ft.*
Sq. Footage	*3,132 sq. ft.*
Foundation	*Basement*
Bedrooms	*Four*
Baths	*2(Full), 1(Half)*

REFER TO PRICE CODE E

An
EXCLUSIVE DESIGN
By Karl Kreeger

- Two-story Foyer adjoins the Parlor/Library and the spectacular Living Room with skylights and a large cozy fireplace

- Gourmet island Kitchen, with a built-in pantry, double sink, and an over abundance of counter and storage space

- Just steps away from the Kitchen is the sunny Breakfast Room and elegant Dining Room with Bay windows and a decorative ceiling

- Stupendous Sun Room with skylights and plant shelves adds solar benefits for all seasons

- First floor Master Suite with decorative ceiling treatment, private Bath with skylights and a room-sized walk-in closet

- Three bedrooms, each with abundant closet space, share the second floor with a walk-in cedar closet and a full Bath

$\mathcal{P}$icturesque Details and Inviting Atmosphere

PLAN INFO:

First Flr.	1,580 sq. ft.
Second Flr.	1,164 sq. ft.
Basement	1,329 sq. ft.
Garage	576 sq. ft.
Sq. Footage	2,744 sq. ft.
Foundation	Basement
Bedrooms	Five
Baths	3(Full), 1(Half)

REFER TO PRICE CODE E

SECOND FLOOR

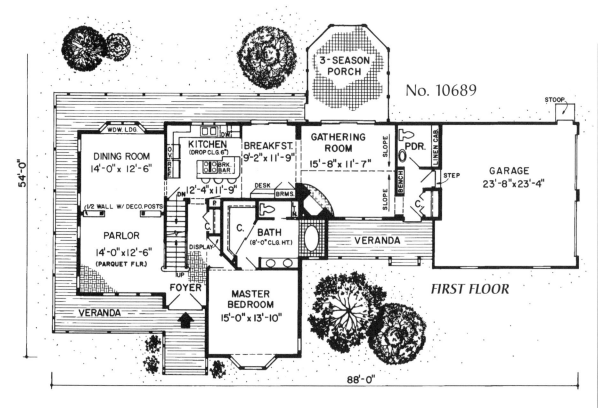

No. 10689

FIRST FLOOR

- ■ *Outdoor living expanded by wrap-around Veranda and three season Porch*

- ■ *Traditional front Parlor and adjoining Dining Room with decorative windows allow for elegant entertaining*

- ■ *Efficient L-shaped Kitchen with cook-top/breakfast bar, built-in pantry and desk easily serves Dining Room, Breakfast area, Gathering Room and Porch beyond*

- ■ *Gathering Room offers cozy, corner fireplace and sliding glass doors to Porch topped by sloped ceiling*

- ■ *First floor Master Bedroom suite accented by lovely bay window and lavish bath with walk-in closet, double vanity and window tub*

- ■ *Second floor boosts three bedrooms Guest Room with ample closets, share two full baths and Study with Veranda*

Pool Accents Center Courtyard

PLAN INFO:

First Flr.	2,194 sq. ft.
Garage	576 sq. ft.
Sq. Footage	2,194 sq. ft.
Foundation	Crawlspace
Bedrooms	Three
Baths	2(Full)

REFER TO PRICE CODE C

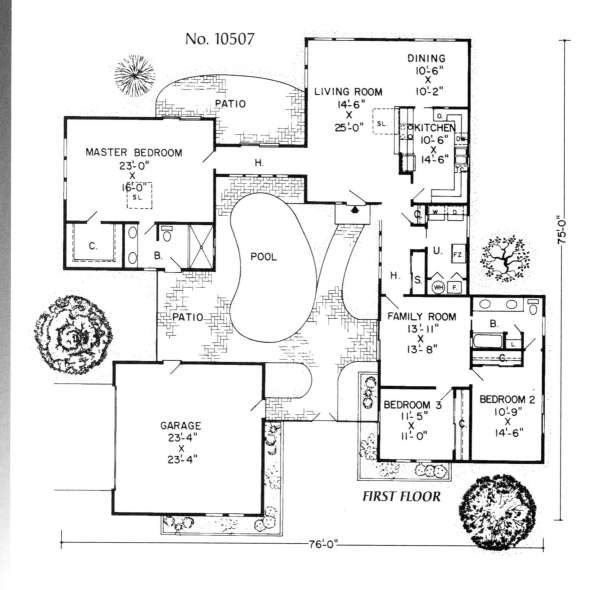

No. 10507

DINING
10'-6"
X
10'-2"

LIVING ROOM
14'-6"
X
25'-0"

PATIO

KITCHEN
10'-6"
X
14'-6"

MASTER BEDROOM
23'-0"
X
16'-0"

H.

POOL

PATIO

C.

B.

U.

FZ.

H.   S.

WH   F.

FAMILY ROOM
13'-11"
X
13'-8"

B.

GARAGE
23'-4"
X
23'-4"

BEDROOM 3
11'-5"
X
11'-0"

BEDROOM 2
10'-9"
X
14'-6"

75'-0"

76'-0"

FIRST FLOOR

- Hub of this warm and hospitable home is Patio with Pool

- Expansive Living Room with corner windows and skylight opens into Dining area for easy entertaining

- Efficient Kitchen with lots of counter and storage space adjoins Dining area, Utilities and Patio

- Private Master Bedroom wing accented by sliding glass door to another Patio, skylight, huge walk-in closet and double-vanity bath with access to pool area

- Family Room central to Patio, two additional bedrooms with ample closets, and double vanity bath

Eye-Catching Exterior For Luxurious Living

PLAN INFO:

First Flr.	1,388 sq. ft.
Second Flr.	1,321 sq. ft.
Basement	1,332 sq. ft.
Garage	680 sq. ft.
Sq. Footage	2,709 sq. ft.
Foundation	Bsmt, Slab, Crawl space
Bedrooms	Four
Baths	2(Full), 1(Half)

No materials list available

REFER TO PRICE CODE E

Master Suite 13-0 x 15-6

whirlpool

make-up   linen

linen

DN

railing

open to below

ledge

Br 4 10-6 x 13-2

desk

Br 3 11-2 x 13-6

Br 2 13-0 x 12-10

SECOND FLOOR

crawl access

Slab, Crawl Space Option

An
EXCLUSIVE DESIGN
By Britt J. Willis

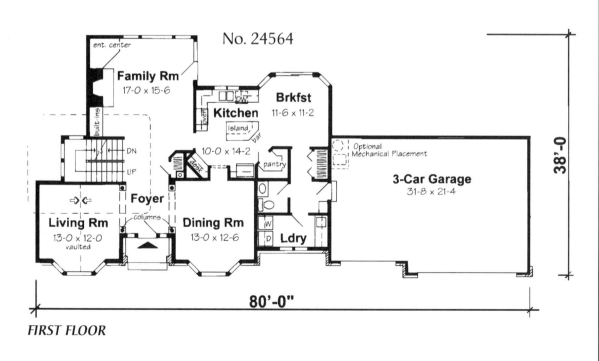

No. 24564

ent. center

Family Rm 17-0 x 15-6

built-ins

DN

UP

Foyer

columns

Living Rm 13-0 x 12-0 vaulted

Kitchen 10-0 x 14-2

island   bar

dw

pantry

desk

Brkfst 11-6 x 11-2

Optional Mechanical Placement

3-Car Garage 31-8 x 21-4

Dining Rm 13-0 x 12-6

W
D

Ldry

38'-0

80'-0"

FIRST FLOOR

- *Sheltered entrance into Foyer framed by columns into formal Dining and Living Rooms with vaulted ceilings crowning bay windows*

- *Family Room features a built-in entertainment center, a huge fireplace and a wall of glass with access to the rear yard*

- *Efficient Kitchen with a work island/eating bar, a walk-in pantry, and a built-in desk accessible to the Breakfast area, the Dining Room, the Laundry and the Garage*

- *Master Suite includes a walk-in closet, a built-in make-up table, a plush bath with a whirlpool tub*

- *Three additional bedrooms with ample closets and decorative windows share double-vanity bath*

$\mathcal{E}$asy Living With Open Layout

PLAN INFO:

First Flr.	1,620 sq. ft.
Second Flr.	858 sq. ft.
Basement	1,110 sq. ft.
Garage	657 sq. ft.
Sq. Footage	2,478 sq. ft.
Foundation	Basement
Bedrooms	Three
Baths	2(Full), 1(Half)

REFER TO PRICE CODE D

An EXCLUSIVE DESIGN
By Energetic Enterprises

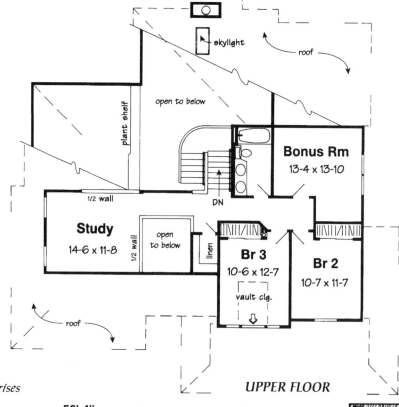

skylight

roof

plant shelf

open to below

Bonus Rm
13-4 x 13-10

1/2 wall

DN

Study
14-6 x 11-8

1/2 wall

open to below

linen

Br 3
10-6 x 12-7

Br 2
10-7 x 11-7

vault clg.

roof

UPPER FLOOR

No. 24252

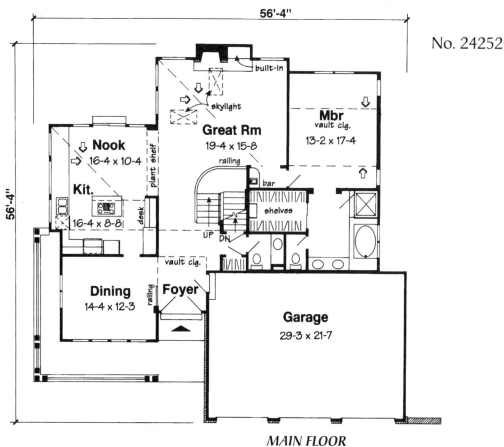

56'-4"

56'-4"

built-in

skylight

Great Rm
19-4 x 15-8

Mbr
vault clg.
13-2 x 17-4

Nook
16-4 x 10-4

plant shelf

railing

bar

Kit.
16-4 x 8-8

desk

shelves

UP DN

vault clg.

Dining
14-4 x 12-3

railing

Foyer

Garage
29-3 x 21-7

MAIN FLOOR

- *Wrap-around porch shelter entrance to vaulted Foyer and curved landing stairway overlooking Great Room*

- *Great Room features cozy fireplace with built-in wood holder between windows and below skylights*

- *Lots of counter and storage space in the Kitchen with a cooktop/work island and a glass eating Nook with access to the rear yard*

- *Private Master Bedroom with vaulted ceiling, walk-in closet and lavish bath with double vanity and garden tub*

- *Two second floor bedrooms with ample closets, share double-vanity bath, Study and Bonus Room with many options*

- *Two walls of windows brighten the Dining Room*

Front Bedroom Features Window Seat

PLAN INFO:

First Flr.	2,027 sq. ft.
Second Flr.	1,476 sq. ft.
Garage	650 sq. ft.
Sq. Footage	3,503 sq. ft.
Foundation	Slab
Bedrooms	Four
Baths	Three

REFER TO PRICE CODE F

SECOND FLOOR

DECK

BEAM

MASTER BEDROOM
20'-6" x 20'-0"

VANITY · SKYLIGHT

SLOPE · SLOPE

SL SL · UP

ROMAN TUB

LIN.

DN

BEDRM. 2
13'-2" x 14'-8"

BEDRM. 3
14'-4" x 14'-2"

SEAT

SEAT

No. 10758

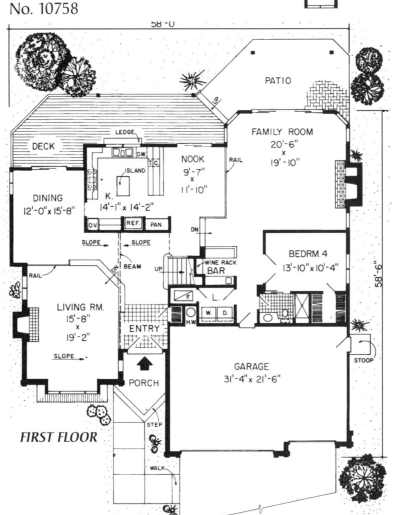

FIRST FLOOR

58'-0

PATIO

FAMILY ROOM
20'-6" x 19'-10"

DECK

LEDGE

DW.

NOOK
9'-7" x 11'-10"

RAIL

ISLAND · T.C.

K.
14'-1" x 14'-2"

DINING
12'-0" x 15'-8"

OV. · REF. · PAN.

SLOPE · SLOPE

BEAM · DN · UP

WINE RACK
BAR

BEDRM. 4
13'-10" x 10'-4"

RAIL

DN

F. · L.

W. D.

LIVING RM.
15'-8" x 19'-2"

ENTRY · H.W.

SLOPE

PORCH

STEP

GARAGE
31'-4" x 21'-6"

STOOP

58'-6"

WALK

- *Sloping roofline creates unusual decorating possibilities in Master Bedroom*

- *Feel the day's cares ease away while relaxing on private deck in Master Suite after reposing in Roman tub in skylit Bath*

- *Soaring ceilings generate airy atmosphere throughout design*

- *Kitchen framed by formal Dining Room and cheery Eating Nook*

- *Two additional Bedrooms on second floor have ample closet space, and share a full Bath*

- *Open railings and single steps separate fireplaced Family and Living Rooms from Entry and Dining Areas*

- *Sliders in Family Room and both Dining Rooms open to rear deck and patio to maximize spacious feeling*

- *Fourth bedroom complete with full Bath tucked behind garage*

Luxury Residence For The Executive Family

PLAN INFO:

First Flr.	*3,798 sq. ft.*
Second Flr.	*1,244 sq. ft.*
Basement	*3,798 sq. ft.*
Garage	*3-car*
Sq. Footage	*5,042 sq. ft.*
Foundation	*Basement*
Bedrooms	*Three*
Baths	*3(Full), 2(Half)*

REFER TO PRICE CODE F

*No materials list available

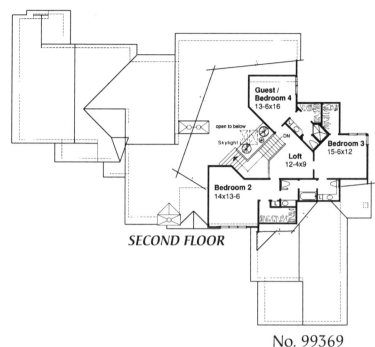

Guest / Bedroom 4
13-6x16

open to below

Skylight

DN

Loft
12-4x9

Bedroom 3
15-6x12

Bedroom 2
14x13-6

SECOND FLOOR

No. 99369

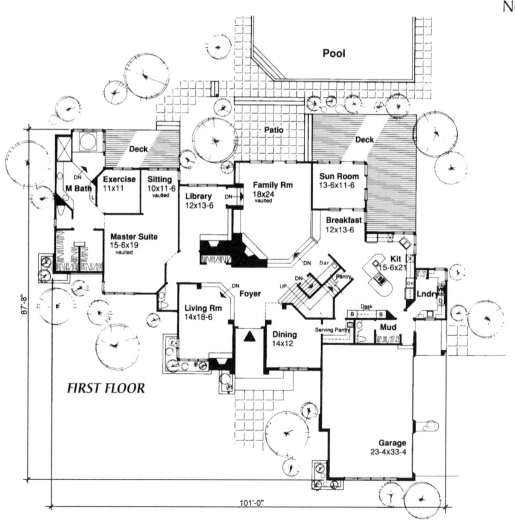

Pool

Patio

Deck

Deck

M Bath

DN

Exercise
11x11

Sitting
10x11-6
vaulted

Library
12x13-6

DN

Family Rm
18x24
vaulted

Sun Room
13-6x11-6

Breakfast
12x13-6

Master Suite
15-6x19
vaulted

DN

Bar

Kit
15-6x21

Pantry

UP

DN

Lndry

DN

Foyer

Living Rm
14x18-6

Desk

B

B

Mud

Serving Pantry

Dining
14x12

Garage
23-4x33-4

87'-8"

FIRST FLOOR

101'-0"

- 70 -

- *Main floor zoned into three main living areas: formal, informal, and Master Suite*

- *Enter formal living/entertaining area from impressive Foyer which opens into the Dining Room with an efficient serving pantry*

- *Master Suite located in a private wing includes a vaulted Sitting Room, Exercise Room, sunken whirlpool tub, and twin walk-in closets*

- *Second floor features a loft and three bedrooms each with personal baths and walk-in closets*

- *Informal zone centers around a large island Kitchen with built-in desk and handy access to the 3-car Garage past the Laundry and Mudroom*

- *Kitchen also oversees the Breakfast area and Sunroom eating areas as well as the sunken Family Room*

Old Style With New Features

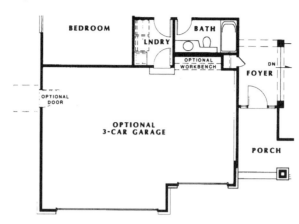

OPTIONAL 3-CAR GARAGE

PLAN INFO:

First Flr.	2,108 sq. ft.
Basement	2,108 sq. ft.
Garage	580 sq. ft.
Sq. Footage	2,108 sq. ft.
Foundation	Bsmt, Slab, Crawl space
Bedrooms	Three
Baths	2(Full)

REFER TO PRICE CODE C

An
EXCLUSIVE DESIGN
By Energetic Enterprises

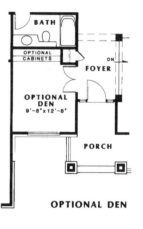

OPTIONAL DEN

No. 24256

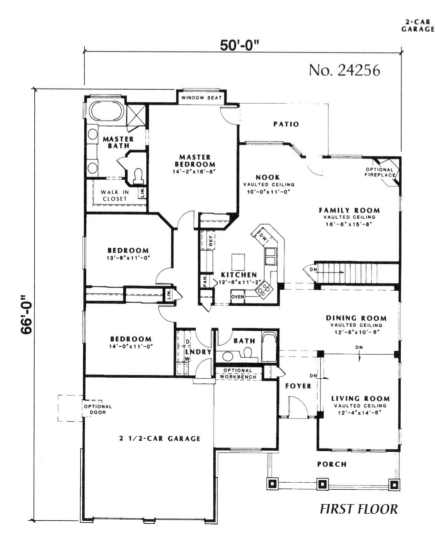

FIRST FLOOR

■ *Welcome entrance into open layout of Living and Dining Rooms defined by pillars and loads of windows*

■ *Central Kitchen with island worktop, built-in pantry and peninsula snackbar easily serves glass Nook, Family and Dining Rooms*

■ *Expansive Family Room with vaulted ceiling topping cozy, corner fireplace between windows and access to Patio*

■ *Comfortable Master Bedroom suite features window seat, lavish bath with corner window tub and two vanities, and access to Patio*

■ *Two additional bedrooms with ample closet space share Laundry and full bath*

■ *Optional Den or third-car Garage customizes this home for you*

Surrounded By Multi-Level Decks

No. 92106

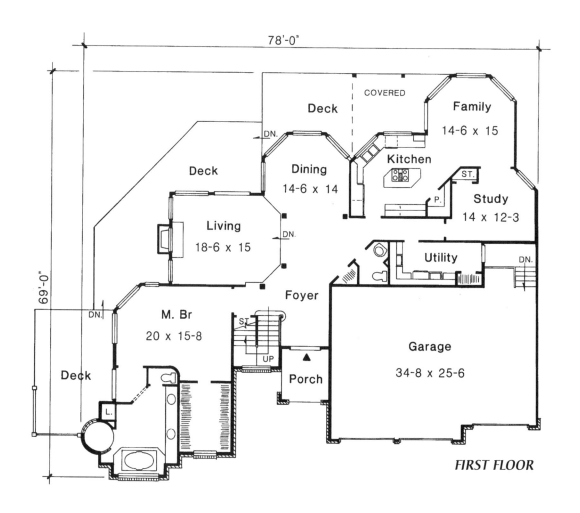

PLAN INFO:

First Flr.	2,358 sq. ft.
Second Flr.	700 sq. ft.
Garage	954 sq. ft.
Sq. Footage	3,058 sq. ft.
Foundation	Crawl space
Bedrooms	Three
Baths	2(Full), 1(Half)

REFER TO PRICE CODE E

SECOND FLOOR

Br #2
14-6 x 12

Br #3
12-6 x 14

LINEN

OPEN TO LIVING BELOW

OPEN TO FOYER BELOW

DN.

FIRST FLOOR

78'-0"

69'-0"

COVERED

Deck

Family
14-6 x 15

Deck

Dining
14-6 x 14

Kitchen

ST.

Study
14 x 12-3

P.

Living
18-6 x 15

DN.

Utility

DN.

Foyer

M. Br
20 x 15-8

ST

UP

DN.

Deck

L.

Porch

Garage
34-8 x 25-6

- *Enter Utility Room with built-in counter and ample closet space from stucco 3-car Garage*

- *Extra lighting and cabinets add to the island Kitchen that opens to a bright sunny Family Room*

- *Unique octagonally-shaped Dining Room leads to immense covered deck and steps down to a fireplaced Living Room*

- *Enjoy the view of the Foyer below from second floor landing with linen closet*

- *Master Bedroom with personal deck features window in walk-in closet and plenty of living and decorating space*

- *Master Bath has his-n-her vanity, linen closet and luxurious circular glass-walled shower*

- *Bedroom Two offers a good-sized closet and breathtaking view an through extra-large window*

- *Bedroom Three includes a sizeable walk-in closet and opens to a shared double vanitied Bath*

Spectacular Display Of Light & Space

PLAN INFO:

First Flr.	1,786 sq. ft.
Second Flr.	1,490 sq. ft.
Basement	1,773 sq. ft.
Garage	579 sq. ft.
Sq. Footage	3,276 sq. ft.
Foundation	Basement
Bedrooms	Four
Baths	2(Full), 1(Half)

REFER TO PRICE CODE F

M. BEDROOM
18'-0"x17'-8"
VAULTED CEILING

JACUZZI

B.

SHWR.

CAB. ABV.

LIN.

C.

C.

B.

DOWN

BOOKS

H.

OPEN TO FOYER

C.

BOOKS

BOOKS

BOOKS

BEDROOM 2
11'-0"x14'-4"

BEDROOM 3
11'-4"x12'-4"

BEDROOM 4
11'-4"x15'-4"

C.

C.

SECOND FLOOR

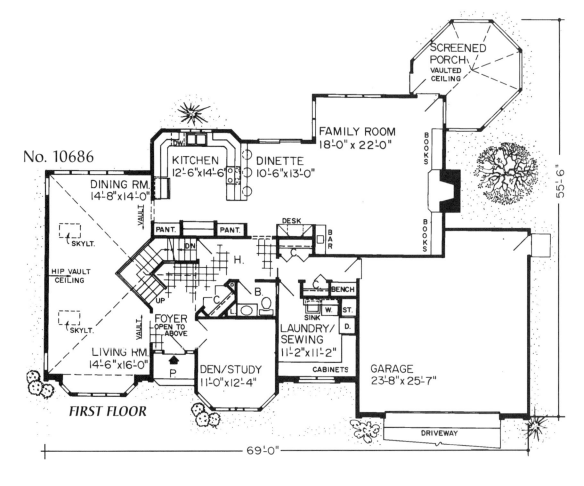

No. 10686

SCREENED PORCH
VAULTED CEILING

FAMILY ROOM
18'-0" x 22'-0"

BOOKS

BOOKS

KITCHEN
12'-6"x14'-6"

DINETTE
10'-6"x13'-0"

DINING RM.
14'-8"x14'-0"

DESK

BAR

PANT.

PANT.

C.

SKYLT.

HIP VAULT CEILING

DN

H.

UP

B.

C.

BENCH

W.

SINK

ST.

D.

SKYLT.

FOYER
OPEN TO ABOVE

LAUNDRY/ SEWING
11'-2"x11'-2"

CABINETS

GARAGE
23'-8"x25'-7"

LIVING RM.
14'-6"x16'-0"

P.

DEN/STUDY
11'-0"x12'-4"

FIRST FLOOR

DRIVEWAY

55'-6"

69'-0"

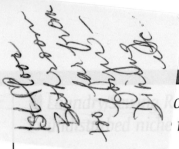

- *Huge two-story Foyer features angular open staircase leading to sleeping quarters on the second floor*

- *Master Bedroom occupies full length of upper level, allowing many luxurious amenities to be included*

- *Master Bath sports a personal jacuzzi for private relaxation*

- *Three additional bedrooms upstairs each possess generous closet area and built-in bookshelving*

- *[...] Room provides [...] niche for special projects*

- *Wide-open family area includes Kitchen, Dinette, and fireplaced Family Room, complete with built-in bar and bookcases*

- *Kitchen features two pantries and lots of counter space as well as easy access to the formal Dining Room*

- *Well-placed skylights and abundant windows bathe every room in sunlight*

$\mathcal{A}$ Truly Stunning Design

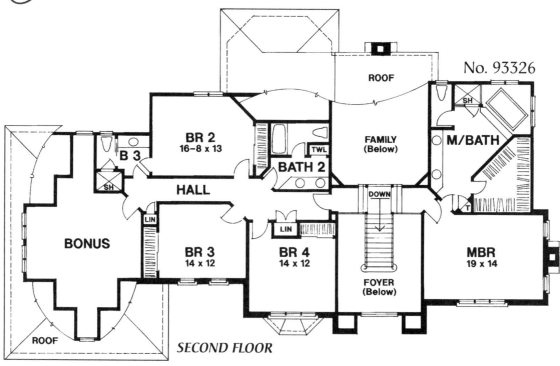

No. 93326

ROOF

BR 2
16-8 x 13

B 3

SH

HALL

BATH 2

TWL

FAMILY
(Below)

M/BATH

SH

DOWN

BONUS

LIN

BR 3
14 x 12

LIN

BR 4
14 x 12

FOYER
(Below)

MBR
19 x 14

ROOF

SECOND FLOOR

PLAN INFO:

First Flr.	*2,228 sq. ft.*
Second Flr.	*1,625 sq. ft.*
Bonus Rm.	*347 sq. ft.*
Basement	*2,228 sq. ft.*
Garage	*816 sq. ft.*
Sq. Footage	*3,853 sq. ft.*
Foundation	*Basement*
Bedrooms	*Four*
Baths	*3(Full), 1(Half)*

No materials list available

REFER TO PRICE CODE F

An
EXCLUSIVE DESIGN
By Patrick Morabito, A.I.A. Architect

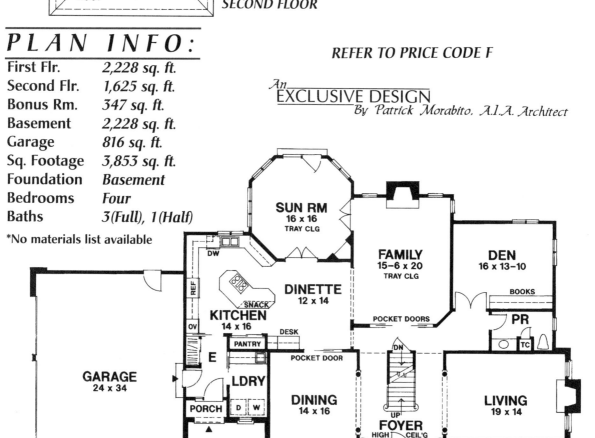

SUN RM
16 x 16
TRAY CLG

FAMILY
15-6 x 20
TRAY CLG

DEN
16 x 13-10

DW

REF

DINETTE
12 x 14

BOOKS

SNACK

KITCHEN
14 x 16

OV

E

DESK

PANTRY

POCKET DOORS

PR

TC

POCKET DOOR

DN

GARAGE
24 x 34

LDRY

DINING
14 x 16

UP

LIVING
19 x 14

PORCH

D **W**

FOYER
HIGH CEIL'G

WIDTH — 84'-0"
DEPTH — 52'-0"
FIRST FLOOR

PORCH

- *Stunning facade of this lovely home with fan-top decorative windows, blocked brick corners and two-story glass entryway attracts admiration*

- *Open Foyer gives ready access to all living areas with its center staircase, pillar entrances to formal Living and Dining rooms, pocket doors into Family room and double doors into Den*

- *Formal Dining Room features a bumped out decorative window and intriguing pocket doors for exclusive entertaining*

- *Spacious Family Room featuring a tray ceiling and another cozy fireplace, opens into the Kitchen area and Sun Room with loads of windows*

- *Gourmet Kitchen has it all; a cooktop/snack bar island, double sink, built-in pantry and desk, a comfortable Dinette area and direct access to the Dining Room, Sun Room, Family Room, Laundry and Garage*

- *Indulgent Master Bedroom Suite, separated on the second floor by a balcony, has a large decorative window viewing the front yard and a lavish Bath with a huge walk-in closet, double vanity and a raised corner window tub*

- *On the other end of the second floor there are three large bedrooms, one with a private bath, and a Bonus room to accommodate any need*

Stone And Stucco Make Striking Sight

SECOND FLOOR

Br 4
11-4 x 10

DN

lin.

foyer below

slope

Br 2
12 x 13-4

slope

slope

Br 3
11 x 13

PLAN INFO:

First Flr.	1,760 sq. ft.
Second Flr.	785, sq. ft.
Basement	1,760 sq. ft.
Garage	797 sq. ft.
Sq. Footage	2,545 sq. ft.
Foundation	Bsmt,Slab, Crawl space
Bedrooms	Four
Baths	3(Full), 1(Half)

REFER TO PRICE CODE D

An
EXCLUSIVE DESIGN
By Karl Kreeger

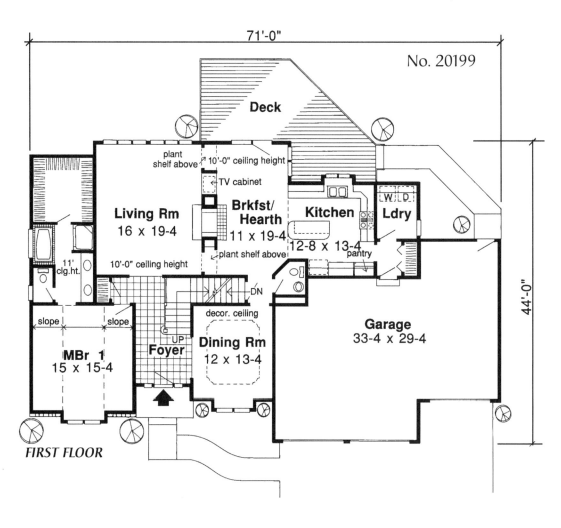

71'-0"

No. 20199

Deck

plant shelf above

10'-0" ceiling height

TV cabinet

Living Rm
16 x 19-4

Brkfst/
Hearth
11 x 19-4

Kitchen
12-8 x 13-4

Ldry

W D

pantry

plant shelf above

11'
clg.ht.

10'-0" ceiling height

DN

slope

slope

decor. ceiling

UP

Foyer

Dining Rm
12 x 13-4

MBr 1
15 x 15-4

Garage
33-4 x 29-4

44'-0"

FIRST FLOOR

- *Impressive tiled Foyer with landing staircase leads into expansive Living Room with wall of windows overlooking rear yard*

- *Efficient U-shaped Kitchen with a work island/snackbar adjoining the Breakfast/Hearth area, Laundry, Garage and Dining Room*

- *Three additional bedrooms, one with private bath, have decorative windows and ample closet space*

- *Decorative ceiling crowns Dining Room with boxed window*

- *Private Master Bedroom Suite highlighted by arched window below sloped ceiling and plush bath with huge walk-in closet, double vanity and window tub*

$\mathcal{A}$rchitectural Details Create $\mathcal{A}$ppeal

PLAN INFO:

First Flr.	2,110 sq. ft.
Basement	2,096 sq. ft.
Garage	714 sq. ft.
Sq. Footage	2,110 sq. ft.
Foundation	Bsmt, Slab, Crawl space
Bedrooms	Three
Baths	2(Full), 1(Half)

*No materials list available

REFER TO PRICE CODE C

An EXCLUSIVE DESIGN
By Britt J. Willis

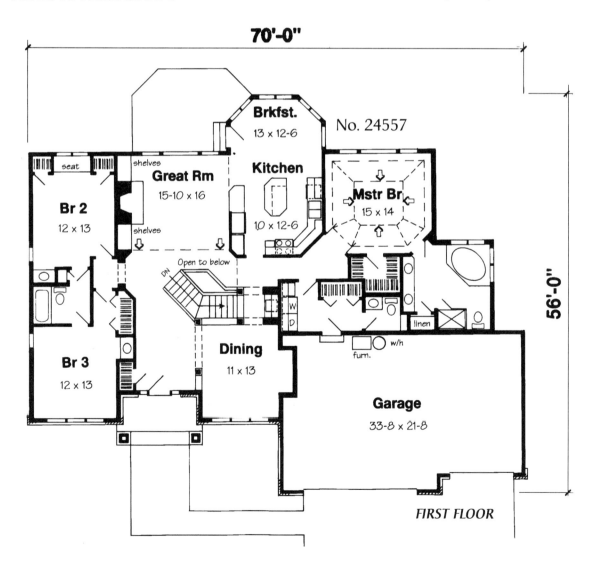

70'-0"

No. 24557

Brkfst.
13 x 12-6

Great Rm
15-10 x 16

Kitchen
10 x 12-6

Mstr Br
15 x 14

Br 2
12 x 13

shelves

shelves

Open to below

DN

Br 3
12 x 13

Dining
11 x 13

linen

w/h

fum.

Garage
33-8 x 21-8

seat

56'-0"

FIRST FLOOR

- *Covered entrance leads into gracious Foyer, Dining Room and Great Room*

- *Dining Room accented by decorative window and recessed area for hutch*

- *Bright and cozy Great Room offers focal point fireplace between built-in shelves and wall of windows overlooking rear yard*

- *Efficient Kitchen features island*

counter/snackbar and glass Breakfast alcove with access to deck

- *Private Master Bedroom suite pampers with decorative ceiling over wall of windows, walk-in closet, and plush bath with double vanity and corner window tub*

- *Two additional bedrooms with closets and private vanities share a full bath*

*S*tunning Manor Sure To Delight You

PLAN INFO:

First Flr.	*2,745 sq. ft.*
Second Flr.	*2,355 sq. ft.*
Garage	*3-car*
Sq. Footage	*5,100 sq. ft.*
Foundation	*Slab*
Bedrooms	*Four*
Baths	*2(Full), 1(Half)*

No materials list available

REFER TO PRICE CODE F

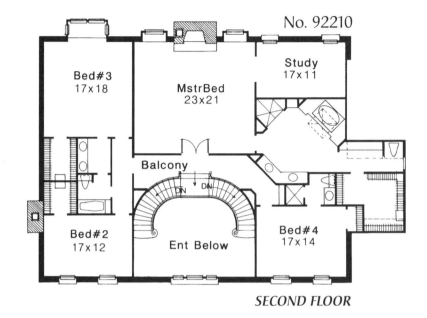

No. 92210

Bed#3
17x18

MstrBed
23x21

Study
17x11

Balcony

Bed#2
17x12

DN   DN

Ent Below

Bed#4
17x14

SECOND FLOOR

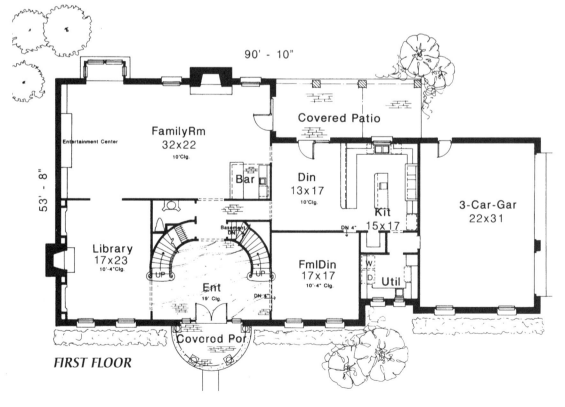

90' - 10"

53' - 8"

Entertainment Center

FamilyRm
32x22
10'Clg.

Covered Patio

Bar

Din
13x17
10'Clg.

Kit
15x17

3-Car-Gar
22x31

Library
17x23
10'-4"Clg.

Basement
DN

UP   UP

Ent
19' Clg

DN

FmlDin
17x17
10'-4" Clg.

W.
D.

Util

Coverod Por

FIRST FLOOR

■ *Distinctive covered porch escorts guests to the Entry highlighted by double curved staircase and 19-foot ceiling*

■ *Fireplaced Library with built-in shelving for extensive collection of books*

■ *Enormous Family Room extends cordial welcome to informal gatherings and private family relaxation with built-in entertainment center, fireplace, and full-sized wetbar*

■ *Spacious island Kitchen with huge walk-in pantry separated from Dinette by eating bar*

■ *Access to the swimming pool via the covered patio through Dinette or Family Room*

■ *Enter your Master Suite through double French doors to discover a personal fireplace, private study and skylit Bath with double sink vanity*

■ *Three additional bedrooms on the second floor feature adjoining Baths*

Distinctive Country Elegance

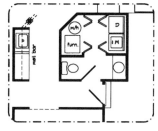

Optional Crawl Space/Slab Plan

PLAN INFO:

First Flr.	2,123 sq. ft.
Second Flr.	714 sq. ft.
Basement	2,123 sq. ft.
Garage	495 sq. ft.
Sq. Footage	2,837 sq. ft.
Foundation	Bsmt, Slab, Crawl space
Bedrooms	Three
Baths	2(Full), 1(Half)

*No materials list available

REFER TO PRICE CODE E

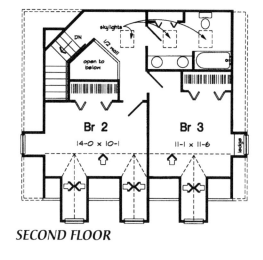

skylights

DN

1/2 hall

open to below

Br 2
14-0 x 10-1

Br 3
11-1 x 11-6

ledge

SECOND FLOOR

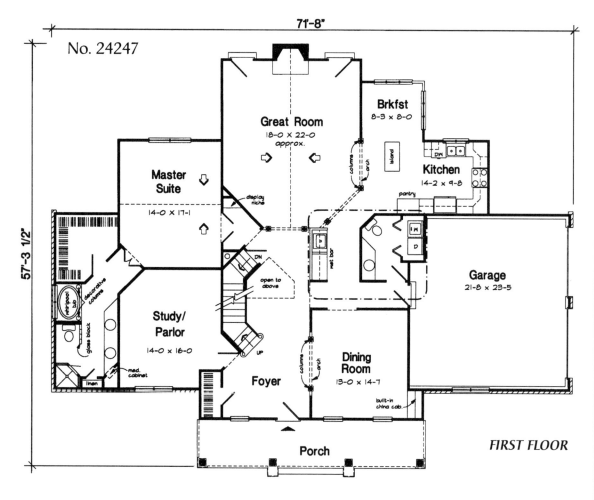

No. 24247

71'-8"

57'-3 1/2"

Great Room
18-0 x 22-0
approx.

display niche

columns
arch

Brkfst
8-3 x 8-0

island

Kitchen
14-2 x 9-8

pantry

Master Suite
14-0 x 17-1

DN

open to above

wet bar

whirlpool tub

decorative columns

glass block

Study/ Parlor
14-0 x 16-0

med. cabinet

linen

UP

Foyer

columns
arch

Dining Room
13-0 x 14-7

built-in china cab.

Garage
21-8 x 23-5

Porch

FIRST FLOOR

- ■ *Stately columns and arched windows enhance front porch leading into open Foyer with lovely, angled staircase*

- ■ *Formal Dining Room accented by built-in china cabinet and arched windows pleasingly repeated by arched entrance*

- ■ *Columns define the expansive Great Room with a large, hearth fireplace between the atrium doors to the rear yard, and a vaulted ceiling*

- ■ *Efficient, U-shaped Kitchen serves the glassed corner Breakfast area, the Great Room and the Dining Room beyond the wet bar*

- ■ *Double door into private Master Bedroom Suite with separate, huge walk-in closet, double vanity and whirlpool tub*

- ■ *Two additional bedrooms on second floor with dormers and over-sized closets share double vanity bath topped by skylights*

- ■ *Wonderful Study/Parlor behind staircase offers many options for living*

Ample Room To Grow As Your Needs Change

PLAN INFO:

First Flr.	*1,703 sq. ft.*
Second Flr.	*1,739 sq. ft.*
Bonus Rm.	*291 sq. ft.*
Garage	*3-car*
Sq. Footage	*3,733 sq. ft.*
Foundation	*Daylight Bsmt*
Bedrooms	*Four*
Baths	*3(Full), 1(Half)*

*No materials list available

REFER TO PRICE CODE F

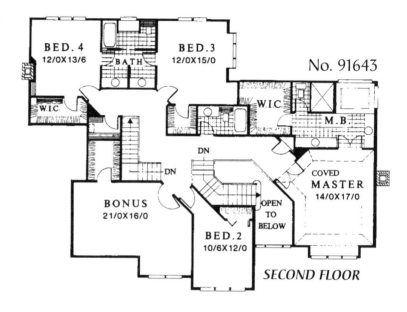

No. 91643

BED. 4
12/0X13/6

BED.3
12/0X15/0

BATH

W.I.C.

W.I.C.

M.B

BONUS
21/0X16/0

DN

DN

COVED
MASTER
14/0X17/0

OPEN
TO
BELOW

BED.2
10/6X12/0

SECOND FLOOR

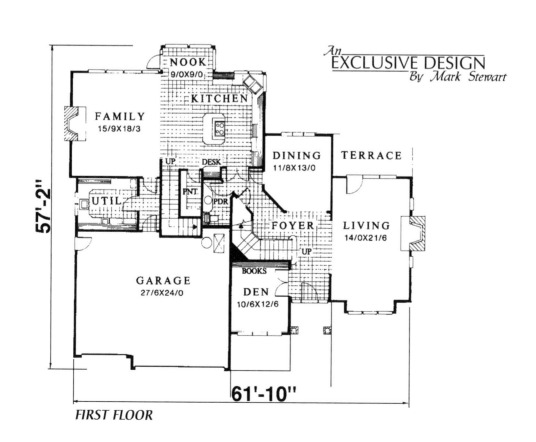

An
EXCLUSIVE DESIGN
By Mark Stewart

NOOK
9/0X9/0

KITCHEN

FAMILY
15/9X18/3

DINING
11/8X13/0

TERRACE

UP

DESK

PNT

PDR

FOYER

LIVING
14/0X21/6

UTIL

UP

GARAGE
27/6X24/0

BOOKS

DEN
10/6X12/6

57'-2"

61'-10"

FIRST FLOOR

- Hip-roofed covered porch enters to Foyer with interesting staircase and open floor plan offset by a convenient Powder Room

- Enormous island Kitchen features large Pantry, well-lighted Nook, cabinets galore and built-in desk for convenient meal-planning

- Bedroom Three and Bedroom Four both feature plenty of windows, walk-in closet, and each have their own vanity in shared full Bath

- Fireplaced Family Room flooded with light from extravagant window wall blends to Kitchen area

- Master Bath with double vanities, shower, tub, and private water closet leads to walk-in closet

- Upstairs hallway has second staircase for convenience and opens to Foyer below

- Huge Bonus Room with walk-in closet on second floor gives space for future expansion

*L*uxury Is *A*lways Popular

PLAN INFO:

First Flr.	2,579 sq. ft.
Second Flr.	997 sq. ft.
Basement	2,579 sq. ft.
Garage/Str.	1,001 sq. ft.
Sq. Footage	3,576 sq. ft.
Foundation	Basement
Bedrooms	Three
Baths	3(Full), 1(Half)

REFER TO PRICE CODE F

SECOND FLOOR

No. 10531

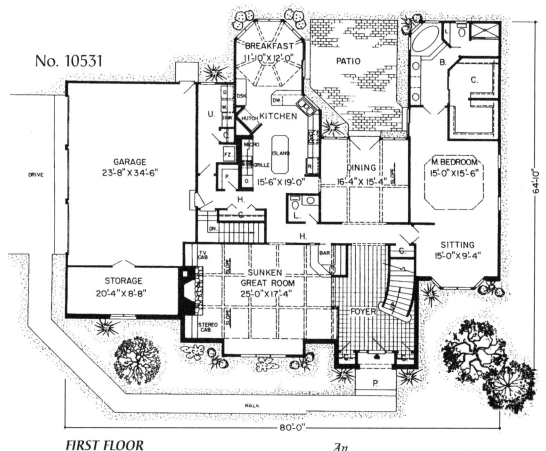

FIRST FLOOR

An
EXCLUSIVE DESIGN
By Karl Kreeger

- Step down to repose in the sunken Great Room featuring a bar, fireplace, and built-in cabinets for TV and stereo

- Fully-equipped Kitchen enjoys a sweeping view of the patio and opens to a stunning Breakfast Nook

- Unusual ceiling treatments in most rooms completes the fabulous impressiveness of this home

- Two additional bedrooms upstairs feature private baths and walk-in closets

- 3-car Garage includes extra storage space

- Bridge-like Balcony on second level overlooks Dining Room to the rear and Foyer on the front

- Luxurious Master Bedroom featuring a sunny Sitting Room with a bay window away from noisy living areas offers quiet solitude

- His-n-her walk-in closets offer plenty of storage space in Master Bedroom

Elegant Touches Add To Comfortable Living

PLAN INFO:

First Flr.	*1,574 sq. ft.*
Second Flr.	*1,098 sq. ft.*
Basement	*1,574 sq. ft.*
Garage	*522 sq. ft.*
Sq. Footage	*2,672 sq. ft.*
Foundation	*Bsmt, Slab, Crawl space*
Bedrooms	*Three or Four*
Baths	*3(Full)*

*No materials list available

REFER TO PRICE CODE E

OPEN TO BELOW

BEDROOM
11'-8"x12'-0"

LIN BATH

OPTIONAL
FIREPLACE

MASTER BEDROOM
VAULTED CEILING
17'-0"x16'-0"

HIS

DN

OPEN
TO
BELOW

BEDROOM
11'-6"x15'-0"

LINEN

MASTER BATH

HERS

SECOND FLOOR

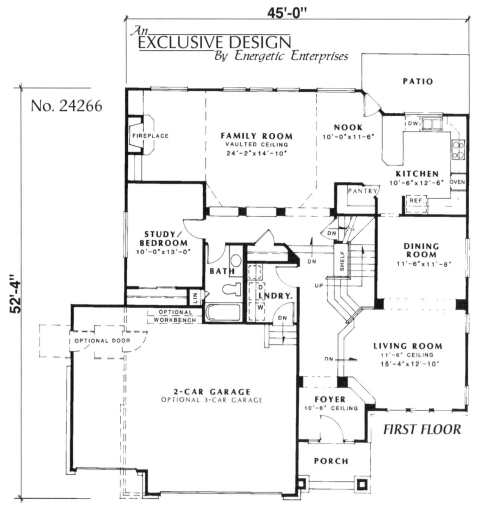

45'-0"

An EXCLUSIVE DESIGN
By Energetic Enterprises

No. 24266

52'-4"

PATIO

FIREPLACE

FAMILY ROOM
VAULTED CEILING
24'-2"x14'-10"

NOOK
10'-0"x11'-6"

DW

KITCHEN
10'-6"x12'-6"

OVEN

PANTRY

REF.

STUDY/
BEDROOM
10'-0"x13'-0"

BATH

DN

SHELF

DN

UP

DINING
ROOM
11'-6"x11'-8"

D LNDRY.
W

LIN

OPTIONAL
WORKBENCH

OPTIONAL DOOR

DN

2-CAR GARAGE
OPTIONAL 3-CAR GARAGE

DN

LIVING ROOM
11'-6" CEILING
15'-4"x12'-10"

FOYER
10'-6" CEILING

FIRST FLOOR

PORCH

- Sheltered entrance leads into Foyer with striking, angled staircase, step-down Living and Dining Rooms

- Efficient Kitchen offers walk-in pantry, peninsula counter and glass eating Nook with access to Patio, opens to Family Room

- Expansive Family Room with vaulted ceiling tops, built-in fireplace and wall of windows overlooking rear yard

- Lavish Master-Bedroom wing accented by corner fireplace, his-n-her closets and over-sized bath with corner garden tub and two vanities

- Two additional bedrooms with large closets share full bath with window tub

- Dramatic windows accent spacious Living and Dining Rooms

*M*aster *B*edroom *T*ruly *A* *S*anctuary

PLAN INFO:

First Flr.	*2,864 sq. ft.*
Garage	*607 sq. ft.*
Sq. Footage	*2,864 sq. ft.*
Foundation	*Slab*
Bedrooms	*Four*
Baths	*3(Full), 1(Half)*

REFER TO PRICE CODE E

No. 10451

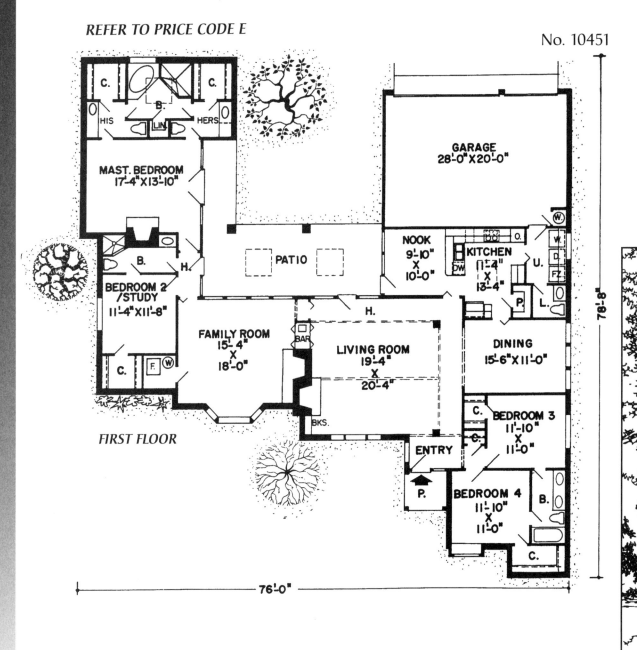

MAST. BEDROOM
17'-4" X 13'-10"

GARAGE
28'-0" X 20'-0"

PATIO

NOOK
9'-10"
X
10'-0"

KITCHEN
11'-4"
X
13'-4"

BEDROOM 2
/STUDY
11'-4" X 11'-8"

FAMILY ROOM
15'-4"
X
18'-0"

BAR

LIVING ROOM
19'-4"
X
20'-4"

DINING
15'-6" X 11'-0"

BKS.

ENTRY

BEDROOM 3
11'-10"
X
11'-0"

P.

BEDROOM 4
11'-10"
X
11'-0"

78'-8"

76'-0"

FIRST FLOOR

■ *A courtyard effect is created by glassed-in living spaces overlooking the central covered patio with skylights*

■ *Dual fireplace in the Family and Living Rooms and a wetbar are the touches that help to set this house apart*

■ *An abundance of amenities and easy access to the Dining Room and the*

Nook area make the Kitchen an efficient, well-appointed room

■ *A secluded sanctuary of your own, the Master Bedroom is a generous space with its charming fireplace, individual dressing rooms, and skylit Bath*

■ *Two additional bedrooms have private access to a full double vanity Bath*

*E*xquisite *A*rchitectural *D*etail *I*n *A* *S*ingle-*L*evel *D*esign

PLAN INFO:

First Flr.	*3,292 sq. ft.*
Garage	*3-car*
Sq. Footage	*3,292 sq. ft.*
Foundation	*Slab*
Bedrooms	*Four*
Baths	*Three*

*No materials list available

REFER TO PRICE CODE F

No. 92209

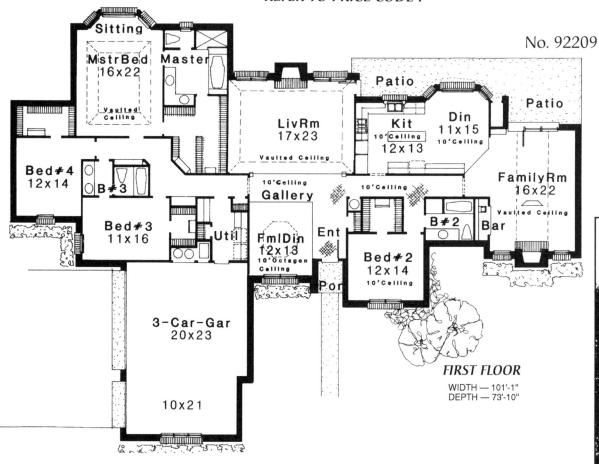

FIRST FLOOR

WIDTH — 101'-1"
DEPTH — 73'-10"

- *Walk through formal Entry to impressive Living Room with fireplace wall framed by unusual window display*

- *Central hallway with 10-foot ceiling escorts one through the Gallery to the quiet sleeping wing*

- *Master Bedroom with a vaulted ceiling enjoys a comfortable Sitting Area with bay window*

- *Expansive split walk-in closet in Master Suite connects to Bath with a twin basin vanity*

- *Two additional bedrooms with walk-in closets share a full Bath*

- *Just steps away from the Kitchen is the Dining Room formalized with a 10-foot octagon ceiling*

- *Large island Kitchen flows into Dinette with bay windows for informal family meals*

- *Family Room sports many amenities such as a wetbar, exclusive access to the backyard patio and uncommon windows framing the fireplace*

High Impact Two-Story Angled Design

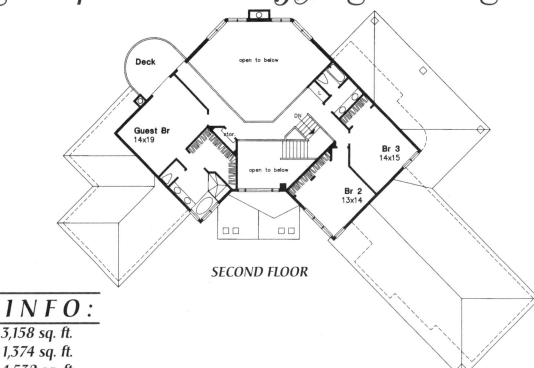

SECOND FLOOR

PLAN INFO:

First Flr.	*3,158 sq. ft.*
Second Flr.	*1,374 sq. ft.*
Sq. Footage	*4,532 sq. ft.*
Foundation	*Slab*
Bedrooms	*Four*
Baths	*3(Full), 1(Half)*

*No materials list available

REFER TO PRICE CODE F

No. 99373

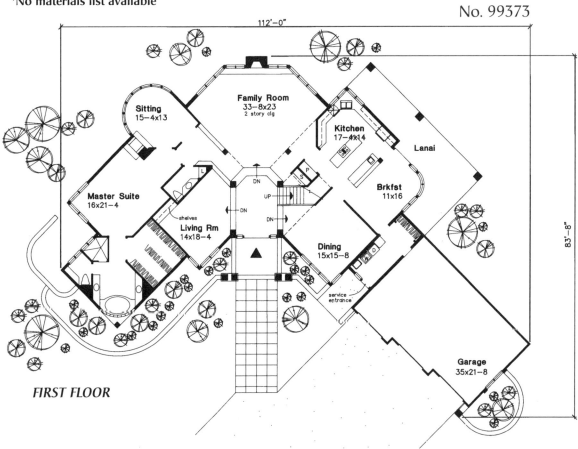

FIRST FLOOR

- *Gracious living abounds in this high impact home with a two-story entry-way and double doors with a full transom*

- *The fireplace and window walls of the large two-story Family Room can been seen from the entrance*

- *Entertaining is a joy in the gourmet Kitchen and Breakfast area that opens to a covered Lanai*

- *Spacious and unique Master Suite has a semi-circular window wall and see-through fireplace perfect for romantic, cozy evenings*

- *A more than accommodating Guest Suite has its own private deck and a walk-in closet*

- *Two additional bedrooms with ample closet space share a full, double vanity hall Bath*

$\mathcal{E}$ye-Catching Keystones

PLAN INFO:

First Flr.	*1,383 sq. ft.*
Second Flr.	*181 sq. ft.*
Bonus	*172 sq. ft.*
Basement	*2, sq. ft.*
Garage/Shop	*675 sq. ft.*
Sq. Footage	*2,564 sq. ft.*
Foundation	*Crawl space*
Bedrooms	*Four*
Baths	*2(Full), 1(Half)*

*No materials list available

REFER TO PRICE CODE D

An EXCLUSIVE DESIGN
By Mark Stewart

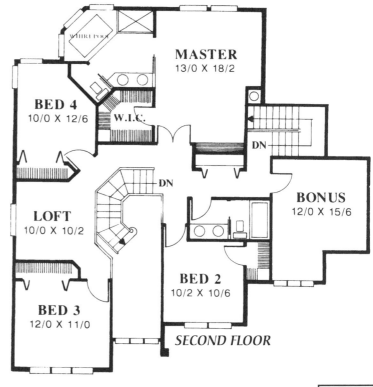

MASTER
13/0 X 18/2

BED 4
10/0 X 12/6

W.I.C.

WHRL POOL

DN

LOFT
10/0 X 10/2

DN

BONUS
12/0 X 15/6

BED 2
10/2 X 10/6

BED 3
12/0 X 11/0

SECOND FLOOR

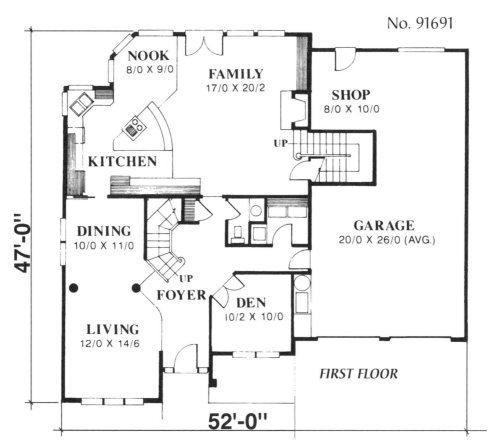

No. 91691

NOOK
8/0 X 9/0

FAMILY
17/0 X 20/2

SHOP
8/0 X 10/0

UP

KITCHEN

GARAGE
20/0 X 26/0 (AVG.)

DINING
10/0 X 11/0

UP

FOYER

DEN
10/2 X 10/0

LIVING
12/0 X 14/6

47'-0"

52'-0"

FIRST FLOOR

- *Impressive glass arched entry leads into the Foyer with a curved stairway and pillars defining the Living and Dining areas*

- *An open, efficient Kitchen with cooktop, snackbar island and ample counter and storage space, easily serves glass eating Nook, Family and Dining Rooms*

- *A Bonus Room offers many options*

- *An expansive Family Room accented by a cozy fireplace, built-in shelves, a wall of glass with access to rear yard and a rear staircase to second floor*

- *A luxurious Master suite features built-in wall, walk-in closet, twin sinks and garden whirlpool tub*

- *Three additional bedrooms with ample closet space share a full bath*

Eye-Catching Glass Turrets

PLAN INFO:

First Flr.	*1,592 sq. ft.*
Second Flr.	*958 sq. ft.*
Bonus Room	*194 sq. ft.*
Basement	*2, sq. ft.*
Garage	*750 sq. ft.*
Sq. Footage	*2,550 sq. ft.*
Foundation	*Crawl space*
Bedrooms	*Three*
Baths	*3(Full)*

REFER TO PRICE CODE D

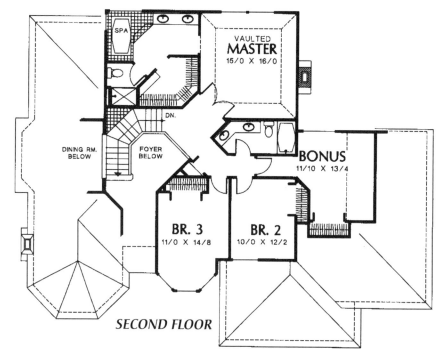

SECOND FLOOR

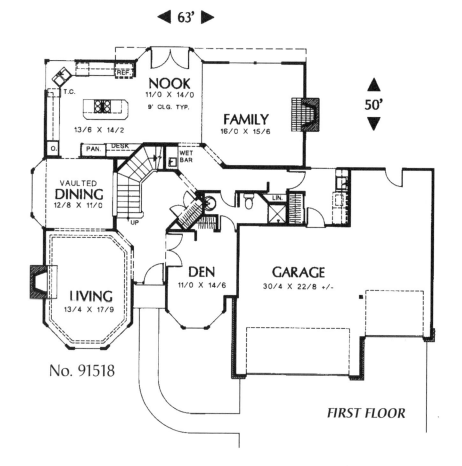

No. 91518

FIRST FLOOR

■ *An elegant two-story Foyer with gracefully curved staircase opens into unique Living Room with an alcove of windows and warm fireplace topped by decorative ceiling*

■ *Another alcove of glass and vaulted ceiling accent open Dining area between Living Room and Kitchen*

■ *A cooktop island snackbar center of dream Kitchen with built-in pantry and desk, ample counter and storage space, and an eating Nook with double door to outdoors*

■ *Expansive Family Room, adjacent to Kitchen area, highlighted by large, hearth fireplace and sliding glass door to rear yard*

■ *Double door leads graciously into Master suite with a vaulted ceiling and ultra bath with walk-in closet, raised spa tub and double vanity*

■ *Two additional bedrooms, one with an alcove of glass, share a full double-vanity bath*

■ *A Bonus Room offers many options*

Arched Windows And Detailed Pediments

PLAN INFO:

First Flr.	*1,245 sq. ft.*
Second Flr.	*1,333 sq. ft.*
Bonus	*181 sq. ft.*
Basement	*1,245 sq. ft.*
Garage	*568 sq. ft.*
Sq. Footage	*2,578 sq. ft.*
Foundation	*Bsmt, Slab,*
	Crawl space
Bedrooms	*Three*
Baths	*2(Full), 1(Half)*

*No materials list available

REFER TO PRICE CODE D

50'-0"

46'-0"

Porch
12-0 x 15-1

Family Rm
18-8 x 15-5

Brkfst
9-6 x 15-5

Kitchen

island

9-0 x 15-5

pantry

desk

Garage
21-5 x 27-0

DN

open to above

UP

Dining Rm
13-5 x 11-9

columns

Foyer

Living Rm
13-5 x 14-0

FIRST FLOOR

An
EXCLUSIVE DESIGN
By Plan One Homes, Inc.

No. 24653

Br 2
11-8 x 12-4

Br 3
11-8 x 12-5

optional skylight

DN

railing

D

W

Common
9-5 x 13-8

open to below

Bonus
11-4 x 15-8

Mstr. Suite
18-4 x 13-4

linen

SECOND FLOOR

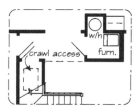

w/h

crawl access

furn.

**Crawl Space/
Slab Option**

- *An enclosed entry leads into two-story Foyer with dramatic, angled staircase and Living Room/Dining Room defined by columns*

- *Gracious Living Room accented by arched window below vaulted ceiling and Dining Room with another decorative window*

- *Large, U-shaped Kitchen features walk-in pantry, built-in desk and work island serving Breakfast area and Family Room beyond*

- *Expansive Family Room accented by hearth fireplace and bay window leads to covered Porch and Garage*

- *Luxurious Master Suite with huge walk-in closet, tray ceiling and plush bath with two vanities and whirlpool window tub*

- *Two additional bedrooms share double-vanity bath, laundry and Common area with skylight*

- *Bonus area offers many options*

$\mathscr{E}$legant Curved Staircase $\mathscr{A}$dds Grace

PLAN INFO:

First Flr.	*1,675 sq. ft.*
Second Flr.	*1,032 sq. ft.*
Bonus	*450 sq. ft.*
Basement	*702 sq. ft.*
Garage	*857 sq. ft.*
Sq. Footage	*2,707 sq. ft.*
Foundation	*Bsmt, Slab,*
	Crawl space
Bedrooms	*Three*
Baths	*2(Full), 1(Half)*

REFER TO PRICE CODE E

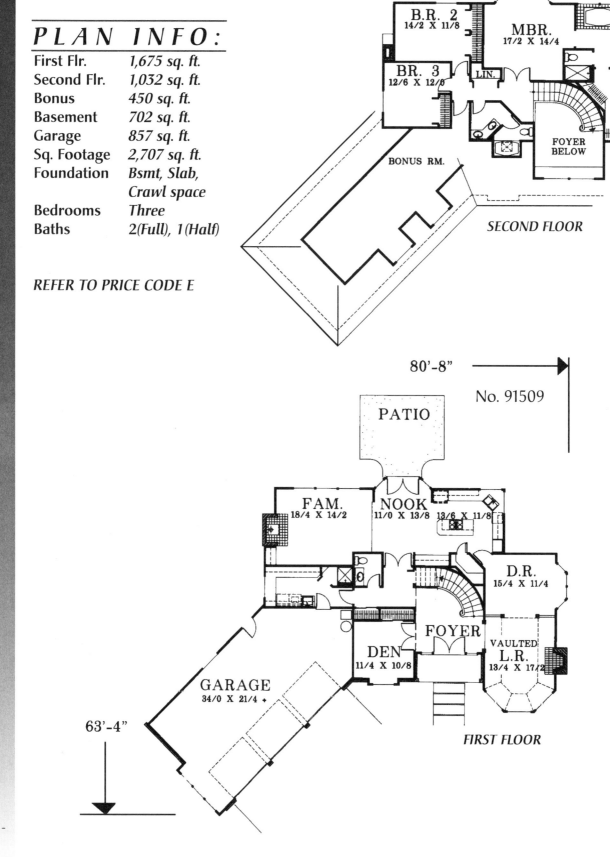

B.R. 2
14/2 X 11/8

MBR.
17/2 X 14/4

B.R. 3
12/6 X 12/8

LIN.

FOYER BELOW

BONUS RM.

SECOND FLOOR

80'-8"

No. 91509

PATIO

FAM.
18/4 X 14/2

NOOK
11/0 X 13/8

13/6 X 11/8

D.R.
15/4 X 11/4

FOYER

DEN
11/4 X 10/8

VAULTED L.R.
13/4 X 17/2

GARAGE
34/0 X 21/4

63'-4"

FIRST FLOOR

■ *Wide, covered entrance into bright two-story Foyer with unique curved staircase*

■ *Gracious entertaining in Living Room with cozy fireplace and alcove windows topped by vaulted ceiling*

■ *Efficient Kitchen with island cooktop and walk-in pantry serves Dining Room, Nook and Patio beyond*

■ *Quiet Den offers many options*

■ *Master Bedroom suite, highlighted by bay window, offers plush bath with double vanity, window tub and huge walk-in closet*

■ *Two additional bedrooms with large closets share double vanity bath and Bonus Room*

Stone & Stucco Give This House Class

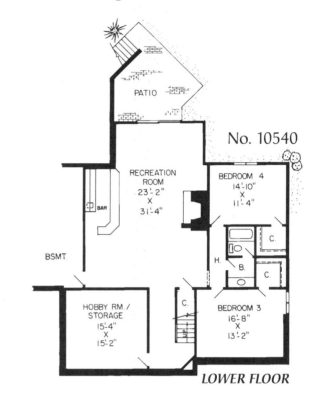

No. 10540

PLAN INFO:

Main Flr.	2,473 sq. ft.
Lower Flr.	1,624 sq. ft.
Basement	732 sq. ft.
Garage/Str.	732 sq. ft.
Sq. Footage	4,097 sq. ft.
Foundation	Basement
Bedrooms	Four
Baths	Three

REFER TO PRICE CODE F

LOWER FLOOR

- RECREATION ROOM 23'-2" X 31'-4"
- BEDROOM 4 14'-10" X 11'-4"
- PATIO
- BAR
- BSMT.
- HOBBY RM. / STORAGE 15'-4" X 15'-2"
- BEDROOM 3 16'-8" X 13'-2"

An
EXCLUSIVE DESIGN
By Karl Kreeger

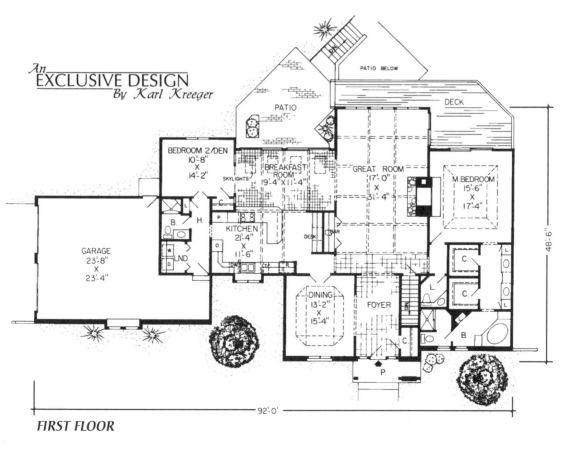

- BEDROOM 2/DEN 10'-8" X 14'-2"
- BREAKFAST ROOM 19'-4" X 11'-4"
- GREAT ROOM 17'-0" X 31'-4"
- M. BEDROOM 15'-6" X 17'-4"
- PATIO
- DECK
- PATIO BELOW
- GARAGE 23'-8" X 23'-4"
- KITCHEN 21'-4" X 11'-6"
- DINING 13'-2" X 15'-4"
- FOYER
- SKYLIGHTS
- DESK
- BAR
- 48'-6"
- 92'-0"

FIRST FLOOR

- *Majestic Foyer creates a stunning first impression and flows into the formal Dining Room and Great Room*

- *A stone fireplace, built-in wetbar and access to a spacious deck add to the convenience and luxury of the Great Room*

- *Large Recreation Room on the lower level includes a built-in wetbar and a fireplace*

- *Dream Kitchen includes a peninsula extension counter, built-in planning center, double sink and an abundance of counter and storage space*

- *A beamed Breakfast Room includes natural illumination from skylights and access to the patio, providing a sunny way to start the morning*

- *Huge Master Suite is equipped with a dressing room with his-n-her walk-in closets and a separate whirlpool Bath*

- *Two additional bedrooms, both with walk-in closets, share a full hall Bath*

Grand Room Designs & An Elegant Facade Spell Luxury

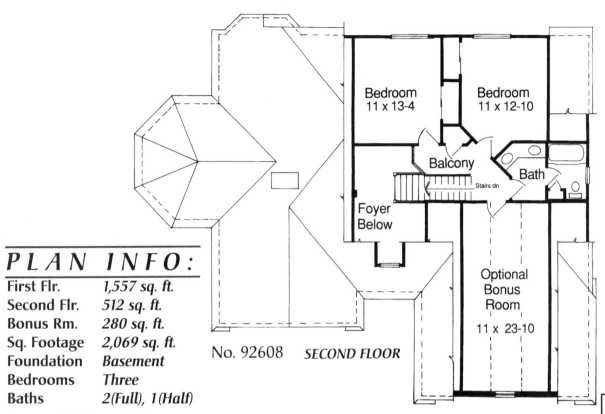

No. 92608   *SECOND FLOOR*

Bedroom
11 x 13-4

Bedroom
11 x 12-10

Balcony

Bath

Foyer Below

Stairs dn

Optional Bonus Room
11 x 23-10

PLAN INFO:

First Flr.	*1,557 sq. ft.*
Second Flr.	*512 sq. ft.*
Bonus Rm.	*280 sq. ft.*
Sq. Footage	*2,069 sq. ft.*
Foundation	*Basement*
Bedrooms	*Three*
Baths	*2(Full), 1(Half)*

*No materials list available

REFER TO PRICE CODE C

1/2 Circle window above

Breakfast
9-6 x 14-8

Kitchen
10 x 16-4

Bath

Lin.

Master Bedroom
15 x 13

Pass thru

Dining Room
14 x 13-2

Pantry

Ent. Ctr.

Hall

Laun.

Walk-in closet

Stairs up

WIDTH 57'-6"
DEPTH 45'-0"

Sunken Great Room
16-4 x 16-4

Slope ceiling → ← Slope ceiling

Foyer

Two-car Garage
20 x 20

FIRST FLOOR

- Naturally lighted by an arched dormer window, the two-story Foyer welcomes guests

- A grand, sunken Great Room has a cathedral ceiling and a stone fireplace

- Dramatic angular views can be seen from the octagonal shaped formal Dining Room

- Central work island, built-in pantry, abundant counter and cabinet space, and a sunny Breakfast Room with outdoor access, make this Kitchen outstanding

- Perfect for empty nesters or families with teenagers, the first floor Master Suite allows parents complete privacy

- Three additional bedrooms, located on the second floor, share a full hall Bath and a Bonus Room

Imposing Traditional Style

PLAN INFO:

First Flr.	*1,717 sq. ft.*
Second Flr.	*1,544 sq. ft.*
Bonus	*230 sq. ft.*
Basement	*1,717 sq. ft.*
Garage	*506 sq. ft.*
Sq. Footage	*3,261 sq. ft.*
Foundation	*Bsmt, Slab, Crawl space*
Bedrooms	*Three*
Baths	*3(Full), 1(Half)*

*No materials list available

REFER TO PRICE CODE F

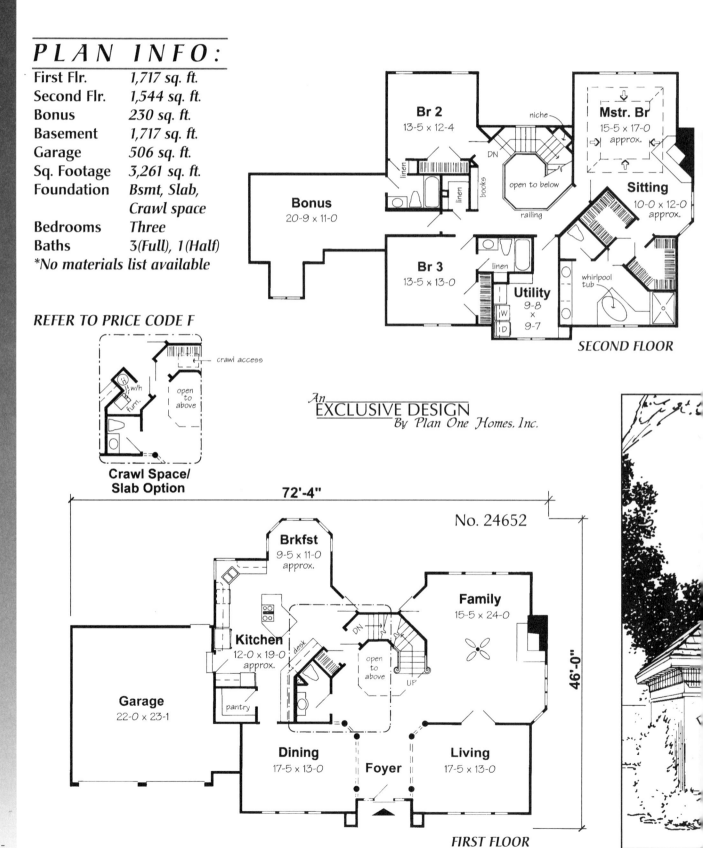

crawl access

w/h

open to above

furn.

Crawl Space/ Slab Option

An
EXCLUSIVE DESIGN
By Plan One Homes, Inc.

Br 2
13-5 x 12-4

niche

Mstr. Br
15-5 x 17-0
approx.

DN

linen

books

linen

open to below

railing

Sitting
10-0 x 12-0
approx.

Bonus
20-9 x 11-0

Br 3
13-5 x 13-0

linen

whirlpool tub

Utility
9-8 x 9-7

W

D

SECOND FLOOR

72'-4"

Brkfst
9-5 x 11-0
approx.

No. 24652

Family
15-5 x 24-0

desk

Kitchen
12-0 x 19-0
approx.

DN

open to above

UP

46'-0"

Garage
22-0 x 23-1

pantry

Dining
17-5 x 13-0

Foyer

Living
17-5 x 13-0

FIRST FLOOR

- *Inviting front door with sidelights sheltered by keystone arch leads into an open Foyer accented by an elegant curved stairway*

- *Formal, but airy Living and Dining rooms with large decorative windows provide ease in entertaining*

- *Double door into Family room reveals a cozy fireplace, another decorative window and access to rear yard*

- *Over-sized, but efficient Kitchen features ample counter and storage space, walk-in pantry and cooktop island serving glassed Breakfast alcove*

- *Spacious Master Bedroom suite accented by tray ceiling and warm fireplace features two walk-in closets and a plush bath with a double vanity and whirlpool garden tub*

- *Two additional bedrooms offer ample closet space and private baths*

- *Bonus Room offers many options*

Designed For Simple, Yet Elegant Living

PLAN INFO:

First Flr.	*1,807 sq. ft.*
Second Flr.	*1,359 sq. ft.*
Basement	*1,807 sq. ft.*
Garage	*576 sq. ft.*
Sq. Footage	*3,166 sq. ft.*
Foundation	*Basement*
Bedrooms	*Three*
Baths	*3(Full), 1(Half)*

REFER TO PRICE CODE E

SECOND FLOOR

No. 20353

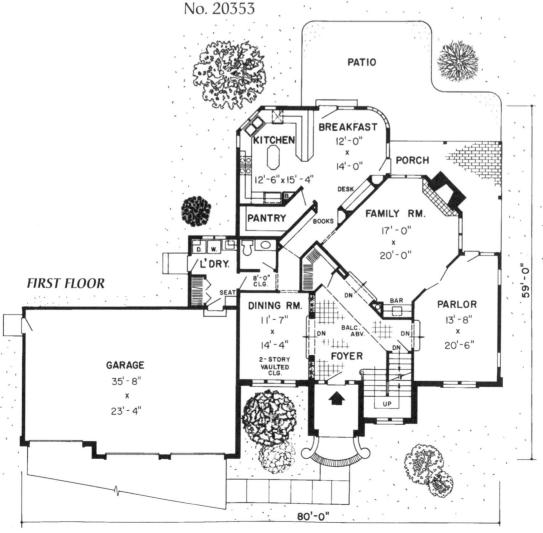

FIRST FLOOR

■ *Magnificent home creates formidable impression after dark*

■ *Numerous arched windows glowing with light extend warm welcome to visitors*

■ *Inside find skylights, vaulted ceilings, and multiple levels rendering an interior equally as exciting as exterior*

■ *Step from the skylit central Foyer into the vaulted Dining Room, cozy Parlor, and Family Room with built-in bar*

■ *Walk down the book-lined hallway to the island Kitchen, Breakfast Nook with built-in desk and unique curved glass wall overlooking backyard patio*

■ *Master Suite complemented by elegant pan vaulted ceiling, fireplace for romantic evenings, private deck, and garden spa*

■ *At either end of the upstairs Balcony, find bedrooms each with individual baths and spacious closets*

Gable And Glass Grace Facade

No. 91640

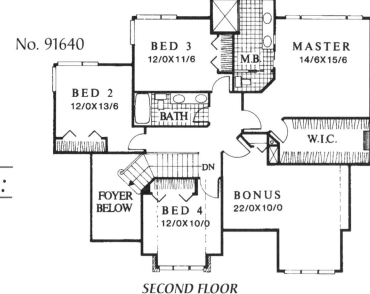

SECOND FLOOR

PLAN INFO:

First Flr.	*1,540 sq. ft.*
Second Flr.	*1,178 sq. ft.*
Bonus Room	*222 sq. ft.*
Sq. Footage	*2,718 sq. ft.*
Foundation	*Post & Beam*
Bedrooms	*Four*
Baths	*2 (Full), 1 (Half)*

*No materials list available

REFER TO PRICE CODE E

An
EXCLUSIVE DESIGN
By Mark Stewart

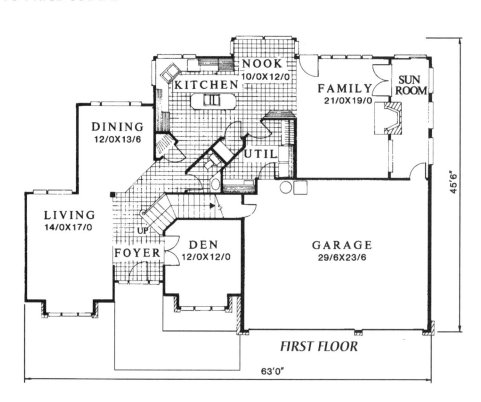

FIRST FLOOR

63'0"

45'6"

- *A stunning blend of Traditional and Contemporary styles create this gracious home*

- *A unique Sun Room opens directly into the Family Room and provides access to an over-sized three car Garage*

- *A modern wrap-around Kitchen with a central island commands the ground floor*

- *Entertaining is both enjoyable and easy because of the design of the Living and Dining Rooms*

- *The imposing Master Suite includes an elegant Bath and a large walk-in closet*

- *Three nice size, additional bedrooms share a full hall Bath*

*W*elcoming *Foyer Makes*
A Lasting Impression

No. 10501

PLAN INFO:

First Flr.	*2,419 sq. ft.*
Second Flr.	*926 sq. ft.*
Basement	*2,419 sq. ft.*
Garage	*615 sq. ft.*
Sq. Footage	*3,345 sq. ft.*
Foundation	*Basement*
Bedrooms	*Four*
Baths	*3(Full), 1(Half)*

REFER TO PRICE CODE F

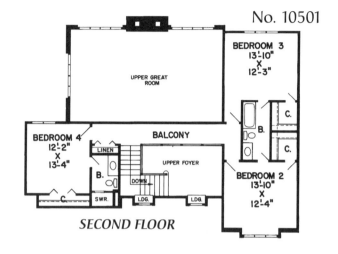

SECOND FLOOR

An
EXCLUSIVE DESIGN
By Karl Kreeger

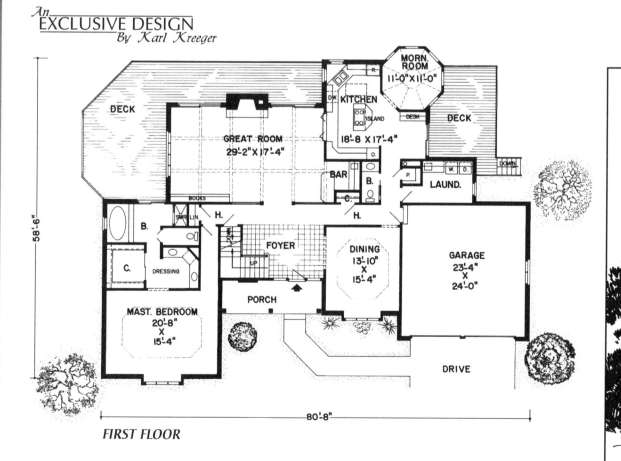

FIRST FLOOR

- *Massive Foyer makes a wonderful first impression in this tastefully appointed design*

- *Fantastic Great Room enlarged by a wrap-around deck and highlighted by a fireplace, built-in shelves and a wetbar*

- *An octagonal Morning Room and a central work island make the Kitchen unique and convenient*

- *Dinner parties will be successful in the formal Dining Room featuring a distinctive box bay window*

- *Inviting Master Suite equipped with a spacious dressing area and a separate and luxurious Bath*

- *A Balcony overlooks the Great Room and the open Foyer and provides access to three bedrooms and two full Bathrooms*

Inviting And Comfortable

PLAN INFO:

First Flr.	1,574 sq. ft.
Second Flr.	1,098 sq. ft.
Basement	1,398 sq. ft.
Garage	522 sq. ft.
Sq. Footage	2,672 sq. ft.
Foundation	Bsmt, Slab, Crawl space
Bedrooms	Three or Four
Baths	3(Full)

REFER TO PRICE CODE E

OPEN TO BELOW

BEDROOM
11'-8"x12'-0"

LIN.   BATH

OPTIONAL FIREPLACE

MASTER BEDROOM
VAULTED CEILING
17'-0"x16'-0"

HIS

DN

OPEN TO BELOW

BEDROOM
11'-6"x15'-0"

LINEN

SECOND FLOOR

MASTER BATH

HERS

An
EXCLUSIVE DESIGN
By Energetic Enterprises

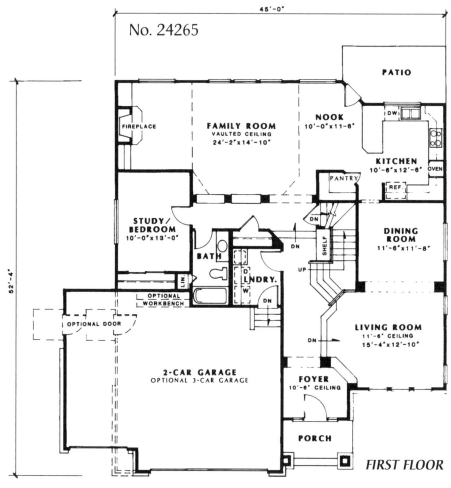

No. 24265

45'-0"

52'-4"

PATIO

FIREPLACE

FAMILY ROOM
VAULTED CEILING
24'-2"x14'-10"

NOOK
10'-0"x11'-6"

DW

KITCHEN
10'-6"x12'-6"

OVEN

PANTRY

REF.

STUDY/
BEDROOM
10'-0"x13'-0"

BATH

D
W

LNDRY.

DN

SHELF

DN

UP

DINING ROOM
11'-6"x11'-8"

OPTIONAL
WORKBENCH

LIN.

DN

LIVING ROOM
11'-6" CEILING
15'-4"x12'-10"

OPTIONAL DOOR

2-CAR GARAGE
OPTIONAL 3-CAR GARAGE

FOYER
10'-6" CEILING

DN

PORCH

FIRST FLOOR

- *Covered Porch highlighted by transom window above front door leads into an open Foyer with dramatic, angled staircase*

- *Open expanse of Living and Dining Rooms with decorative windows offers easy but elegant entertaining*

- *An efficient Kitchen features walk-in pantry and peninsula counter serving eating Nook Family Room and Patio*

- *Spacious Family Room with a wall of windows and cozy fireplace between built-ins topped by vaulted ceiling*

- *Quiet Study/Bedroom on first floor provides multiple uses*

- *Luxurious Master Bedroom suite accented by vaulted ceiling and huge Master Bath with corner, garden tub, double vanity and his and her closets*

- *Two additional bedrooms share a full bath*

*J*Heavenly Kitchen For The Gourmet Of The House

PLAN INFO:

First Flr.	*3,307 sq. ft.*
Second Flr.	*837 sq. ft.*
Porch/Patio	*382 sq. ft.*
Garage	*646 sq. ft.*
Sq. Footage	*4,144 sq. ft.*
Foundation	*Slab*
Bedrooms	*Five*
Baths	*4(Full), 1(Half)*

REFER TO PRICE CODE F

No. 10417

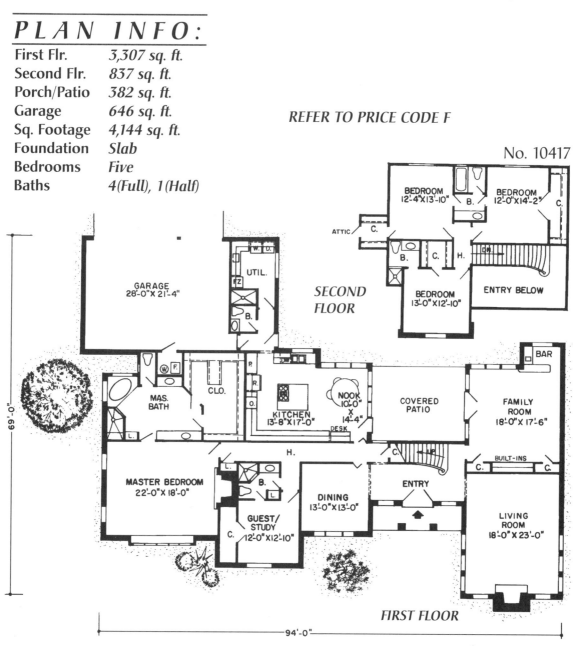

SECOND FLOOR

BEDROOM 12'-4"X13'-10"
BEDROOM 12'-0"X14'-2"
ATTIC
C.
B.
B.
C.
H.
BEDROOM 13'-0"X12'-10"
ENTRY BELOW

FIRST FLOOR

GARAGE 28'-0"X 21'-4"
UTIL.
W. D.
FZ.
B.
MAS. BATH
CLO.
W. F.
P.
R.
O.
KITCHEN 13'-8"X17'-0"
DESK
NOOK 10'-0" X 14'-4"
COVERED PATIO
BAR
FAMILY ROOM 18'-0"X 17'-6"
BUILT-INS
C.
C.
MASTER BEDROOM 22'-0"X 18'-0"
L.
B.
H.
GUEST/ STUDY 12'-0"X12'-10"
C.
DINING 13'-0"X13'-0"
ENTRY
LIVING ROOM 18'-0" X 23'-0"

69'-0"
94'-0"

- Kitchen affords 60 square feet of counter space

- Step-saving cooking island adds more culinary area

- Windowed Eating Nook and nearby patio extend convenience and brilliance to spacious Kitchen

- Large Master Bedroom with walk-in closet situated away from noisy living areas

- Study easily doubles as Guest Room

- Ten-foot ceilings throughout lower level

- Nine-foot ceilings upstairs add to spaciousness created by large rooms

- Double doors usher you into two-story Entry with staircase curving gently to second-level rooms

Country Touches Throughout
This Modern Design

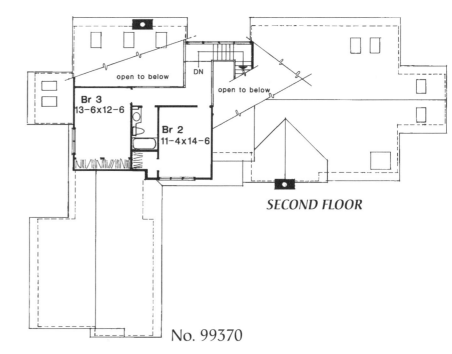

SECOND FLOOR

Br 3
13-6x12-6

Br 2
11-4x14-6

open to below

open to below

DN

PLAN INFO:

First Flr.	*2,389 sq. ft.*
Second Flr.	*673 sq. ft.*
Basement	*1,348 sq. ft.*
Garage	*2-car*
Sq. Footage	*3,062 sq. ft.*
Foundation	*Basement*
Bedrooms	*Three*
Baths	*Three*

No. 99370

REFER TO PRICE CODE E

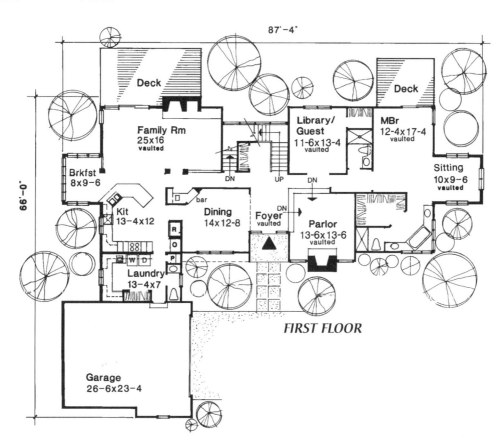

87'-4"

66'-0"

Deck

Deck

Family Rm
25x16
vaulted

Library/
Guest
11-6x13-4
vaulted

MBr
12-4x17-4
vaulted

Brkfst
8x9-6

Sitting
10x9-6
vaulted

Kit
13-4x12

bar

Dining
14x12-8

Foyer
vaulted

Parlor
13-6x13-6
vaulted

UP

DN

DN

DN

Laundry
13-4x7

Garage
26-6x23-4

FIRST FLOOR

- *Front projections and gables give a custom look and the special interior finishes and flourishes are plentiful*

- *Impressive Foyer with a view through to the backyard features an angular staircase*

- *Invite guests to step down into your vaulted Parlor*

- *Uniquely shaped Kitchen includes many modern conveniences*

- *Breakfast alcove juts out between the island Kitchen and Family Room for early morning repast*

- *Vast Family Room with a vaulted ceiling, fireplace, and wetbar offers the perfect place for entertaining*

- *Library located in quiet side of house can double as a Guest Room with ample closet space*

- *Master Suite has an adjoining Sitting Room, secluded luxurious Bath and a walk-in wardrobe*

- *Second floor houses two additional bedrooms with individual closets and an adjoining Bath*

Bay Windows With Seats Overlook Porch

PLAN INFO:

First Flr.	1,584 sq. ft.
Second Flr.	1,277 sq. ft.
Basement	1,584 sq. ft.
Garage	550 sq. ft.
Sq. Footage	2,861 sq. ft.
Foundation	Bsmt, Slab, Crawl space
Bedrooms	Four
Baths	2(Full), 1(Half)

No materials list available

REFER TO PRICE CODE E

An
EXCLUSIVE DESIGN
By Britt J. Willis

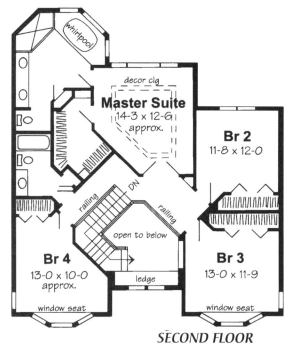

Master Suite
14-3 x 12-6
approx.

decor clg

whirlpool

Br 2
11-8 x 12-0

DN

railing   railing

open to below

Br 4
13-0 x 10-0
approx.

Br 3
13-0 x 11-9

ledge

window seat   window seat

SECOND FLOOR

No. 24563

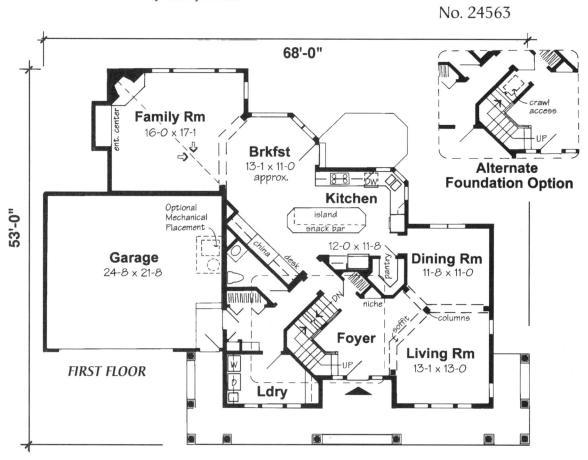

68'-0"

Family Rm
16-0 x 17-1

ent. center

Brkfst
13-1 x 11-0
approx.

Kitchen
island
snack bar

crawl access

UP

Alternate Foundation Option

Optional Mechanical Placement

china   desk

Garage
24-8 x 21-8

12-0 x 11-8

pantry

Dining Rm
11-8 x 11-0

niche

DN

soffit

columns

53'-0"

Foyer

UP

W

D

Living Rm
13-1 x 13-0

FIRST FLOOR

Ldry

- *Open layout between Living and Dining Rooms, and Kitchen, Breakfast and Family Room creates easy living and entertaining space*

- *Efficient, L-shaped Kitchen with walk-in pantry, built-in desk and china cabinet, and island/snack bar readily serve bright Breakfast area, rear yard, Family and Dining Rooms*

- *Corner fireplace and entertainment area accent Family Room*

- *Master Suite offers pampered privacy with decorative ceiling, walk-in closet and plush bath with double vanity and atrium whirlpool tub*

- *Three additional bedrooms, two with wonderful bay window seats, share full bath*

- *Friendly porch leads into open Foyer with graceful staircase and columns framing Living and Dining Rooms*

Traditional Elements In A Modern Design

PLAN INFO:

First Flr.	3,438 sq. ft.
Garage	610 sq. ft.
Sq. Footage	3,438 sq. ft.
Foundation	Slab
Bedrooms	Four
Baths	3(Full), 1(Half)

REFER TO PRICE CODE F

No. 10749

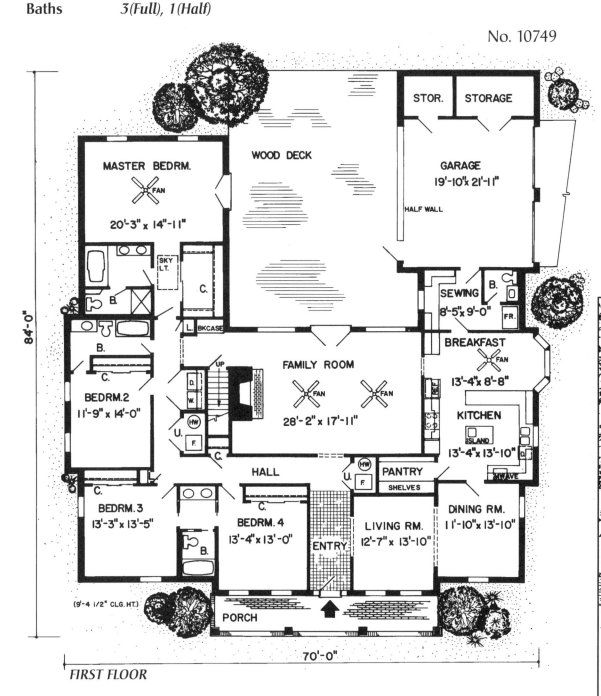

STOR. | STORAGE

WOOD DECK

GARAGE
19'-10" x 21'-11"

MASTER BEDRM.
FAN
20'-3" x 14"-11"

HALF WALL

SKY LT.

C.

B.

SEWING
8'-5" x 9'-0"

FR.

BKCASE

L.

BREAKFAST
FAN
13'-4" x 8'-8"

B.

C.

BEDRM.2
11'-9" x 14'-0"

UP

D.
W.

HW

U.

F.

C.

FAMILY ROOM
FAN   FAN
28'-2" x 17'-11"

REF.

KITCHEN
ISLAND
13'-4" x 13'-10"

MWAVE

C.

BEDRM. 3
13'-3" x 13'-5"

HALL

C.

BEDRM. 4
13'-4" x 13'-0"

ENTRY

HW
U.
F.

PANTRY
SHELVES

B.

LIVING RM.
12'-7" x 13'-10"

DINING RM.
11'-10" x 13'-10"

(9'-4 1/2" CLG. HT.)

PORCH

84'-0"

70'-0"

FIRST FLOOR

■ *Classic elements from yesteryear: columned porch, high ceilings with cooling fans and loads of built-in storage make this home special*

■ *Distinctive interior plan uses a contemporary sleeping wing and central location for family living*

■ *Formal and family areas are served with equal ease from the conveniently placed island Kitchen*

■ *A massive fireplace is included in the Family Room, which overlooks the outdoor wood deck*

■ *Every bedroom adjoins a bath, and the skylit Master Suite enjoys access to the deck*

Luxurious Living On One Level

PLAN INFO:

First Flr.	2,242 sq. ft.
Basement	2,303 sq. ft.
Garage	744 sq. ft.
Sq. Footage	2,242 sq. ft.
Foundation	Bsmt, Slab, Crawl Space
Bedrooms	Three
Baths	2(Full)

REFER TO PRICE CODE D

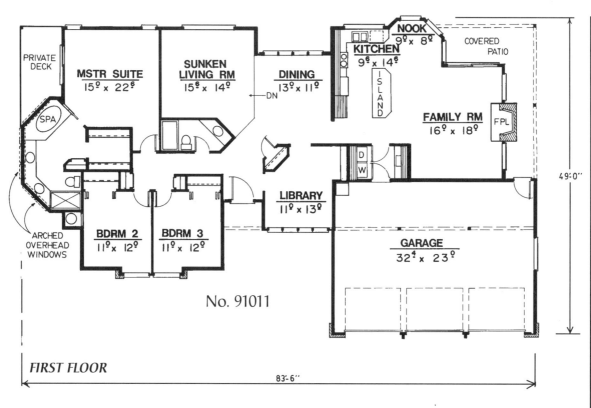

PRIVATE DECK

SPA

MSTR SUITE
15⁰ x 22⁶

SUNKEN LIVING RM
15⁶ x 14⁰

DINING
13⁰ x 11⁰

DN

KITCHEN
9⁶ x 14⁶

NOOK
9⁰ x 8⁰

COVERED PATIO

ISLAND

FAMILY RM
16⁰ x 18⁰

FPL

ARCHED OVERHEAD WINDOWS

BDRM 2
11⁰ x 12⁰

BDRM 3
11⁰ x 12⁰

D W

LIBRARY
11⁰ x 13⁰

GARAGE
32⁴ x 23⁰

No. 91011

FIRST FLOOR

49'-0"

83'-6"

- *Sheltered Entry leads into the bright Library with built-in shelves, a Sunken Living Room and a Dining Room with a wall of windows*

- *Master Suite offers a private Deck, a large walk-in closet and a plush bath with a double vanity and a luxurious spa tub*

- *Two additional bedroom with decorative windows and large closets, share a full bath*

- *Efficient, L-shaped Kitchen with an island/snackbar, opening to the glass eating Nook, the Family Room with a huge fireplace, a covered Patio and a Laundry area*

PLAN INFO:

First Flr.	*2,546 sq. ft.*
Basement	*1,409 sq. ft.*
Garage	*623 sq. ft.*
Sq. Footage	*2,546 sq. ft.*
Foundation	*Bsmt, Slab, Crawl space*
Bedrooms	*Four*
Baths	*2(Full)*

REFER TO PRICE CODE D

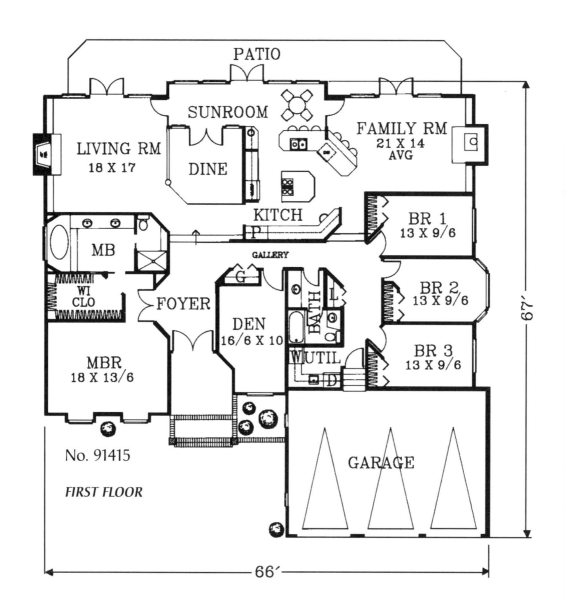

PATIO

SUNROOM

LIVING RM
18 X 17

DINE

FAMILY RM
21 X 14
AVG

KITCH

BR 1
13 X 9/6

MB

GALLERY

WI
CLO

FOYER

G

BATH

BR 2
13 X 9/6

DEN
16/6 X 10

W UTIL

BR 3
13 X 9/6

MBR
18 X 13/6

No. 91415

GARAGE

FIRST FLOOR

67'

66'

■ *An open Kitchen features cooktop work island, built-in pantry and desk , and unique eating bar serving both Sunroom and Family Room*

■ *Central Dining area offers easy entertaining between Living Room and Kitchen, plus double door into Sunroom and Patio beyond*

■ *Three additional bedrooms with ample closets and decorative windows share a full bath*

■ *A quiet Den off Gallery offers many options*

■ *Secluded Master Bedroom suite accented by decorative windows features walk-in closet and luxurious bath with double vanity and raised-window tub*

■ *Double door entrance into Foyer leads to formal Living Room with raised hearth fireplace, built-in shelves and French doors to Patio*

Contemporary With Unique Curves

PLAN INFO:

First Flr.	1,985 sq. ft.
Second Flr.	715 sq. ft.
Basement	2, sq. ft.
Garage	545 sq. ft.
Sq. Footage	2,700 sq. ft.
Foundation	Bsmt, Slab, Crawl Sapce
Bedrooms	Three
Baths	2(Full), 1(Half)

REFER TO PRICE CODE E

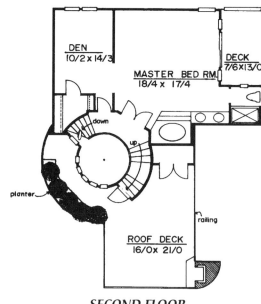

SECOND FLOOR

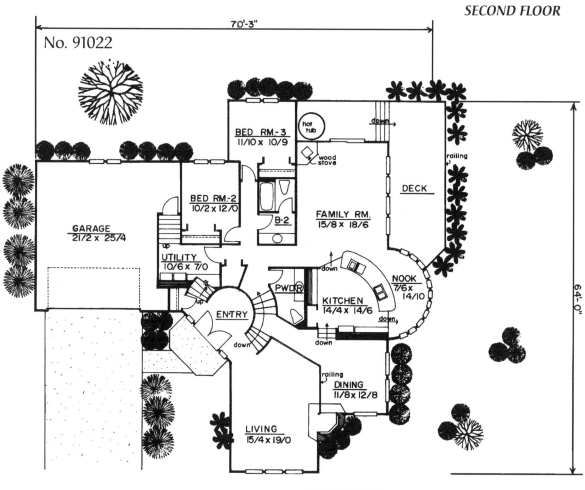

No. 91022

70'-3"

64'-0"

FIRST FLOOR

- *Impressive Entry with circular staircase leads into Living and Dining Rooms with lots of windows*

- *Bright, efficient Kitchen with circular cooktop counter and eating Nook, located next to Dining Room and opens to Family Room*

- *Expansive Family Room with wall of windows, wood stove in corner and sliding glass door to hot tub on upper Deck*

- *Secluded and luxurious Master Bedroom suite offers private Deck, Den, walk-in closet and whirlpool tub*

- *Two additional bedrooms with ample closet space share full bath*

Relax And Enjoy This
Magnificent Stucco Design

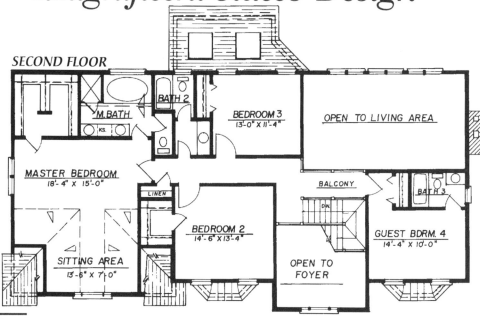

SECOND FLOOR

- BATH 2
- M.BATH
- KS.
- MASTER BEDROOM 18'-4" X 15'-0"
- LINEN
- SITTING AREA 13'-6" X 7'-0"
- BEDROOM 3 13'-0" X 11'-4"
- OPEN TO LIVING AREA
- BALCONY
- DN
- BATH 3
- BEDROOM 2 14'-6" X 13'-4"
- OPEN TO FOYER
- GUEST BDRM. 4 14'-4" X 10'-0"

PLAN INFO

First Flr.	1,695 sq. ft.
Second Flr.	1,620 sq. ft.
Basement	1,695 sq. ft.
Garage	572 sq. ft.
Sq. Footage	3,315 sq. ft.
Foundation	Basement
Bedrooms	Four
Baths	3(Full), 1(Half)

*No materials list available

REFER TO PRICE CODE F

An **EXCLUSIVE DESIGN**
By Jannis Vann & Associates, Inc.

No. 93273

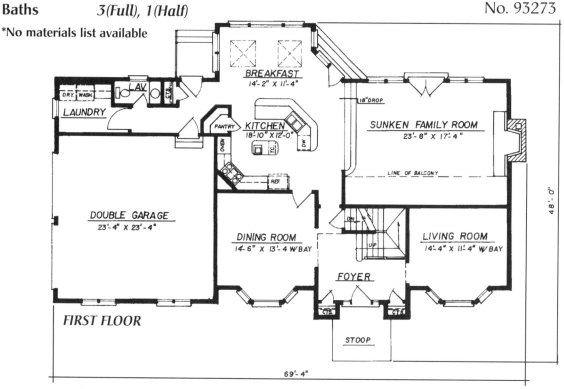

FIRST FLOOR

- DRY. WASH. AV. CT.
- LAUNDRY
- PANTRY
- KITCHEN 18'-10" X 12'-0"
- OVEN
- REF.
- DW
- DOUBLE GARAGE 23'-4" X 23'-4"
- BREAKFAST 14'-2" X 11'-4"
- 18" DROP
- SUNKEN FAMILY ROOM 23'-8" X 17'-4"
- LINE OF BALCONY
- DINING ROOM 14'-6" X 13'-4 W/ BAY
- FOYER
- DN
- UP
- LIVING ROOM 14'-4" X 11'-4" W/ BAY
- CTS
- STOOP
- 48'-0"
- 69'-4"

■ *Quiet elegance greets one and all into this classic home with a two-story, open Foyer leading to the formal Living Room and Dining Room high-lighted with bay windows*

■ *Expansive sunken Family Room offers comfort and convenience with its large, hearth fireplace, a wall of glass leading outdoors and its proximity from the kitchen*

■ *Two work islands, one with a snack bar in the Kitchen and a walk-in pantry, make this well-appointed room even more efficient*

■ *Bright and sunny Breakfast area offers a cheerful way to start the day with skylights, windows on three sides and easy access to the outdoors*

■ *Comfortable Master Bedroom Suite featuring views on three sides, contains a unique Sitting Area, a double walk-in closet, and a private Bath with window tub and double vanity*

■ *Three additional bedrooms, one with a private bath, have ample closet space*

Contemporary With Many Comforts

PLAN INFO:

First Flr.	1,550 sq. ft.
Second Flr.	1,001 sq. ft.
Basement	1,550 sq. ft.
Garage	750 sq. ft.
Sq. Footage	2,551 sq. ft.
Foundation	Basement or Crawl space
Bedrooms	Three or Four
Baths	3(Full)

REFER TO PRICE CODE D

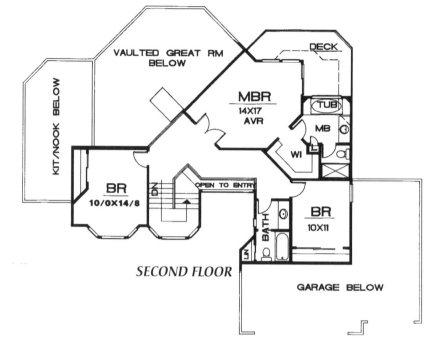

SECOND FLOOR

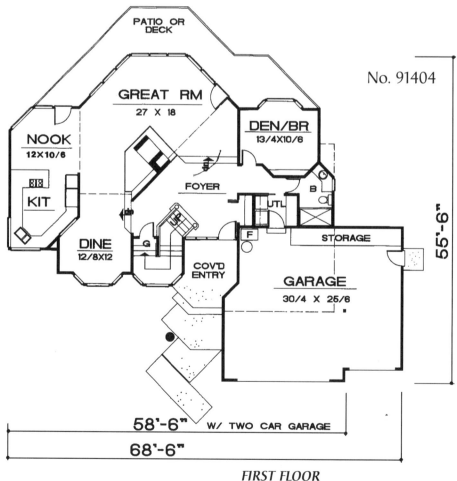

No. 91404

55'-6"

58'-6" W/ TWO CAR GARAGE

68'-6"

FIRST FLOOR

- Glassed Entry into central two-story Foyer with impressive, landing staircase framed by two-story bay window

- Steps down to Dining Room with another bay window and Great Room alcove of windows, access to Patio or Deck

- Cozy, two-way fireplace warms Great Room, and Dining and Nook areas

- Efficient Kitchen features corner window, pass-through counter and cooktop peninsula serving Nook and Dining area with ease

- Quiet Den/Bedroom offers many options

- Luxurious Master Bedroom suite accented by private Deck, walk-in closet and plush bath with garden tub

- Two additional bedrooms, one with bay window, share full bath

*A*n Open Concept *F*loor *P*lan
Makes *F*or Convenient *L*iving

PLAN INFO:

First Flr.	*2,511 sq. ft.*
Garage	*690 sq. ft.*
Sq. Footage	*2,511 sq. ft.*
Foundation	*Slab, Crawl space***
Bedrooms	*Four*
Baths	*Two*

*No materials list available

**Please specify when ordering

An
EXCLUSIVE DESIGN
By Belk Home Designs

No. 93050

REFER TO PRICE CODE D

WIDTH 69'-0"
DEPTH 63'-6"

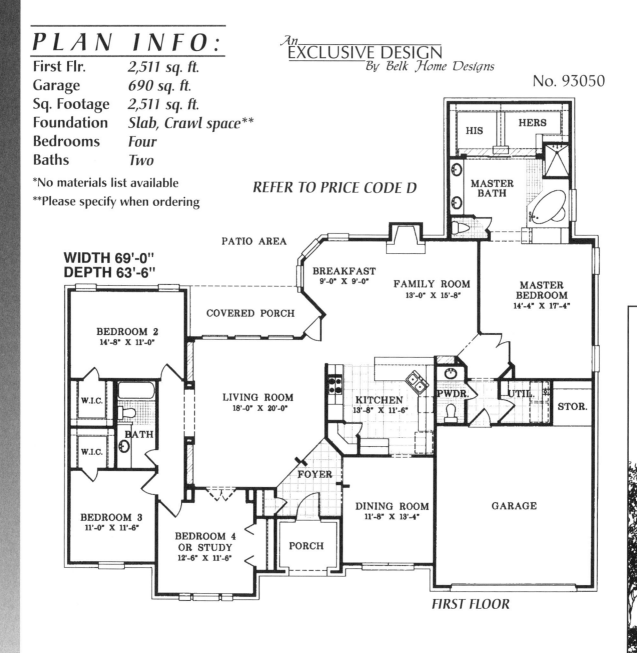

HIS   HERS

MASTER
BATH

PATIO AREA

BREAKFAST
9'-0" X 9'-0"

FAMILY ROOM
13'-0" X 15'-8"

MASTER
BEDROOM
14'-4" X 17'-4"

COVERED PORCH

BEDROOM 2
14'-8" X 11'-0"

LIVING ROOM
18'-0" X 20'-0"

KITCHEN
13'-8" X 11'-6"

PWDR.

UTIL.

STOR.

W.I.C.

BATH

W.I.C.

FOYER

BEDROOM 3
11'-0" X 11'-6"

BEDROOM 4
OR STUDY
12'-6" X 11'-6"

PORCH

DINING ROOM
11'-8" X 13'-4"

GARAGE

FIRST FLOOR

■ *Covered front entrance to tiled Foyer leads directly to the open Living Room and formal Dining Room with a decorative front window*

■ *Living Room offers built-in shelves, a wall of windows and easy access to the covered Porch and Breakfast Room/Family Room*

■ *A well-appointed Kitchen with ample cabinet space, a peninsula counter and a walk-in pantry opens to both the Breakfast Room/Family Room and the Dining Room*

■ *Bay window area of the Breakfast Room and the warm, hearth fireplace in the Family Room make this area perfect for family gatherings*

■ *Double French doors open into the private Master Bedroom Suite high-lighted by a pampering Bath with a corner whirlpool garden tub, double vanity and his-n-her walk-in closets*

■ *Three additional bedrooms on the same level located on the other side of the home have walk-in closets and share a full hall Bath*

Comfortable Elegance With Country Kitchen

PLAN INFO:

First Flr.	1,552 sq. ft.
Second Flr.	1,064 sq. ft.
Basement	1,552 sq. ft.
Garage	708 sq. ft.
Sq. Footage	2,616 sq. ft.
Foundation	Bsmt, Slab, Crawl space
Bedrooms	Three or Four
Baths	3(Full)

*No materials list available

REFER TO PRICE CODE E

An
EXCLUSIVE DESIGN
By Britt J. Willis

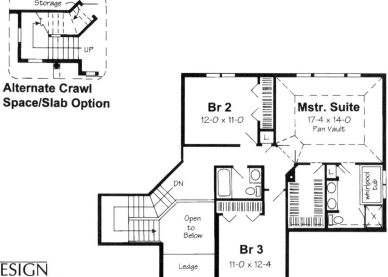

Alternate Crawl
Space/Slab Option

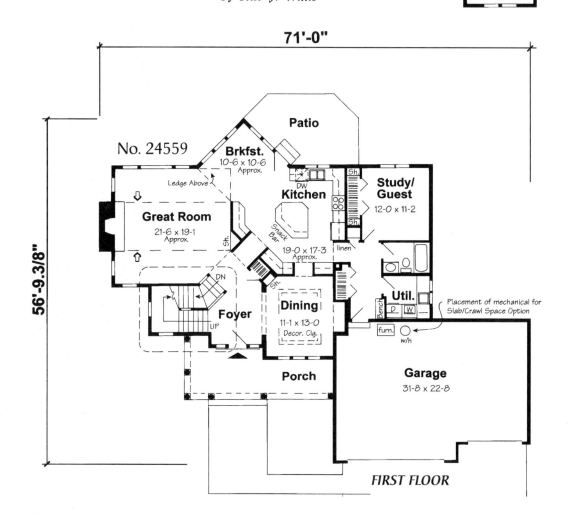

No. 24559

FIRST FLOOR

- Columns accent front Porch leading into two-story Foyer with impressive, landing staircase and expansive Great Room beyond

- Formal Dining Room accented by decorative ceiling above hutch alcove and triple window

- Huge, hearth fireplace surrounded by windows below vaulted ceiling accents Great Room which opens into Kitchen area

- Great Kitchen with loads of counter and storage space, work island/snack-bar and glass Breakfast area accessible to Patio, Great Room, Dining Room, Utility and Garage

- Private Master Suite features triple window below pan vault ceiling, walk-in closet and luxury bath with double vanity and whirlpool tub

- Two additional bedrooms with large closets share full bath

Classic Symmetry On This Columned Facade

SECOND FLOOR

PLAN INFO:

First Flr.	3,116 sq. ft.
Second Flr.	1,997 sq. ft.
Sq. Footage	5,113 sq. ft.
Foundation	Basement
Bedrooms	Four
Baths	4(Full), 1(Half)

REFER TO PRICE CODE F

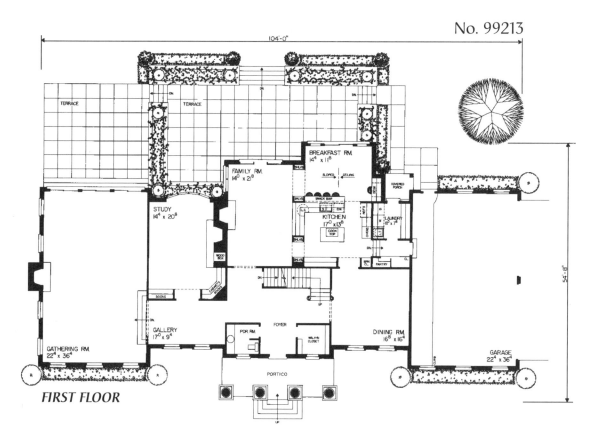

No. 99213

FIRST FLOOR

■ *Grand Foyer welcomes guests into the home and leads into the Gallery*

■ *Extremely spacious, yet made cozy by the large fireplace, the Gathering Room stands ready to accommodate any entertaining endeavor*

■ *Study offers a special place to sit by the fireplace and read surrounded by built-in shelves and a bow window view of the outdoor terrace*

■ *Centrally located Kitchen, with a cooktop island, built-in pantry and*

planning desk, plenty of counter space and snack bar easily serves both the formal Dining Room and informal Breakfast Room.

■ *Whirlpool tub, a fourth fireplace and his-n-her closets are just a few of the reasons this second floor Master Bedroom suite will become a favorite retreat*

■ *Three additional bedrooms, each with a private bath, are also located on the second floor*

This Modern Tudor Is Hard To Resist

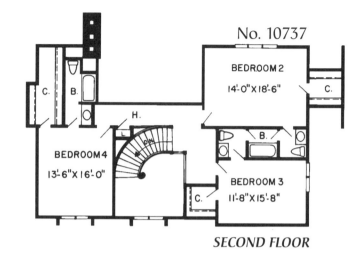

No. 10737

PLAN INFO:

First Flr.	2,457 sq. ft.
Second Flr.	1,047 sq. ft.
Sun Room	213 sq. ft.
Basement	2,457 sq. ft.
Garage	837 sq. ft.
Sq. Footage	3,504 sq. ft.
Foundation	Basement
Bedrooms	Four
Baths	3(Full), 1(Half)

REFER TO PRICE CODE F

SECOND FLOOR

FIRST FLOOR

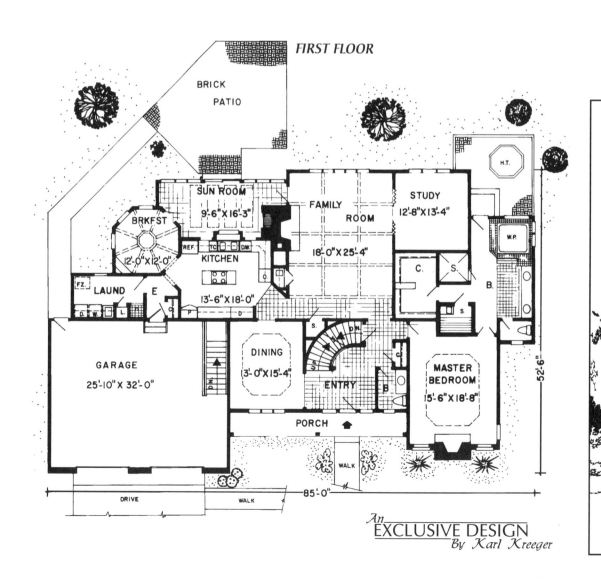

An
EXCLUSIVE DESIGN
By Karl Kreeger

- *Partake of morning coffee in the seven-sided, Breakfast Room*

- *Island Kitchen affords easy access to Dining Room*

- *Family room features exposed wood beams adding atmosphere to this impressive home*

- *Energy-saving Sun Room and unobtrusive Study flank Family Room for convenience*

- *Balcony at top of stairs overlooks grand Entry*

- *Master Bedroom with recessed ceiling encompasses entire wing for spacious living*

- *Master Bath encourages pampering with double vanity, walk-in closet, sauna, whirlpool bath, and hot tub*

- *Graceful curving staircase enhances exciting tiled Entry with a two-story ceiling*

- *Three additional bedrooms on the second floor feature individual walk-in closets for plenty of personal storage*

$\mathcal{A}$ Grand Presence

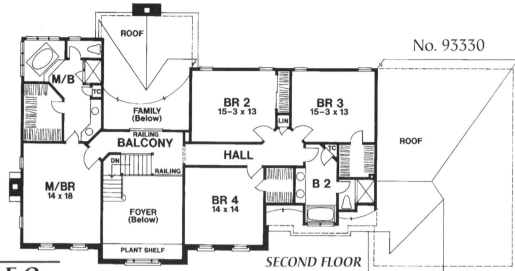

No. 93330

SECOND FLOOR

PLAN INFO:

First Flr.	2,093 sq. ft.
Second Flr.	1,527 sq. ft.
Basement	2,093 sq. ft.
Garage	816 sq. ft.
Sq. Footage	3,620 sq. ft.
Foundation	Basement
Bedrooms	Four
Baths	2(Full), 1(Half)

*No materials list available

REFER TO PRICE CODE F

An
EXCLUSIVE DESIGN
By Patrick Morabito, A.I.A. Architect

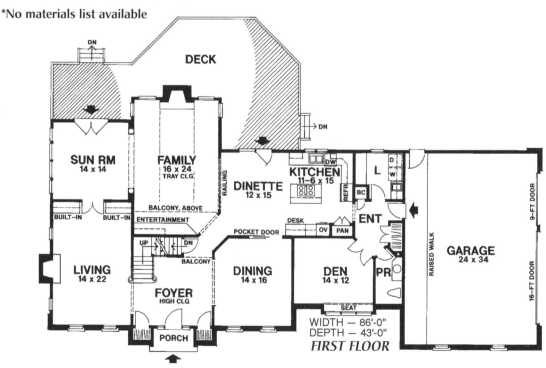

FIRST FLOOR

WIDTH — 86'-0"
DEPTH — 43'-0"

■ *Imposing and symmetrical in design, this spacious home welcomes family and friends through an impressive entrance into an open Foyer leading easily into all living areas*

■ *Formal Living Room offers a warm fireplace centered between two large windows and built-in shelves on each side of double doors leading into the Sun Room*

■ *Pocket Door separates the formal Dining Room from the Kitchen area, providing privacy and disappearing into the wall when not needed*

■ *Gourmet Kitchen is equipped with a cooktop island, built-in pantry and planning desk, and adjoining Dinette area with a glass door to the outdoor Deck*

■ *Expansive Family Room has a second fireplace surrounded by windows, a built-in entertainment center, and a tray ceiling with a balcony above*

■ *A luxurious Bath highlights the private Master Bedroom Suite with a raised corner window tub, step-in shower, double vanity and walk-in closet*

■ *Three large, additional bedrooms share a full hall Bath with a window tub and another double vanity*

*F*rench Country *D*esign
*W*ith *E*legant *A*menities

No. 91658

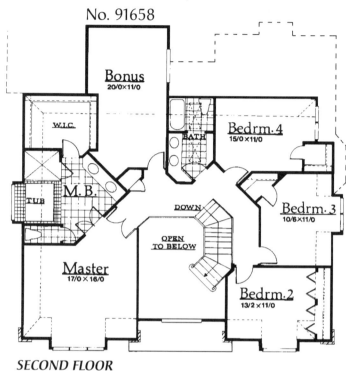

SECOND FLOOR

PLAN INFO:

First Flr.	*1,718 sq. ft.*
Second Flr.	*1,340 sq. ft.*
Bonus Rm.	*220 sq. ft.*
Sq. Footage	*3,278 sq. ft.*
Foundation	*Crawl space*
Bedrooms	*Four*
Baths	*2(Full), 1(Half)*

*No materials list available

REFER TO PRICE CODE F

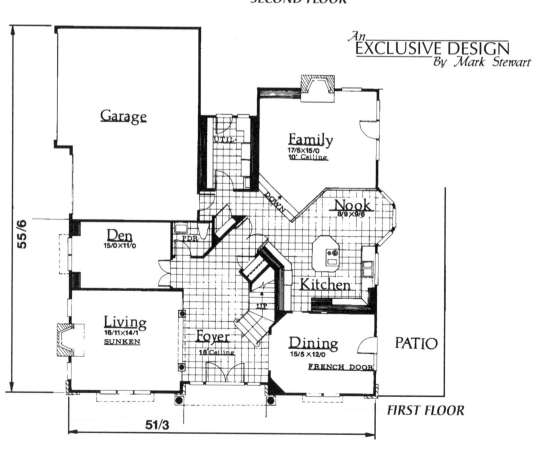

An
EXCLUSIVE DESIGN
By Mark Stewart

FIRST FLOOR

- Pleasant grace surrounds this corner French country home with its double front doors, two-story glass and tile Foyer, and curved stairway

- Sunken formal Living Room is enhanced by an arched Entry and a large hearth fireplace

- Formal dining takes place in the elegant Dining Room that features French doors to the Patio

- Double French doors lead to the informal living areas, including a sunken Family Room with a cozy fireplace for all to gather around on cold winter nights

- Fabulous island Kitchen includes an abundance of counter and storage space and a Nook Area for informal eating

- Master Bedroom suite highlighted by a window seat and luxurious Bath with atrium tub, double vanity and large walk-in closet

- Three additional bedrooms and a large Bonus room share the full, double vanity hall Bath

*T*wo-Story Glass Entrance...
Need We Say More!

REFER TO PRICE CODE E

PLAN INFO:

First Flr.	1,720 sq. ft.
Second Flr.	1,305 sq. ft.
Basement	1,720 sq. ft.
Garage	768 sq. ft.
Sq. Footage	3,025 sq. ft.
Foundation	Basement
Bedrooms	Four
Baths	2(Full), 1(Half)

*No materials list available

An
EXCLUSIVE DESIGN
By Patrick Morabito, A.I.A. Architect

No. 93322

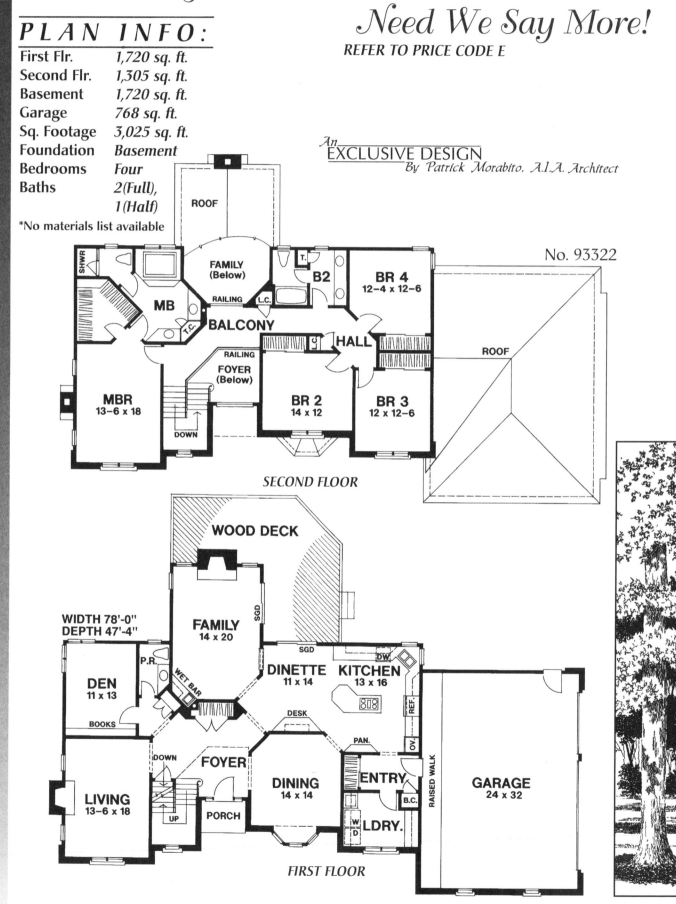

ROOF

SHWR

MB

FAMILY (Below)

RAILING

B2

BR 4
12-4 x 12-6

ROOF

T.C.

BALCONY

L.C.

HALL

MBR
13-6 x 18

RAILING

FOYER (Below)

L.C.

BR 2
14 x 12

BR 3
12 x 12-6

DOWN

SECOND FLOOR

WOOD DECK

WIDTH 78'-0"
DEPTH 47'-4"

FAMILY
14 x 20

SGD

SGD

DINETTE
11 x 14

KITCHEN
13 x 16

DW

DEN
11 x 13

P.R.

WET BAR

REF.

OV.

BOOKS

DESK

PAN.

FOYER

DINING
14 x 14

ENTRY

B.C.

RAISED WALK

GARAGE
24 x 32

DOWN

LIVING
13-6 x 18

UP

PORCH

W
D

LDRY.

FIRST FLOOR

■ *Enter this gracious home through a two-story, glass entrance that leads to all living areas from the expansive Foyer*

■ *Formal Living Room features an inviting hearth fireplace to set the mood in formal entertaining*

■ *Bay window adds elegance and natural illumination to the formal Dining Room*

■ *Spacious Family Room equipped with sliders to a deck, built-in wetbar and a cozy fireplace, provides a perfect place for informal entertaining*

■ *Expansive Kitchen offers a cooktop island/eating bar, corner double sink, built-in pantry and desk as well as a Dinette area leading to the Family Room and outdoor Deck*

■ *Cozy Den offers built-in book shelves and a quiet corner on the first floor*

■ *Ultra Bath with a raised window tub and two vanities adds to the attraction of the Master Bedroom Suite*

■ *Three additional bedrooms with ample closet space share a full hall Bath with a double vanity*

Classic Style With Impressive Portico

PLAN INFO:

First Flr.	1,860 sq. ft.
Second Flr.	803 sq. ft.
Basement	2, sq. ft.
Garage	506 sq. ft.
Sq. Footage	2,663 sq. ft.
Foundation	Bsmt, Slab, Crawl space
Bedrooms	Four
Baths	2(Full), 1(Half)

*No materials list available

REFER TO PRICE CODE E

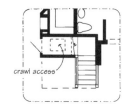

crawl access

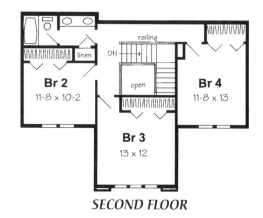

Br 2
11-8 x 10-2

linen

DN

railing

open

Br 4
11-8 x 13

Br 3
13 x 12

SECOND FLOOR

An
EXCLUSIVE DESIGN
By Britt J. Willis

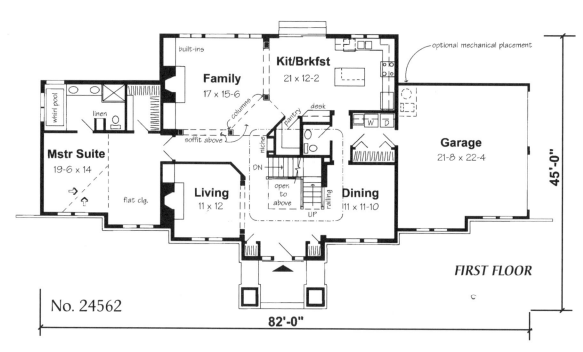

built-ins

Family
17 x 15-6

Kit/Brkfst
21 x 12-2

optional mechanical placement

whirl pool

linen

columns

soffit above

pantry

desk

W   D

niche

Garage
21-8 x 22-4

Mstr Suite
19-6 x 14

flat clg.

Living
11 x 12

DN

open to above

UP

railing

Dining
11 x 11-10

45'-0"

No. 24562

82'-0"

FIRST FLOOR

- *An elegant entrance into an open layout for easy entertaining in Living and Dining room areas*

- *A spacious Kitchen/Breakfast Room offers walk-in pantry, built-in desk, work island/snackbar and adjoining Family Room, rear yard, laundry/mud-room, Garage and Dining room*

- *A cozy fireplace between built-ins, a wall of glass and columns accent open Family room*

- *A secluded Master Suite wing features an expansive main area, walk-in closet and luxurious bath with double vanity and whirlpool tub*

- *Three additional bedrooms on second floor with ample closet space share a full double vanity bath*

*O*utdoor Views Abound Indoors

PLAN INFO:

First Flr.	1,418 sq. ft.
Second Flr.	1,066 sq. ft.
Bonus Area	230 sq. ft.
Basement	1,418 sq. ft.
Garage	720 sq. ft.
Sq. Footage	2,484 sq. ft.
Foundation	Basement
Bedrooms	Three
Baths	3(Full)

REFER TO PRICE CODE D

An
EXCLUSIVE DESIGN
By Energetic Enterprises

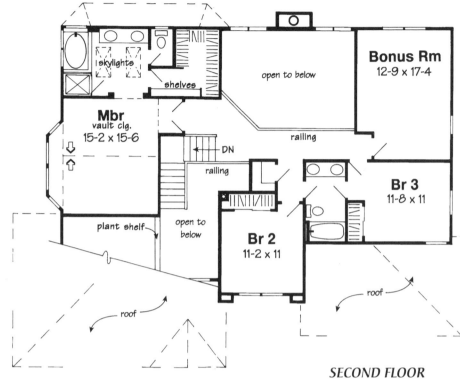

Bonus Rm
12-9 x 17-4

open to below

Mbr
vault clg.
15-2 x 15-6

skylights

shelves

DN

railing

railing

Br 3
11-8 x 11

plant shelf

open to below

Br 2
11-2 x 11

roof

roof

SECOND FLOOR

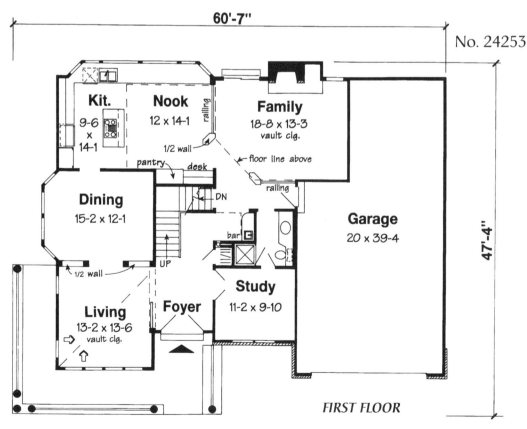

60'-7"

No. 24253

47'-4"

Kit.
9-6 x 14-1

Nook
12 x 14-1

railing

Family
18-8 x 13-3
vault clg.

1/2 wall

pantry

desk

floor line above

railing

DN

Dining
15-2 x 12-1

bar

Garage
20 x 39-4

UP

1/2 wall

Living
13-2 x 13-6
vault clg.

Foyer

Study
11-2 x 9-10

FIRST FLOOR

- *Wrap-around porch invites you into Foyer with graceful, landing staircase, and bright Living Room with vaulted ceiling over decorative windows*

- *Impressive Dining Room with alcove of windows opens into Living Room*

- *Quiet Study with double window offers many options*

- *Efficient Kitchen with cooktop/snack-bar island, built-in pantry, desk and Nook opens to Family Room*

- *Family Room features hearth fireplace with wood bin and sliding glass door to rear yard topped by vaulted ceiling*

- *Secluded Master Bedroom suite appointed by vaulted ceiling over large bay window and plush bath with skylights and corner window tub*

- *Two additional bedrooms share double-vanity bath and Bonus Room*

The Luxury Of A Library

PLAN INFO:

First Flr.	1,746 sq. ft.
Second Flr.	1,472 sq. ft.
Basement	1,746 sq. ft.
Garage	521 sq. ft.
Sq. Footage	3,218 sq. ft.
Foundation	Bsmt, Slab, Crawl space
Bedrooms	Four
Baths	2(Full), 1(Half)

*No materials list available

REFER TO PRICE CODE F

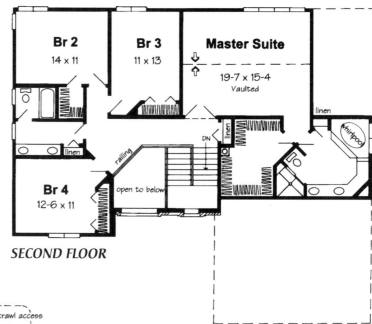

Br 2 14 x 11

Br 3 11 x 13

Master Suite 19-7 x 15-4 Vaulted

linen

whirlpool

linen

DN

railing

open to below

Br 4 12-6 x 11

SECOND FLOOR

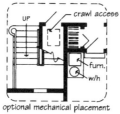

UP
crawl access
fum.
w/h

optional mechanical placement

An **EXCLUSIVE DESIGN** *By Greg Stafford*

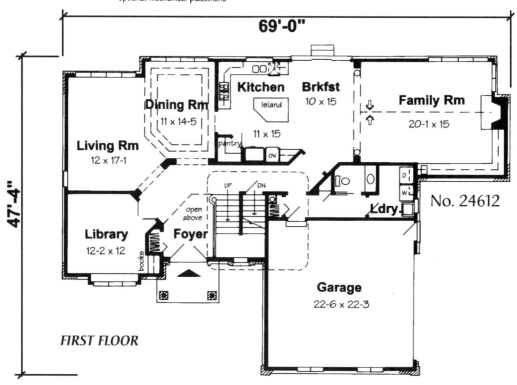

69'-0"

47'-4"

Living Rm 12 x 17-1

Dining Rm 11 x 14-5

Kitchen island

Brkfst 10 x 15

Family Rm 20-1 x 15

11 x 15

pantry

ov.

UP   DN

open above

Library 12-2 x 12

books

Foyer

Ldry.

No. 24612

Garage 22-6 x 22-3

FIRST FLOOR

- *An elegant two-story entrance into Foyer with abundance of light leading to open Living and Dining Rooms accented by more windows*

- *Quiet Library offers built-in bookshelves and grand front window*

- *Expansive Family Room includes a cozy fireplace*

- *The Breakfast Room has a terrific relaxed family living space*

- *Master Suite topped by vaulted ceiling features room-size closet and plush bath with whirlpool tub*

- *Three additional bedrooms with over-sized closets share double vanity bath*

- *Efficient Kitchen with island counter, walk-in pantry, and Breakfast area adjoins Dining Room, rear yard, Family Room, Laundry and Garage*

$\mathcal{D}$elightful Decorative Ceilings

PLAN INFO:

First Flr.	*1,544 sq. ft.*
Second Flr.	*1,214 sq. ft.*
Basement	*1,544 sq. ft.*
Garage	*796 sq. ft.*
Sq. Footage	*2,758 sq. ft.*
Foundation	**Basement**
Bedrooms	*Four*
Baths	*2(Full), 1(Half)*

REFER TO PRICE CODE E

An
EXCLUSIVE DESIGN
By Britt J. Willis

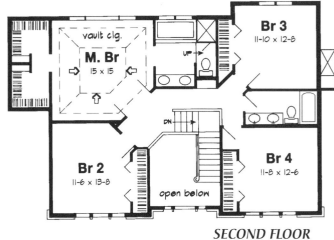

SECOND FLOOR

No. 24555

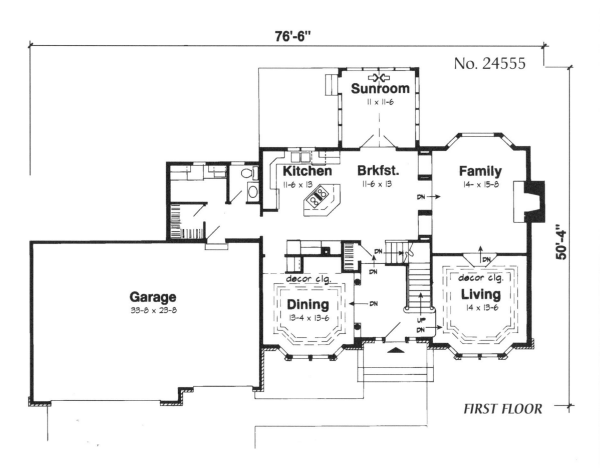

FIRST FLOOR

- Grand front door with sidelights leads into the Foyer, with a graceful, landing staircase

- Efficient Kitchen with island cooktop/snackbar and Breakfast area, ideally located near Laundry, Garage, Dining Room and Family Room

- Double doors from the Breakfast area lead into a wonderful Sunroom with steps to the outdoors

- Gracious Master-Bedroom suite accented by vaulted ceiling, double, walk-in closet and private bath with double vanity and window tub

- Three additional bedrooms with over-sized closets and decorative windows share double-vanity bath

- Step down into elegant Living and Dining Rooms with decorative ceilings over bay windows

- Comfortable Family Room highlighted by large, hearth fireplace and lovely bay window

Grand Colonial Design With Entrance Court

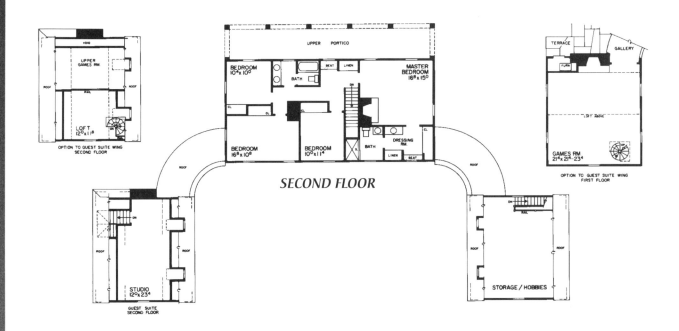

SECOND FLOOR

PLAN INFO:

First Flr.	*1,152 sq. ft.*
Second Flr.	*2,146 sq. ft.*
Bonus Room	*525 sq. ft.*
Garage	*483 sq. ft.*
Sq. Footage	*3,298 sq. ft.*
Foundation	*Basement*
Bedrooms	*Four*
Baths	*3(Full), 1(Half)*

REFER TO PRICE CODE F

No. 99236

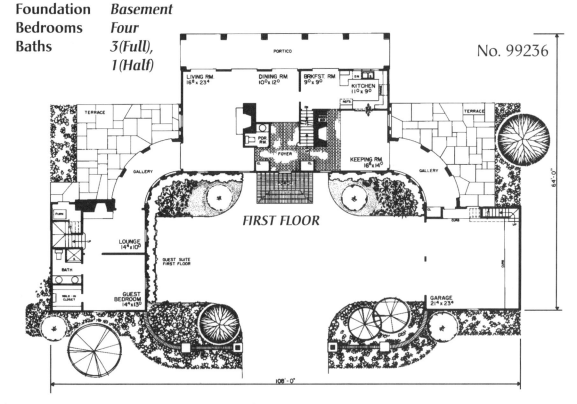

FIRST FLOOR

- *Courtyard entry makes an appropriate impression for the luxurious living awaiting within*

- *Central brick floored Foyer leads into a Traditional Keeping Room equipped with a fireplace and a brick bread oven*

- *Charming curvilinear galleries lead to a double Garage on one side, Lounge and Studio/Guest Suite on the other*

- *Efficient Kitchen adjoins the Breakfast Room for convenient informal meals*

- *A combined formal Living and Dining Room is extremely spacious and features a central fireplace*

- *Large hearth fireplace and separate dressing and bath areas are highlighted in the oversized Master Suite*

- *Three additional bedrooms share a full hall Bath*

- *Optional ideas for guest and garage wings offered*

$\mathcal{M}$any Options Offered On One Level

PLAN INFO:

First Flr.	2,108 sq. ft.
Basement	2,108 sq. ft.
Garage	462 sq. ft.
Sq. Footage	2,108 sq. ft.
Foundation	Bsmt, Slab, Crawl space
Bedrooms	Three
Baths	2(Full)

REFER TO PRICE CODE C

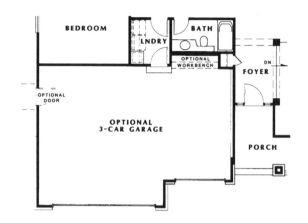

OPTIONAL 3-CAR GARAGE

An EXCLUSIVE DESIGN
By Energetic Enterprises

No. 24257

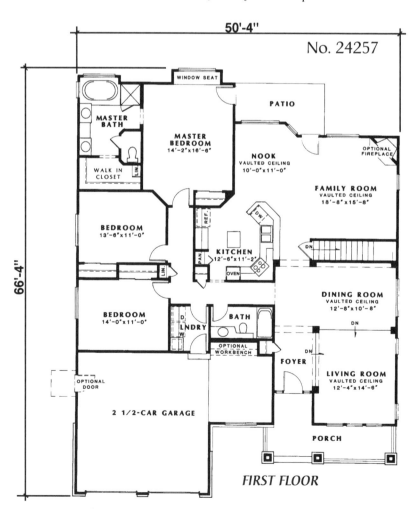

FIRST FLOOR

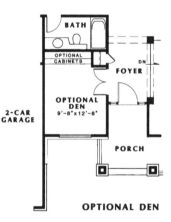

OPTIONAL DEN

■ *A covered Porch leads into an open Foyer and Living and Dining Rooms with pillars topped by vaulted ceilings*

■ *A central and efficient Kitchen with pantry, work island and peninsula snackbar easily serves Dining Room, Nook and Family Room*

■ *A wall of glass below vaulted ceilings in Nook and Family Room with corner*

fireplace offers easy outdoor access

■ *A window seat accents the Master Bedroom suite with atrium tub and double vanity.*

■ *Two additional bedrooms with ample closet space share a full bath*

■ *Optional Den offers potential home office or three-car Garage*

Traditional Facade Hides Modern Layout

PLAN INFO:

First Flr.	2,542 sq. ft.
Garage	510 sq. ft.
Sq. Footage	2,542 sq. ft.
Foundation	Slab
Bedrooms	Four
Baths	2(Full), 1(Half)

REFER TO PRICE CODE D

An
EXCLUSIVE DESIGN
By Jannis Vann & Associates, Inc.

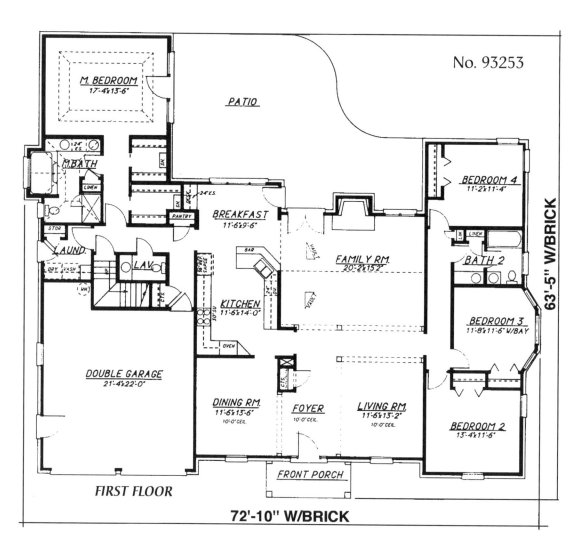

No. 93253

M. BEDROOM
17'-4"x13'-6"

PATIO

M.BATH

LINEN

STOR

LAUND.

DRY WASH

LAV.

BREAKFAST
11'-6"x9'-6"

PANTRY

KITCHEN
11'-6"x14'-0"

BAR

OVEN

VAULT

FAMILY RM.
20'-2"x15'-2"

BEDROOM 4
11'-2"x11'-4"

LINEN

BATH 2

BEDROOM 3
11'-8"x11'-6" W/BAY

63'-5" W/BRICK

DOUBLE GARAGE
21'-4"x22'-0"

DINING RM.
11'-6"x13'-6"
10'-0" CEIL.

FOYER
10'-0" CEIL.

LIVING RM.
11'-6"x13'-2"
10'-0" CEIL.

BEDROOM 2
13'-4"x11'-6"

FRONT PORCH

FIRST FLOOR

72'-10" W/BRICK

- ■ *Front Porch opens into Dining Room, Living Room and Family Room defined by pillars dormer windows and vaulted ceiling*

- ■ *Focal point fireplace between sliding glass doors to Patio accents Family Room*

- ■ *Kitchen with peninsula counter/snack-bar serving glass Breakfast area, Patio and Dining Room*

- ■ *Lavish Master Bedroom wing with atrium door to Patio features decorative ceiling, two walk-in closets and vanities, garden tub and adjacent Laundry*

- ■ *Three additional bedrooms with large closets and decorative windows share full bath with two vanities*

An Angled Design Wrapped Around The Perfect Executive Suite

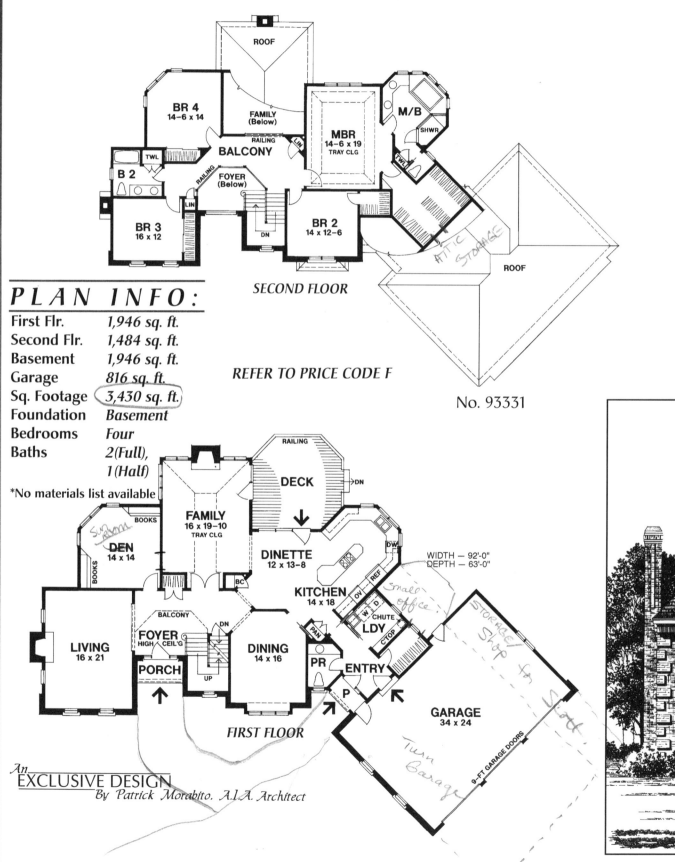

SECOND FLOOR

REFER TO PRICE CODE F

No. 93331

PLAN INFO:

First Flr.	1,946 sq. ft.
Second Flr.	1,484 sq. ft.
Basement	1,946 sq. ft.
Garage	816 sq. ft.
Sq. Footage	3,430 sq. ft.
Foundation	Basement
Bedrooms	Four
Baths	2(Full), 1(Half)

*No materials list available

WIDTH — 92'-0"
DEPTH — 63'-0"

FIRST FLOOR

An
EXCLUSIVE DESIGN
By Patrick Morabito, A.I.A. Architect

- *Windows around the front door, a wide landing staircase and a balcony overlooking the Foyer create a great first impression of this elegant home*

- *Hearth Fireplace centered between two windows invites company from the Foyer*

- *Formal Dining Room offers a decorative bumped out window and a quite place for elegant entertaining*

- *Unusual Den features a corner of windows overlooking the back and side yard, and surrounded by built-in book shelves*

- *Hexagon-shaped Kitchen equipped with a cooktop island/snack bar and a built-in pantry, loads of counter space and an open Dinette area with sliding glass doors to Deck, make this room ideal for cooking and entertaining*

- *A tray ceiling, a huge fireplace surrounded by windows plus access to an outdoor deck make this Family Room ideal for informal gatherings*

- *Luxurious Master Bedroom Suite features a tray ceiling, triple windows, a room-size walk-in closet, and a lavish Bath with an atrium tub, oversized shower and double vanity*

- *Three additional bedrooms with ample closets, off the balcony, share a full hall Bath*

ℙrivate Court Outside Master Bedroom

No. 10534

PLAN INFO:

First Flr.	2,486 sq. ft.
Second Flr.	954 sq. ft.
Basement	2,486 sq. ft.
Garage	576 sq. ft.
Sq. Footage	3,440 sq. ft.
Foundation	Basement
Bedrooms	Four
Baths	3(Full), 1(Half)

REFER TO PRICE CODE F

SECOND FLOOR

An
EXCLUSIVE DESIGN
By Karl Kreeger

*No materials list available

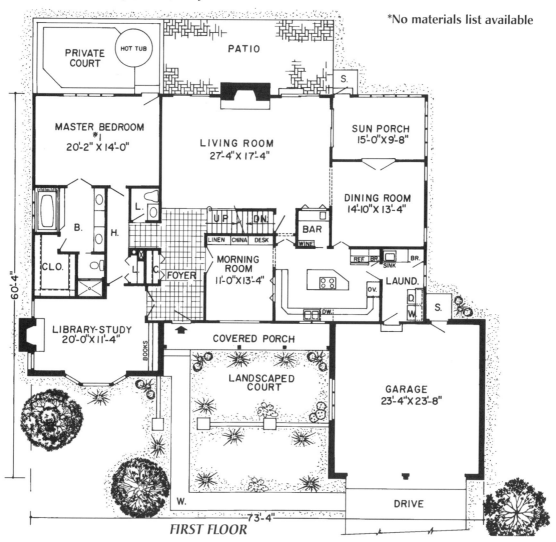

FIRST FLOOR

- Secluded from the rest of the first floor, the Master Bedroom Suite includes an oversized walk-in closet and personal Bath

- Adjoining the luxurious Master Bedroom is a private courtyard complete with hot tub

- Enter the cozy Library through French doors from Foyer

- Comfortable Morning Room features built-in linen closet, china cabinet and desk

- Focal point of spacious Living Room is the warm welcoming fireplace

- Wine storage area behind bar in Living Room for convenience

- Walk out to Sun Porch through French doors in Dining Room

- Overlook the Living Room from the second-floor railing

- Three additional bedrooms, two baths, and plenty of closet space adorn upstairs level

Library And Sunroom Among Many Extras

PLAN INFO:

First Flr.	1,747 sq. ft.
Second Flr.	1,276 sq. ft.
Basement	1,747 sq. ft.
Garage	687 sq. ft.
Sq. Footage	3,023 sq. ft.
Foundation	Bsmt, Slab, Crawl space
Bedrooms	Three
Baths	2(Full), 1(Half)

*No materials list available

REFER TO PRICE CODE E

An
EXCLUSIVE DESIGN
By Britt J. Willis

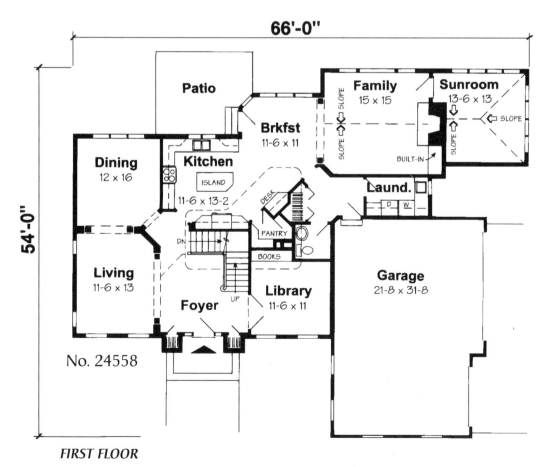

SECOND FLOOR

- WHIRLPOOL TUB
- NICHE
- LINEN
- SH.
- **Mstr. Suite** 14 x 17
- VAULT CLG.
- RAILING
- DN
- LINEN
- **Br 2** 12-6 x 11
- OPEN TO FOYER
- **Br 3** 11-7 x 11
- LEDGE

Optional Crawl/Slab Plan

- STORAGE
- W/H
- FURN

FIRST FLOOR

66'-0"

54'-0"

- **Patio**
- **Brkfst** 11-6 x 11
- **Family** 15 x 15
- SLOPE
- **Sunroom** 13-6 x 13
- **Dining** 12 x 16
- **Kitchen**
- ISLAND 11-6 x 13-2
- DESK
- BUILT-IN
- **Laund.** D W
- DN
- PANTRY
- BOOKS
- **Living** 11-6 x 13
- **Foyer**
- UP
- **Library** 11-6 x 11
- **Garage** 21-8 x 31-8

No. 24558

■ *Elegant entrance into two-story Foyer with graceful landing staircase and triple window leads into front to back Living and Dining Rooms for easy entertaining*

■ *Double door entrance into quiet Library with built-in bookshelves*

■ *Central Kitchen with walk-in pantry, built-in desk and work island easily serves Dining Room, Breakfast and Patio, Family and Sunroom with*

Laundry and Garage close by

■ *Family Room with warm, hearth fireplace and built-in shelves below sloped ceiling offers access to airy Sunroom*

■ *Master Suite crowned by vaulted ceiling features large walk-in closet and plush bath with double vanity and atrium tub*

■ *Two additional bedrooms with large closets share double vanity bath*

$\mathcal{P}$alatial Splendor With Grand Detail

PLAN INFO:

First Flr.	*2,224 sq. ft.*
Second Flr.	*1,841 sq. ft.*
Basement	*2,212 sq. ft.*
Garage	*746 sq. ft.*
Sq. Footage	*4,065 sq. ft.*
Foundation	*Bsmt, Slab, Crawl space*
Bedrooms	*Five*
Baths	*2 (Full), 1 (Half)*

*No materials list available

REFER TO PRICE CODE F

An
EXCLUSIVE DESIGN
By Britt J. Willis

SECOND FLOOR

Mstr Br 17-6 x 15 approx. — pan clg.
2-sided fireplace
open to below
railing
Br 2 14-8 x 12-6 10'-4" clg.
open to below — railing
niche
linen
Br 5 13 x 15-2 approx.
desk
Br 4 12 x 13 10'-4" clg.
linen — shelves
Br 3 13 x 11-8 10'-4" clg.

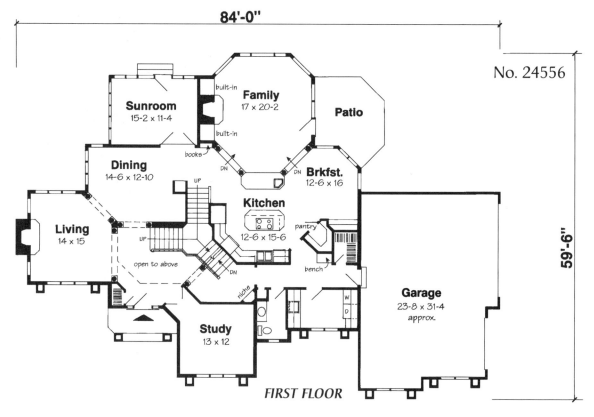

84'-0"

No. 24556

59'-6"

Sunroom 15-2 x 11-4
built-in — Family 17 x 20-2 — Patio
books — built-in
Dining 14-6 x 12-10
UP — DN — Brkfst. 12-6 x 16
Living 14 x 15 — Kitchen 12-6 x 15-6 — pantry
UP — open to above — DN — bench
niche — W D — Garage 23-8 x 31-4 approx.
Study 13 x 12

FIRST FLOOR

- Decorative windows framed by stacked pediments create impressive facade

- Inviting Foyer with grand staircase leads into quiet Study and open Living and Dining Rooms defined by pillars and accented by hearth fireplace and detailed windows

- Grand Kitchen hub of activity with walk-in pantry, cooktop island/snack-bar and separate serving counter opens to glass Breakfast area, Family Room with Patio beyond, Laundry and Garage

- Secluded Master Bedroom suite lavishly accented by two-sided fireplace and pan ceiling offers walk-in closet, double vanity and garden-window tub

- Four additional bedrooms with ample closets share balconies and double-vanity bath

- Entertain elegantly with spacious layout between Dining Room, Living Room, Sunroom, Kitchen and Family Room

Contemporary Drama

No. 99366

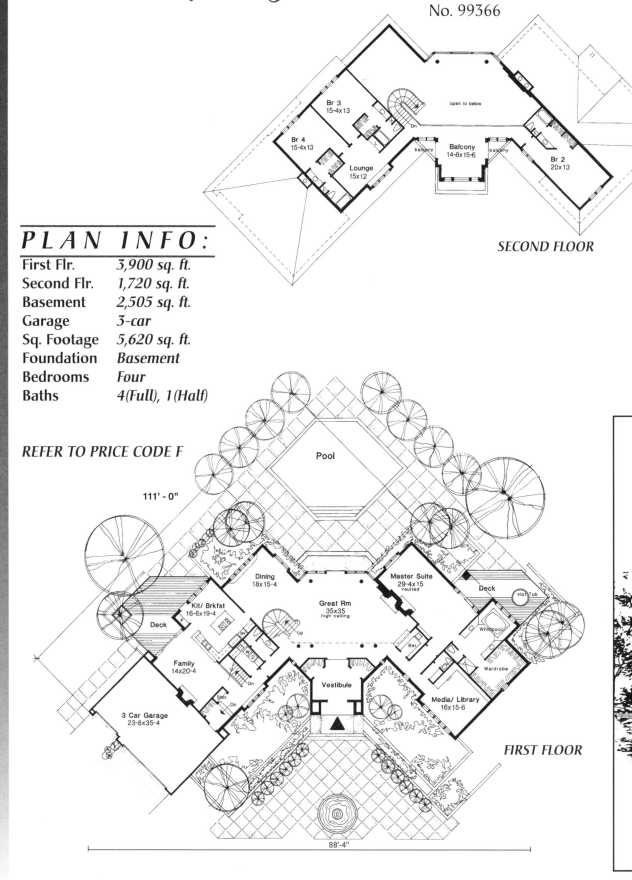

SECOND FLOOR

Br 3
15-4x13

Br 4
15-4x13

open to below

Lounge
15x12

balcony

Balcony
14-8x15-6

balcony

Br 2
20x13

PLAN INFO:

First Flr.	*3,900 sq. ft.*
Second Flr.	*1,720 sq. ft.*
Basement	*2,505 sq. ft.*
Garage	*3-car*
Sq. Footage	*5,620 sq. ft.*
Foundation	*Basement*
Bedrooms	*Four*
Baths	*4(Full), 1(Half)*

REFER TO PRICE CODE F

111' - 0"

Pool

Dining
18x15-4

Master Suite
29-4x15
vaulted

Deck

Hot Tub

Kit/ Brkfst
16-6x19-4

Deck

Great Rm
35x35
high ceiling

Whirlpool

Family
14x20-4

Bar

Wardrobe

3 Car Garage
23-8x35-4

Stor.

Vestibule

Media/ Library
16x15-6

FIRST FLOOR

88'-4"

■ *Special dramatics focused on the grand stairway and balcony above Great Room*

■ *Columned arcade directs traffic from Vestibule to Master Suite and Library wing on left; Family and Kitchen areas on right*

■ *Entrance offers impressive view of the double-height Great Room with a detailed fireplace wall*

■ *Vast Master Suite has walk-in closet and whirlpool tub with twin vanities in the Master Bath*

■ *Private access through the Master Suite allows intimate evenings relaxing in your hot tub on the deck*

■ *Dining Room is open, yet in its own alcove, to savor same spatial elegance*

■ *L-shaped Kitchen opens to the Breakfast area with sliding glass doors to the second deck*

■ *Three additional bedrooms on the second level each sport personal baths and plenty of closet space*

Spacious Loft Ideal As A Playroom, Library, Etc.

PLAN INFO:

First Flr.	*2,887 sq. ft.*
Second Flr.	*1,488 sq. ft.*
Basement	*2,888 sq. ft.*
Garage	*843 sq. ft.*
Sq. Footage	*4,375 sq. ft.*
Foundation	*Basement*
Bedrooms	*Four*
Baths	*3(Full), 2(Half)*

REFER TO PRICE CODE F

BEDROOM 2
14'-2" X 16'-0"

BEDROOM 3
13'-8" X 16'-0"

C.

B.

BEDROOM 4
15'-0" X 22'-10"

SLOPE

DN

LOFT
16'-4" X 24'-0"

C.

B.

C.

SECOND FLOOR

No. 10734

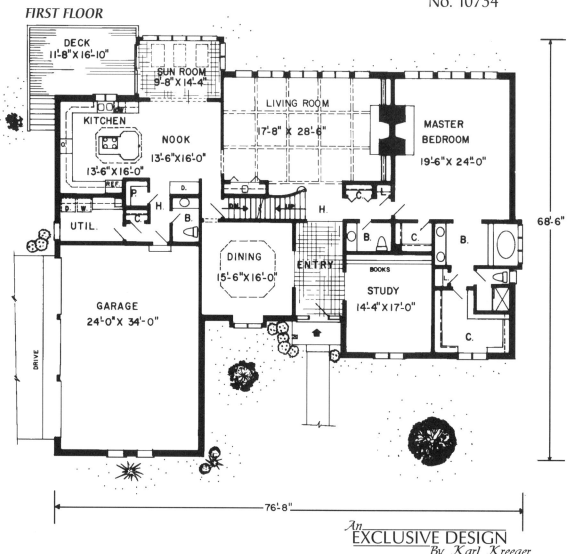

FIRST FLOOR

DECK
11'-8" X 16'-10"

SUN ROOM
9'-8" X 14'-4"

LIVING ROOM
17'-8" X 28'-6"

MASTER BEDROOM
19'-6" X 24'-0"

KITCHEN

NOOK
13'-6" X 16'-0"

13'-6" X 16'-0"

REF.

P.

D.

H.

UTIL.

C.

B.

DN

H.

C.

DINING
15'-6" X 16'-0"

ENTRY

B.

C.

B.

GARAGE
24'-0" X 34'-0"

BOOKS

STUDY
14'-4" X 17'-0"

C.

DRIVE

68'-6"

76'-8"

An
EXCLUSIVE DESIGN
By Karl Kreeger

- *Large, tiled Entry provides easy access to spacious upstairs Loft, offering the perfect playroom for children*

- *Informal meals are enjoyable in the Sun Room, Nook or on the outdoor wood deck*

- *An adjacent Kitchen is designed for efficiency, equipped with a cook top island, more than ample counter space and a built-in pantry*

- *Wood beams and a glowing fireplace in the Living Room make for a cozy escape*

- *First floor Master Suite provides a relaxing atmosphere with its own fireplace and a whirlpool bath*

- *Children's rooms are equipped with their own baths and a double vanity*

Two Story Living Areas Lend A Spacious Air To This Home

No. 93323

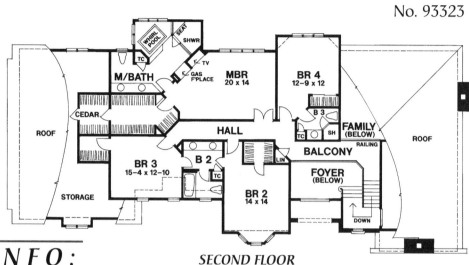

SECOND FLOOR

PLAN INFO:

First Flr.	2,388 sq. ft.
Second Flr.	1,660 sq. ft.
Basement	2,338 sq. ft.
Garage	816 sq. ft.
Sq. Footage	4,048 sq. ft.
Foundation	Basement
Bedrooms	Four
Baths	4(Full), 1(Half)

*No materials list available

REFER TO PRICE CODE F

An
EXCLUSIVE DESIGN
By Patrick Morabito, A.I.A. Architect

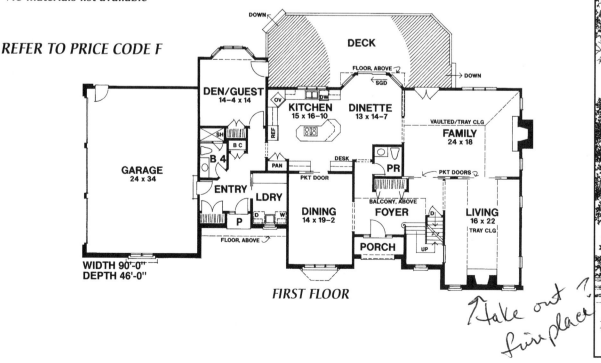

FIRST FLOOR

WIDTH 90'-0"
DEPTH 46'-0"

- *Grand entrance created by a detailed door with sidelights and window transom lead into an open Foyer with window stair landing*

- *Decorative ceiling treatments add drama and fireplaces add warmth to the Living Room and the Family Room*

- *Formal Dining Room enhanced by expansive front window and pocket door leads directly to the Kitchen*

- *Family Room provides access to the Foyer and Living Room with pocket doors, to the outdoor deck by French doors and to the Kitchen area with sliding doors*

- *Efficient Kitchen offers a cooktop island and eating bar, a built-in pantry and planning desk open to a Dinette area with a bay access to outdoor deck*

- *Luxurious second floor Master Bedroom suite has a gas fireplace, a huge walk-in closet, separate cedar closet and large storage area, and a private Bath with a whirlpool, corner tub, over-sized shower and double vanity*

- *Three additional bedrooms, one with a private Bath, the other two sharing a Bath with private accesses*

Customize The Kitchen To Your Liking

PLAN INFO:

First Flr.	1,241 sq. ft.
Second Flr.	1,170 sq. ft.
Basement	1,241 sq. ft.
Garage	512 sq. ft.
Sq. Footage	2,411 sq. ft.
Foundation	Bsmt, Slab, Crawlspace
Bedrooms	Four
Baths	2(Full), 1(Half)

*No materials list available

REFER TO PRICE CODE D

No. 24264

An **EXCLUSIVE DESIGN**
By Energetic Enterprises

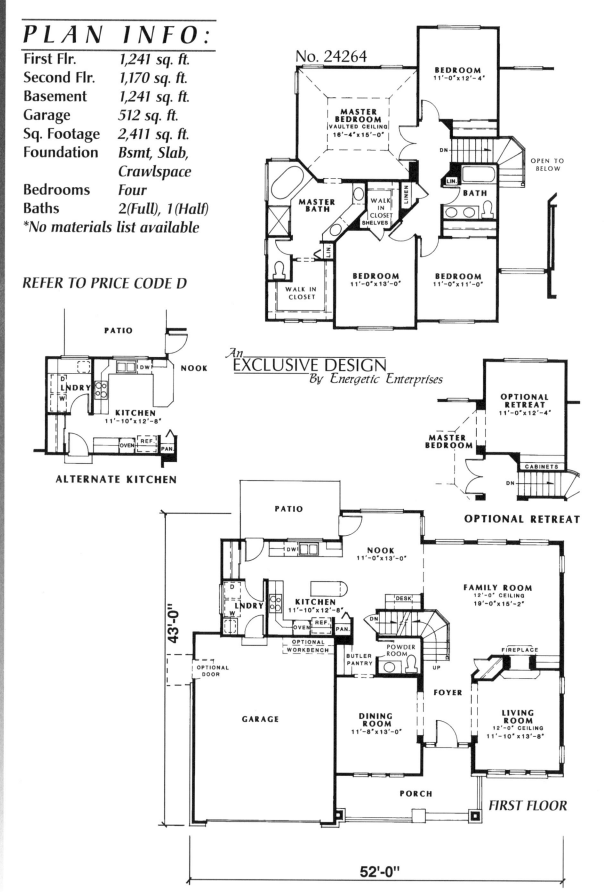

BEDROOM 11'-0"x12'-4"

MASTER BEDROOM VAULTED CEILING 16'-4"x15'-0"

OPEN TO BELOW

MASTER BATH

WALK IN CLOSET SHELVES

LINEN

DN

LIN.

BATH

LIN.

WALK IN CLOSET

BEDROOM 11'-0"x13'-0"

BEDROOM 11'-0"x11'-0"

PATIO

NOOK

D W

LNDRY

DW

KITCHEN 11'-10"x12'-8"

OVEN | REF. | PAN.

ALTERNATE KITCHEN

OPTIONAL RETREAT 11'-0"x12'-4"

MASTER BEDROOM

CABINETS

DN

OPTIONAL RETREAT

43'-0"

PATIO

DW

NOOK 11'-0"x13'-0"

D W

LNDRY

KITCHEN 11'-10"x12'-8"

OVEN | REF. | PAN.

OPTIONAL WORKBENCH

OPTIONAL DOOR

GARAGE

BUTLER PANTRY

DESK

DN

POWDER ROOM

UP

FAMILY ROOM 12'-0" CEILING 19'-0"x15'-2"

FIREPLACE

FOYER

DINING ROOM 11'-8"x13'-0"

LIVING ROOM 12'-0" CEILING 11'-10"x13'-8"

PORCH

FIRST FLOOR

52'-0"

- *Dramatic stone arch leads into open Foyer with curved stairway beyond formal Dining and Living Rooms*

- *Elegant entertaining with decorative windows accenting Dining Room and Living Room with see-through fireplace*

- *Efficient L or U-shaped Kitchen with easy access to Patio, Laundry and Garage serves glassed Nook and Dining Room through Butler Pantry*

- *Luxurious Master Bedroom suite with double door entry below vaulted ceiling offers oversized walk-in closet, two vanities and corner garden tub*

- *Three additional bedrooms with oversized closets share double vanity bath*

- *Huge Family Room with wall of windows overlooking rear yard, ideally next to Kitchen area*

Great Room, Great Hub

PLAN INFO:

First Flr.	*2,010 sq. ft.*
Basement	*2,010 sq. ft.*
Garage	*482 sq. ft.*
Sq. Footage	*2,010 sq. ft.*
Foundation	*Bsmt, Slab, Crawl space*
Bedrooms	*Three*
Baths	*2(Full)*

REFER TO PRICE CODE C

An
EXCLUSIVE DESIGN
By Energetic Enterprises

OPTIONAL DEN
12'-0"x12'-0"
LIN.
OPTIONAL CABINETS

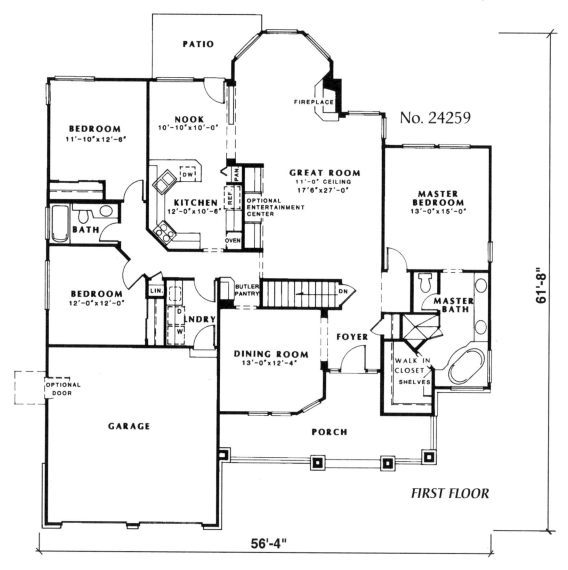

No. 24259

PATIO

FIREPLACE

BEDROOM
11'-10"x12'-6"

NOOK
10'-10"x10'-0"

DW

KITCHEN
12'-0"x10'-6"

REF.
PAN.

OPTIONAL ENTERTAINMENT CENTER

OVEN

GREAT ROOM
11'-0" CEILING
17'6"x27'-0"

MASTER BEDROOM
13'-0"x15'-0"

BATH

BEDROOM
12'-0"x12'-0"

LIN.

D
W

LNDRY

BUTLER PANTRY

DN

MASTER BATH

DINING ROOM
13'-0"x12'-4"

FOYER

WALK IN CLOSET
SHELVES

OPTIONAL DOOR

GARAGE

PORCH

61'-8"

56'-4"

FIRST FLOOR

- *An inviting, covered Porch leads into an open Foyer and Great Room beyond*

- *Gracious entertaining in formal Dining Room with unique decorative windows and butler pantry nearby*

- *Expansive Great Room features an entertainment center and warm, hearth fireplace set between more decorative windows overlooking rear yard*

- *An efficient Kitchen with built-in pantry and a peninsula counter serving Nook area and Patio beyond adjoins Laundry, Garage and Dining Room*

- *Private Master Bedroom suite offers expansive view of rear yard and plush bath with double vanity, walk-in closet and corner garden tub*

- *Two additional bedrooms with over-sized closets share full bath*

Striking, Notable And Very Impressive

No. 91670

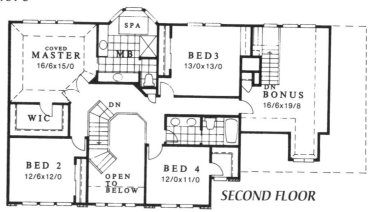

SECOND FLOOR

PLAN INFO:

First Flr.	*1,586 sq. ft.*
Second Flr.	*1,433 sq. ft.*
Bonus Rm.	*305 sq. ft.*
Garage	*632 sq. ft.*
Total Sq. Footage	*3,019 sq. ft.*
Foundation	*Crawl space*
Bedrooms	*Four*
Baths	*2(Full), 1(Half)*

*No materials list available

REFER TO PRICE CODE E

An
EXCLUSIVE DESIGN
By Mark Stewart

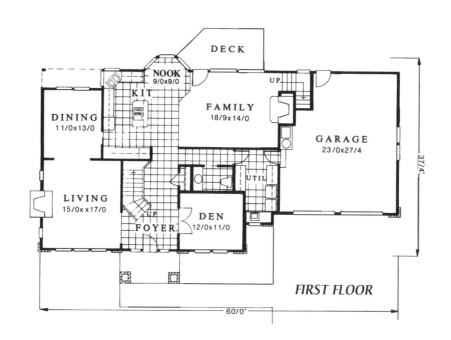

FIRST FLOOR

- *Exciting French Contemporary exterior conceals a simple building form*

- *Spacious formal Living Room, located off the Foyer, includes a large hearth fireplace as a terrific focal point*

- *Formal dining is a delight in the elegant Dining Room that flows from the Living Room and is located next to the Kitchen*

- *Large and expansive Kitchen is equipped with a center, cooktop island, more than ample counter and storage space, plus a sunny Breakfast Nook*

- *Open to the Kitchen and Nook, the Family Room feels even more spacious and includes another great fireplace as well as direct access to the outdoor deck*

- *Cozy Den provides a private area for late night work or just time alone*

- *A coved ceiling crowns the Master Suite that includes a large walk-in closet, and lavish Bath with a spa tub, separate shower and two vanities*

- *Three additional second floor bedrooms share a full, double vanity hall Bath*

Dignified Drama Exudes
From This Charmer

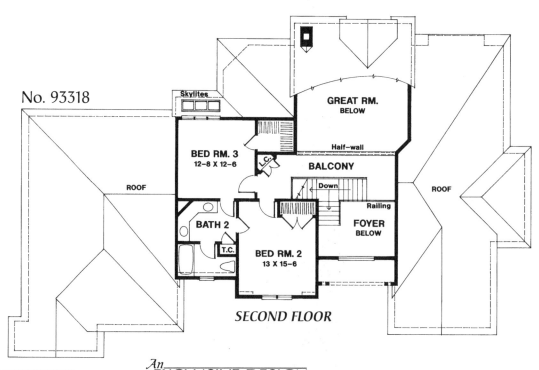

No. 93318

Skylites

GREAT RM.
BELOW

BED RM. 3
12-8 X 12-6

C.

BALCONY

Half-wall

ROOF

Down

Railing

ROOF

BATH 2

T.C.

BED RM. 2
13 X 15-6

FOYER
BELOW

SECOND FLOOR

An
EXCLUSIVE DESIGN
By Patrick Morabito, A.I.A. Architect

PLAN INFO:

First Flr.	*1,984 sq. ft.*
Second Flr.	*633 sq. ft.*
Basement	*1,984 sq. ft.*
Garage	*884 sq. ft.*
Sq. Footage	*2,617 sq. ft.*
Foundation	*Basement*
Bedrooms	*Three*
Baths	*2(Full), 1(Half)*

*No materials list available

REFER TO PRICE CODE E

WIDTH 80'-4"
DEPTH 50'-10"

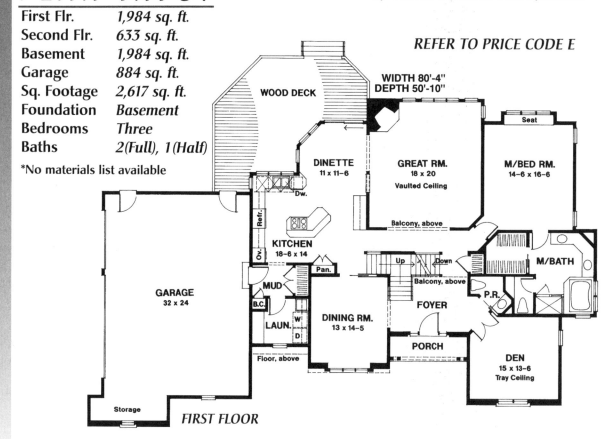

WOOD DECK

DINETTE
11 x 11-6

GREAT RM.
18 x 20
Vaulted Ceiling

Balcony, above

M/BED RM.
14-6 x 16-6

Seat

Dw.

Refr.

KITCHEN
18-6 x 14

Ov.

Pan.

Up

Down

Balcony, above

M/BATH

GARAGE
32 x 24

MUD

B.C.

LAUN.

W
D

DINING RM.
13 x 14-5

FOYER

P.R.

Floor, above

PORCH

DEN
15 x 13-6
Tray Ceiling

Storage

FIRST FLOOR

■ *Columned entrance invites guests into a bright two-story Foyer with a split stairway and impressive balcony*

■ *Vaulted ceiling, glass wall and a corner fireplace in the Great Room provides a spacious but cozy place for family gatherings*

■ *Brightened by skylights above the sink and made convenient by a built-in pantry, center island with cooktop and abundant cabinet space, this Kitchen is sure to please the any gourmet cook*

■ *Quiet corner Den with tray ceiling and decorative front window presents a getaway for daytime projects and late night reading*

■ *Romantic window seat, walk-in closet, luxurious Bath with a double vanity, and a raised window tub allow the Master Suite to become a personal hide-away*

■ *Two additional bedrooms share a large, segmented Bath on second floor*

Pleasing Combination Of Brick And Wood

PLAN INFO:

First Flr.	1,370 sq. ft.
Second Flr.	1,000 sq. ft.
Bonus Room	194 sq. ft.
Basement	1,370 sq. ft.
Garage	667 sq. ft.
Sq. Footage	2,370 sq. ft.
Foundation	Basement
Bedrooms	Three
Baths	2(Full), 1(Half)

REFER TO PRICE CODE D

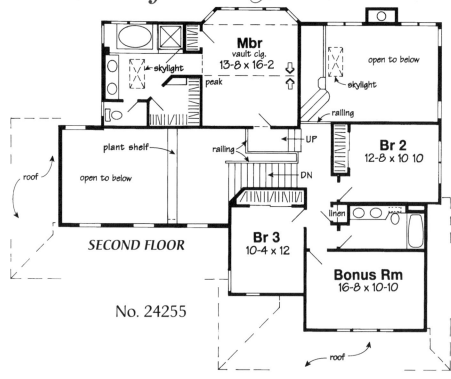

No. 24255

SECOND FLOOR

An EXCLUSIVE DESIGN *By Energetic Enterprises*

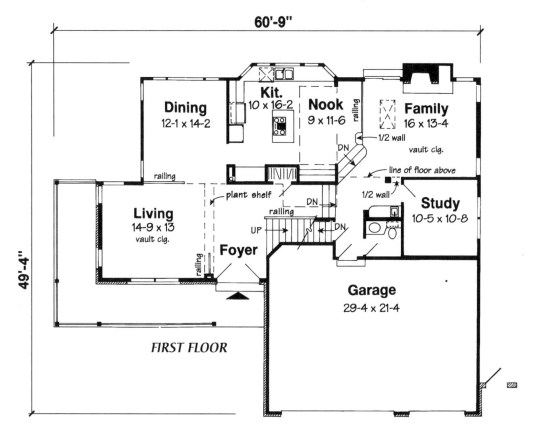

FIRST FLOOR

- *Gracious double door entry from friendly, wrap-around Porch leads into open Foyer with plants and railings defining Living and Dining rooms*

- *Decorative windows and open layout offer easy entertaining in Living and Dining areas*

- *Bright, efficient Kitchen features cooktop serving island, Nook and adjacent Family Room*

- *Comfortable Family Room with vaulted ceiling and cozy fireplace tucked between views and access to rear yard*

- *Plush Master Bedroom suite with private stairway, wall of windows below vaulted ceiling, two closets, skylit bath with double vanity and garden tub*

- *Two additional bedrooms with oversized closets share double-vanity bath*

Two-Story Daylight Basement Design

PLAN INFO:

First Flr.	1,888 sq. ft.
Second Flr.	1,613 sq. ft.
Basement	1,365 sq. ft.
Garage	955 sq. ft.
Sq. Footage	4,866 sq. ft.
Foundation	Bsmt, Crawl space
Bedrooms	Four
Baths	3(Full), 1(Half)

No. 92111

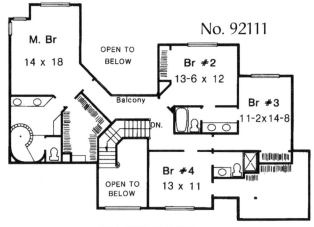

SECOND FLOOR

REFER TO PRICE CODE F

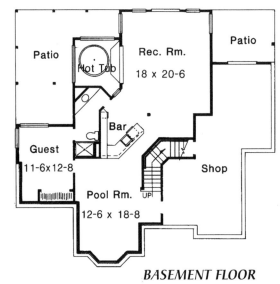

BASEMENT FLOOR

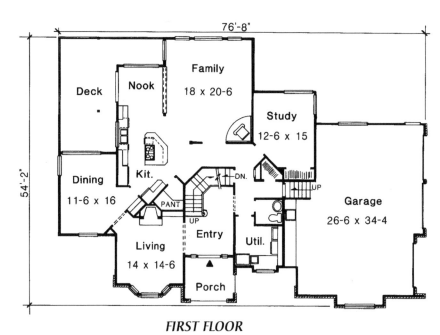

FIRST FLOOR

- *Step-down to the 3-car Garage hidden by a graceful arched window treatment*

- *Secluded Study with corner window affords peaceful atmosphere*

- *Exceptional Family Room has elegant corner fireplace and additional light floods in from door to deck*

- *Private Guest room with ample closet space opens to expansive patio*

- *Island Kitchen features a pantry for extra storage and bright sunny Nook with access to rear deck*

- *Recreation Room with wetbar, private Bath including convenient shower stall, luxurious hot tub, and angled vanity features a Pool Room*

- *Basement complemented by a handy-man Shop located next to the Recreation Room with access to a backyard patio*

Come Inside And Experience
Luxurious Living

PLAN INFO:

First Flr.	2,277 sq. ft.
Second Flr.	1,838 sq. ft.
Basement	2,277 sq. ft.
Garage	1,196 sq. ft.
Sq. Footage	4,115 sq. ft.
Foundation	Basement
Bedrooms	Four
Baths	3(Full), 1(Half)

*No materials list available

REFER TO PRICE CODE F

No. 93328

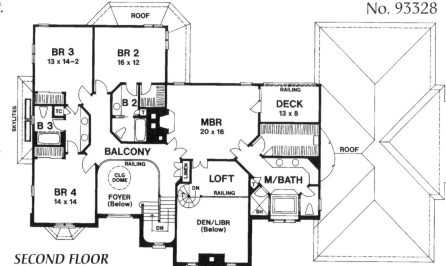

SECOND FLOOR

An
EXCLUSIVE DESIGN
By Patrick Morabito, A.I.A. Architect

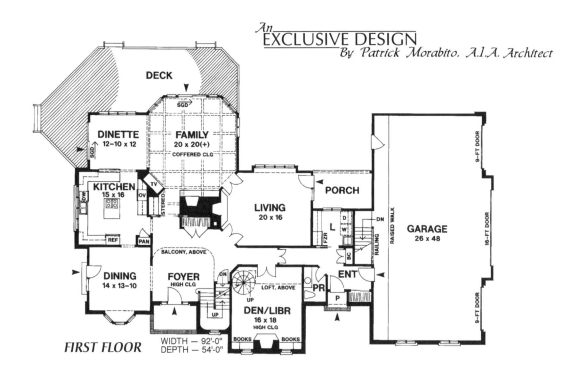

WIDTH — 92'-0"
DEPTH — 54'-0"

FIRST FLOOR

- *Graceful and imposing, this home presents intricate brick detailing, fan top windows and a double front door topped with a arched transom window inviting everyone to come inside*

- *Formal Living Room, accessed by French doors from the Foyer and Family Room, features a huge fireplace, expansive view of the backyard and a private covered Porch to expand living space in warmer weather*

- *Formal Dining Room with a bay window, glass door to the side yard, and adjacent Kitchen allows elegant but efficient entertaining*

- *Convenient Den/Library offers a cozy fireplace set between windows and built-in book shelves, and a unique spiral staircase to a reading Loft*

- *Expansive Family Room provides a wonderful gathering place with a coffered ceiling, huge fireplace, built-in entertainment center, a wall of window with a sliding glass door to the backyard, and open to Dinette area*

- *Gourmet Kitchen located between the Dining Room and Dinette is equipped with a cooktop island, built-in pantry and an abundance of counter and cabinet space*

- *Lavish Master Bedroom Suite includes a cozy fireplace, private deck, large walk-in closet, exclusive access to reading Loft, and an ideal Bath with a raised window tub, step-in shower and double vanity*

- *Three additional large bedrooms have private access to full baths*

Elegance From Any Direction

PLAN INFO:

First Flr.	*1,966 sq. ft.*
Second Flr.	*872 sq. ft.*
Garage	*569 sq. ft.*
Sq. Footage	*2,838 sq. ft.*
Foundation	*Slab, Crawl space*
Bedrooms	*Four*
Baths	*Three*

*No materials list available

REFER TO PRICE CODE E

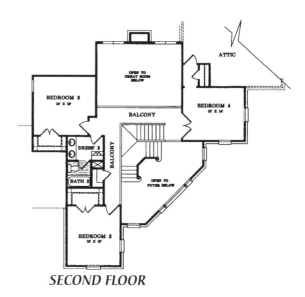

SECOND FLOOR

No. 93034

An
EXCLUSIVE DESIGN
By Belk Home Designs

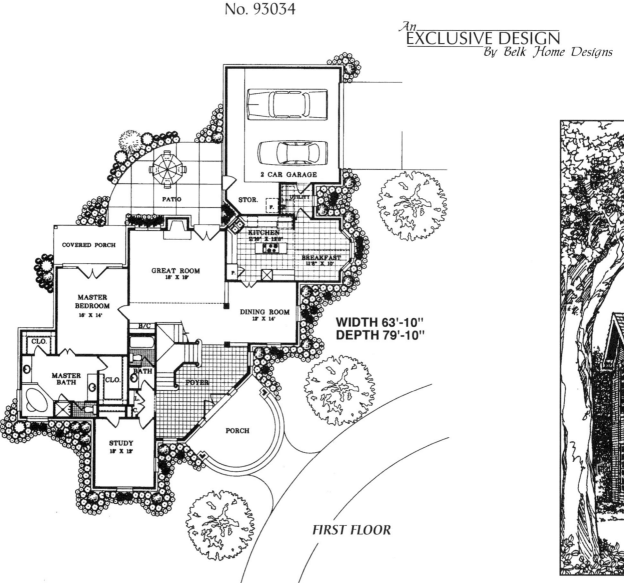

WIDTH 63'-10"
DEPTH 79'-10"

FIRST FLOOR

- *Designed for a corner or pie-shaped lot, this beautiful brick home provides lots of natural light and comfort*

- *Spectacular split staircase moves upward floor from the two-story, glass and tile Foyer*

- *Entrance to the Dining Room features square columns accenting the elegance of the room*

- *Cook top work island and angled window sink help to make this well equipped Kitchen even more efficient*

- *Distinctive Breakfast area accented by a vaulted ceiling and expansive bay window*

- *Sumptuous retreat for the homeowner, the Master Suite includes his-n-her closets and vanities, and a corner whirlpool tub with a separate shower*

- *Three additional bedrooms on the second floor share a double vanity Bath*

$\mathcal{F}$amily Preferred Features In Tudor Design

No. 10568

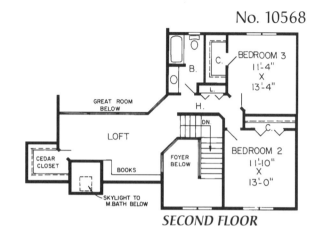

SECOND FLOOR

PLAN INFO:

First Flr.	2,167 sq. ft.
Second Flr.	755 sq. ft.
Basement	2,224 sq. ft.
Garage	690 sq. ft.
Sq. Footage	2,922 sq. ft.
Foundation	Basement
Bedrooms	Three
Baths	3(Full), 1(Half)

REFER TO PRICE CODE E

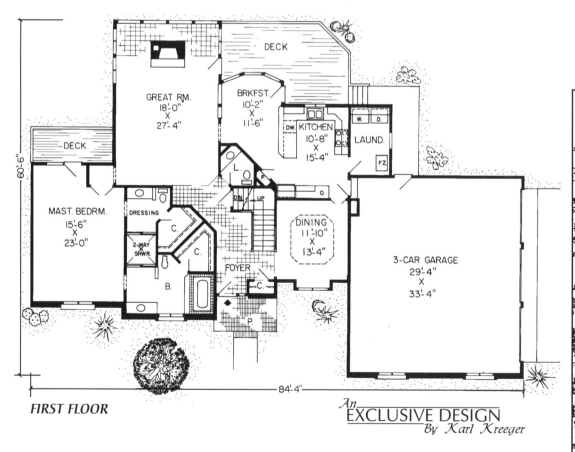

FIRST FLOOR

An
EXCLUSIVE DESIGN
By Karl Kreeger

- *Energy-efficient Foyer leads into an expansive Great Room, featuring a wood-burning fireplace and easy access to the Breakfast Nook and a large deck*

- *A U-shaped Kitchen efficiently located close to both the sunny Breakfast Nook and the elegant formal Dining Room*

- *Deluxe Master Suite includes a private wood deck, two way shower and his and her bathroom, space with separate facilities*

- *Terrific cedar closet located on the second floor is an easy solution to the storage of winter clothing*

- *Special Loft area serves as a balcony over the Great Room*

- *Two additional bedrooms share a full hall Bath*

$\mathcal{D}$istinguished $\mathcal{F}$our $\mathcal{B}$edroom

PLAN INFO:

First Flr.	*1,516 sq. ft.*
Second Flr.	*1,148 sq. ft.*
Basement	*2, sq. ft.*
Garage	*440 sq. ft.*
Sq. Footage	*2,664 sq. ft.*
Width	*59'-6"*
Depth	*40'-0"*
Foundation	*Basement*
Bedrooms	*Four*
Baths	*2(Full), 1(Half)*

*No materials list available

REFER TO PRICE CODE E

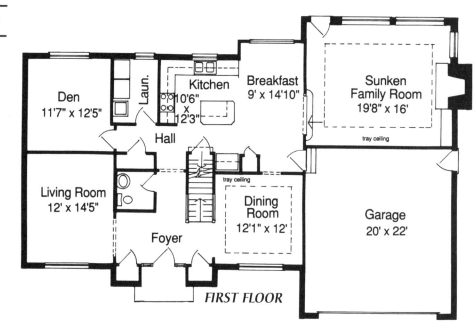

Den
11'7" x 12'5"

Laun.

Kitchen
10'6"
x
12'3"

Breakfast
9' x 14'10"

Sunken
Family Room
19'8" x 16'

tray ceiling

Hall

Living Room
12' x 14'5"

tray ceiling

Dining
Room
12'1" x 12'

Garage
20' x 22'

Foyer

FIRST FLOOR

No. 92616

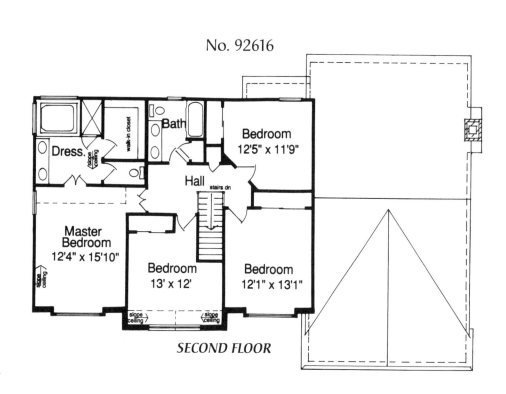

Dress.

slope ceiling

walk-in closet

Bath

Bedroom
12'5" x 11'9"

Hall

stairs dn

Master
Bedroom
12'4" x 15'10"

slope ceiling

Bedroom
13' x 12'

Bedroom
12'1" x 13'1"

slope ceiling

slope ceiling

SECOND FLOOR

- *Covered entrance with sidelights welcomes everyone into Foyer and adjacent Living and Dining Rooms accented by double windows*

- *Work island/snack bar highlights the efficient Kitchen serving the Dining Room, open to the Breakfast area and the Family Room beyond*

- *Three additional bedrooms share a double-vanity bath*

- *Sunken Family Room features a cozy fireplace and a wall of windows with access to the rear yard topped by a tray ceiling*

- *Quiet corner Den offers multiple options for living space*

- *Luxurious Master Bedroom suite offers huge Dressing area with walk-in closet, double vanity and corner-window tub*

Sleek French Contemporary

No. 93047

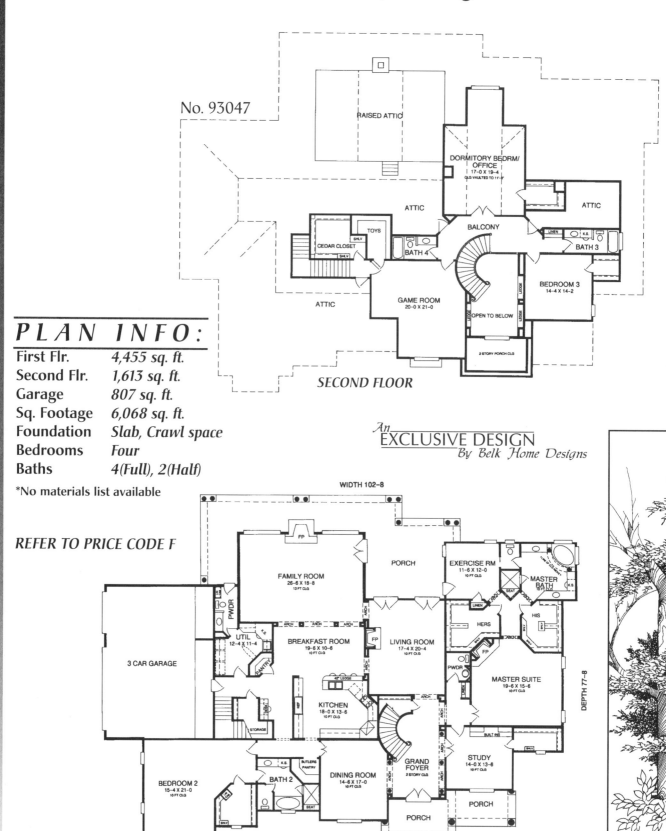

RAISED ATTIC

ATTIC

DORMITORY BEDRM/ OFFICE
17-0 X 19-4
CLG VAULTED TO 11'-0"

ATTIC

BALCONY

TOYS

CEDAR CLOSET

SHLV

SHLV

BATH 4

LINEN

K.S.

BATH 3

ATTIC

GAME ROOM
20-0 X 21-0

OPEN TO BELOW

LEDGE

LEDGE

BEDROOM 3
14-4 X 14-2

2 STORY PORCH CLG

ATTIC

SECOND FLOOR

PLAN INFO:

First Flr.	*4,455 sq. ft.*
Second Flr.	*1,613 sq. ft.*
Garage	*807 sq. ft.*
Sq. Footage	*6,068 sq. ft.*
Foundation	*Slab, Crawl space*
Bedrooms	*Four*
Baths	*4(Full), 2(Half)*

*No materials list available

REFER TO PRICE CODE F

An
EXCLUSIVE DESIGN
By Belk Home Designs

WIDTH 102-8

FP

FAMILY ROOM
26-6 X 18-8
13 FT CLG

PORCH

EXERCISE RM
11-6 X 12-0
10 FT CLG

MASTER BATH

PWDR

UTIL
12-4 X 11-4

K.S.

PANTRY

BREAKFAST ROOM
19-6 X 10-6
10 FT CLG

FP

LIVING ROOM
17-4 X 20-4
10 FT CLG

LINEN

HERS

HIS

3 CAR GARAGE

42" LEDGE

KITCHEN
18-0 X 13-6
10 FT CLG

FP

PWDR

MASTER SUITE
19-6 X 15-6
10 FT CLG

STORAGE

GRAND FOYER
2 STORY CLG

ARCH

BUILT INS

SHLV

STUDY
14-0 X 13-6
10 FT CLG

BEDROOM 2
15-4 X 21-0
10 FT CLG

K.S.

BUTLERS PANTRY

BATH 2

DINING ROOM
14-6 X 17-0
10 FT CLG

SEAT

PORCH

PORCH

DEPTH 77-8

SHLV

WINDOW SEAT

FIRST FLOOR

-202-

- Grand Foyer offers a gracefully, curved staircase, and elegant curved arches into the Formal Dining Room, Study and Living Room

- Formal Living Room features a center fireplace with arches to the Breakfast and Family Rooms as well as direct access to an expansive Porch

- Kitchen, Breakfast Room and an enormous Family Room open to one another to provide a great place for family gatherings

- Luxurious Master Suite with a cozy corner fireplace, his-n-her walk-in closets, an Exercise Room, and elegantly appointed Master Bath will pamper your every need

- A first floor Bedroom with a private large Bath and walk-in closet accommodates guests with privacy

- Two additional bedrooms on the second floor with walk-in closets have access to a full Bath

$\mathcal{T}$imeless Elegance Exudes From This Design

PLAN INFO:

First Flr.	2,080 sq. ft.
Second Flr.	1,051 sq. ft.
Basement	2,080 sq. ft.
Garage	666 sq. ft.
Sq. Footage	3,131 sq. ft.
Foundation	Basement
Bedrooms	Four
Baths	3(Full), 1(Half)

REFER TO PRICE CODE E

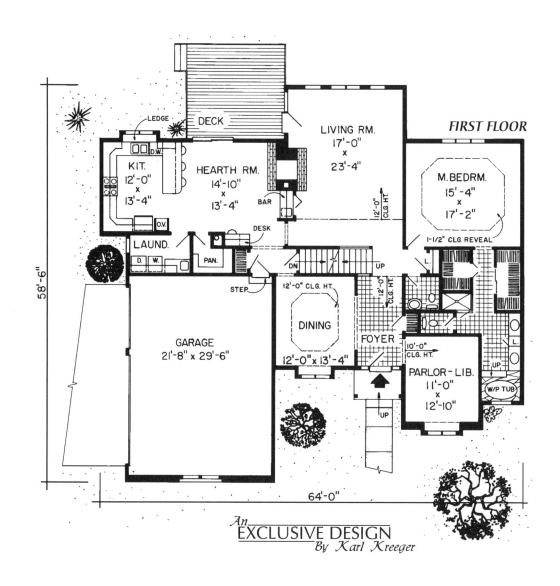

No. 20105

BEDRM. 4
15'-10" x 11'-4"

BEDRM. 2
17'-2" x 11'-0"

SLOPE

BALCONY

DN

HALF WALL

SHELVES

BEDRM. 3
21'-4" x 11'-0"

SLOPE

TO ATTIC

SECOND FLOOR

FIRST FLOOR

LEDGE

DECK

LIVING RM.
17'-0"
x
23'-4"

D.W.

KIT.
12'-0"
x
13'-4"

HEARTH RM.
14'-10"
x
13'-4"

M. BEDRM.
15'-4"
x
17'-2"

BAR

12'-0" CLG. HT.

1-1/2" CLG. REVEAL

O.V.

LAUND.

DESK

DN

UP

D. W.

PAN.

STEP

12'-0" CLG. HT.

12'-0" CLG. HT.

GARAGE
21'-8" x 29'-6"

DINING
12'-0" x 13'-4"

FOYER

10'-0"
CLG. HT.

UP

PARLOR - LIB.
11'-0"
x
12'-10"

W/P TUB

UP

58'-6"

64'-0"

An
EXCLUSIVE DESIGN
By Karl Kreeger

■ *Step through the Foyer past stairway into the massive Living Room characterized by high ceiling, abundant windows, and access to private rear deck*

■ *Both Living and Hearth Rooms share easy entertaining and cozy atmosphere with two-way access to the wetbar and fireplace*

■ *Steal away to quiet solitude in the Parlor/Library for serious contemplation or light conversation with good friends*

■ *Recessed ceiling, twin walk-in closets and a luxurious Bath adorn first floor Master Suite*

■ *Three ample bedrooms enjoy walk-in closets and neighboring baths upstairs*

■ *Overlook the tiled Foyer and Living Room from balcony above*

■ *Revealed ceiling in Dining Room adds sophistication to formal meals*

■ *Adjoining Kitchen with handy breakfast bar and nearby pantry is marvel of convenience*

Two Story Farmhouse With A Wrap-Around Porch

PLAN INFO:

First Flr.	1,590 sq. ft.
Second Flr.	1,344 sq. ft.
Basement	1,271 sq. ft.
Garage	2-car
Sq. Footage	2,934 sq. ft.
Foundation	Basement
Bedrooms	Four
Baths	2(Full), 1(Half)

REFER TO PRICE CODE E

SECOND FLOOR

No. 99205

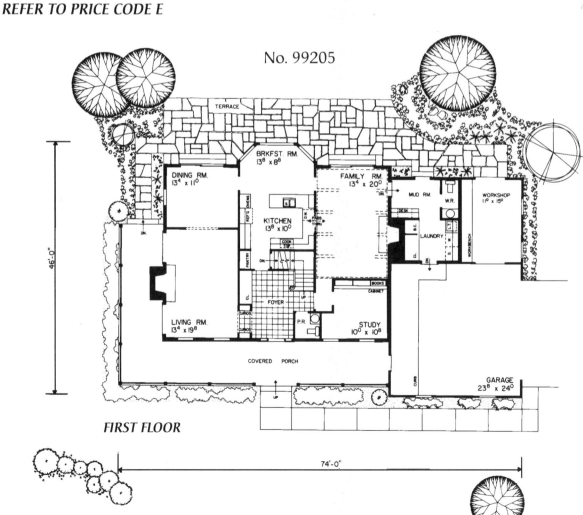

FIRST FLOOR

- *Wrap-around covered porch gives good old-fashioned air of comfort and relaxation*

- *Welcoming Foyer features angled staircase, huge closet, built-in curio shelves and access to a convenient Powder Room*

- *Extra-large Workshop has a built-in workbench for tool organization*

- *Oversized Master Bedroom opens to a Dressing Room with make-up vanity, old-fashioned window seat and his-n-her walk-in closets*

- *Spacious Kitchen with plenty of cabinet and counter space and a cook-top opens to bright sunny Breakfast Room overlooking the backyard terrace*

- *Exceptionally large Family Room with a fireplace and convenient pass-thru to the Kitchen exits to the patio or steps down to Mudroom with a Washroom and handy built-in desk*

- *Three Bedrooms share a full Bath with a double vanity, tub, linen closet and extra towel storage*

Classic Louisiana Raised Cottage

PLAN INFO:

First Flr.	2,551 sq. ft.
Garage	484 sq. ft.
Sq. Footage	2,551 sq. ft.
Foundation	Slab or Crawl space
Bedrooms	Four
Baths	2(Full), 1(Half)

REFER TO PRICE CODE D

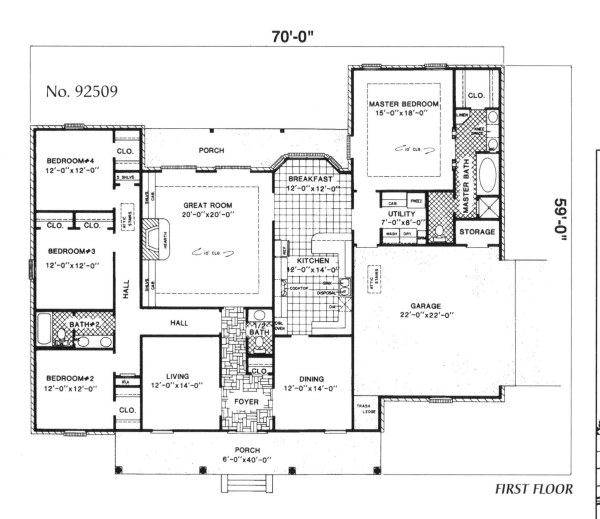

No. 92509

70'-0"

59'-0"

FIRST FLOOR

■ *Wide, covered entrance into bright two-story Foyer with unique curved staircase*

■ *Gracious entertaining in Living Room with cozy fireplace and alcove windows topped by vaulted ceiling*

■ *Efficient Kitchen with island cooktop and walk-in pantry serves Dining Room, Nook and Patio beyond*

■ *Quiet Den offers many options*

■ *Master Bedroom suite, highlighted by bay window, offers plush bath with double vanity, window tub and huge walk-in closet*

■ *Two additional bedrooms with large closets share double-vanity bath and Bonus Room*

Vaulted Ceilings Make This Home Special

PLAN INFO:

First Flr.	4,014 sq. ft.
Second Flr.	727 sq. ft.
Garage	657 sq. ft.
Sq. Footage	4,741 sq. ft.
Foundation	Slab
Bedrooms	Five
Baths	Five

REFER TO PRICE CODE F

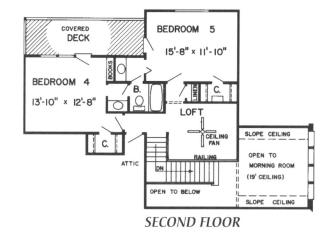

SECOND FLOOR

No. 10698

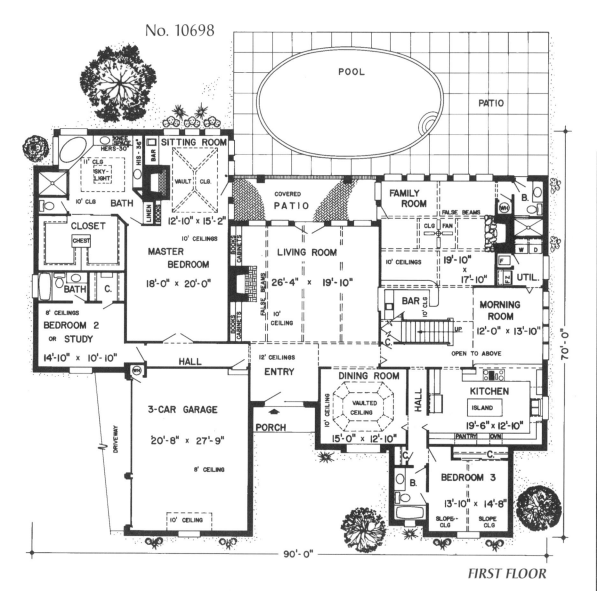

FIRST FLOOR

- *Survey two-story Morning Room and yard beyond from vantage point upstairs*

- *Stately Dining Room displays special ceiling works*

- *Island Kitchen separated from Morning Room by counter bar*

- *Delight in pool vistas from covered patio*

- *Master Suite opens into spacious king-size Bedroom flowing into awesome Sitting Room with built-in bar and fireplace*

- *Two bedrooms adjoining full bath and covered deck share upper level with Loft*

- *Skylit Master Bath features his-n-her basins and leads directly into double walk-in closet*

- *Additional Bedroom adjacent to Master Suite doubles as Study*

- *Both Family Room and Living Room include beamed, ten-foot ceilings, massive fireplaces, and share a wetbar and access to patio*

Five Fireplaces Add A Distinctive Flair

SECOND FLOOR

PLAN INFO:

First Flr.	4,104 sq. ft.
Second Flr.	979 sq. ft.
Basement	2,110 sq. ft.
Garage	2-car
Sq. Footage	5,083 sq. ft.
Foundation	Basement
Bedrooms	Four
Baths	4(Full), 1(Half)

REFER TO PRICE CODE F

No. 99204

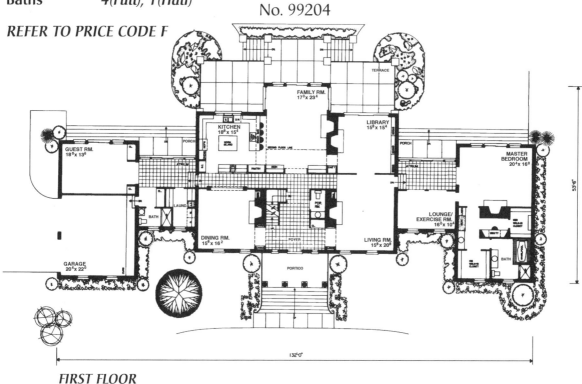

FIRST FLOOR

- *Sprawling portico opens to a two-story Foyer with a sweeping view of the overhead balcony*

- *Fireplaced Dining and Living Rooms allow for formal entertaining*

- *Towering Family Room leads out to an expansive rear terrace*

- *Rear-facing rooms linked to the backyard by charming atrium doors*

- *Centrally located island Kitchen for easy service to active areas*

- *Huge Master suite has a fireplace, luxurious walk-in closets, plush Bath, and extends into a unique exercise room*

- *Upstairs bedrooms feature twin walk-in closets and private baths*

- *Design topped with decorative glass-walled cupola to reflect air of elegance*

- *Guest room has desirable privacy and the added comfort of an adjoining Bath – perfect for entertaining visitors*

$\mathcal{D}$ormers Top Classic Brick Home

PLAN INFO:

First Flr.	2,577 sq. ft.
Second Flr.	68 sq. ft.
Bonus Room	619 sq. ft.
Basement	2,561 sq. ft.
Garage	560 sq. ft.
Sq. Footage	2,645 sq. ft.
Foundation	Bsmt, Slab, Crawl space
Bedrooms	Four
Baths	2(Full), 1(Half)

An
EXCLUSIVE DESIGN
By Jannis Vann & Associates. Inc.

REFER TO PRICE CODE E

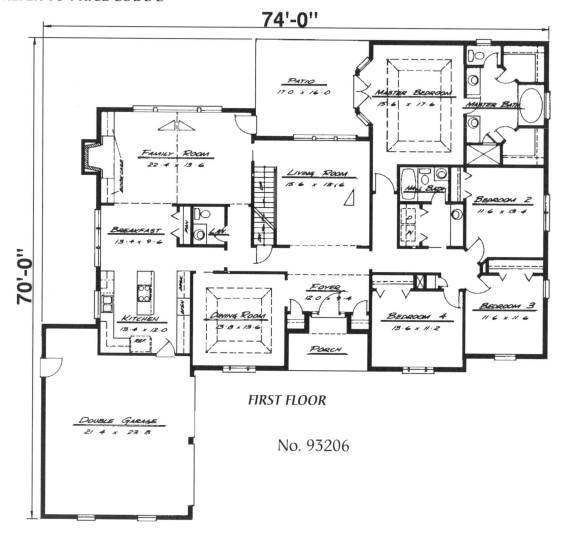

74'-0"

70'-0"

PATIO
17.0 x 16.0

MASTER BEDROOM
15.6 x 17.6

MASTER BATH

FAMILY ROOM
22.4 x 13.6

LIVING ROOM
15.6 x 13.6

HALL BATH

BEDROOM 2
11.6 x 13.4

BREAKFAST
13.4 x 9.6

LAV.

KITCHEN
13.4 x 12.0

DINING ROOM
13.8 x 13.6

FOYER
12.0 x 9.4

BEDROOM 4
13.6 x 11.2

BEDROOM 3
11.6 x 11.6

PORCH

DOUBLE GARAGE
21.4 x 23.8

FIRST FLOOR

No. 93206

- *A covered entrance leads into open Foyer and formal Living Room with a wall of glass overlooking Patio and rear yard*

- *Tray ceiling crowns formal Dining Room giving an elegant atmosphere for entertaining*

- *Kitchen offers cooktop island, ample counter and storage space, ideally adjacent to Breakfast nook, Family Room, Dining Room and Garage*

- *Spacious Family Room made cozy by huge fireplace between built-in shelves*

- *and airy by a wall of windows below vaulted ceiling*

- *Private Master Bedroom suite offers French doors to Patio, a decorative ceiling and a lavish Master Bath with twin vanities, walk-in closets and a garden tub*

- *Three additional bedrooms with ample closet space share a full bath*

- *An unfinished second floor offers plenty of room for expansion*

$\mathcal{U}$nique Octagon Sunroom

PLAN INFO:

First Flr.	*1,799 sq. ft.*
Second Flr.	*1,318 sq. ft.*
Basement	*1,799 sq. ft.*
Garage	*768 sq. ft.*
Sq. Footage	*3,117 sq. ft.*
Foundation	*Basement*
Bedrooms	*Four*
Baths	*2(Full), 1(Half)*

*No materials list available

REFER TO PRICE CODE E

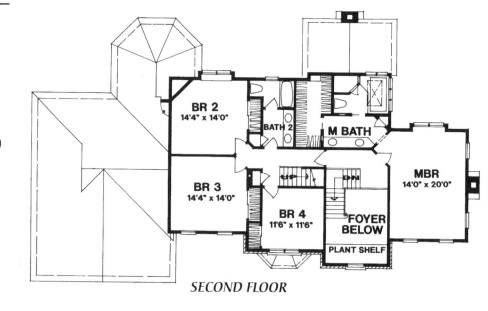

SECOND FLOOR

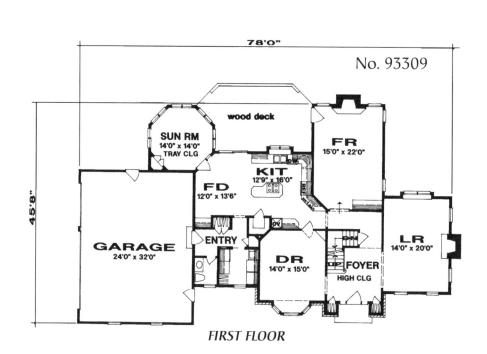

No. 93309

FIRST FLOOR

An
EXCLUSIVE DESIGN
By Patrick Morabito, A.I.A. Architect

- *Arched entrance into two-story Foyer with landing staircase, coat closets and easy access to formal Living and Dining Rooms*
- *Beautiful bay window in formal Dining Room and decorative windows in Living Room with fireplace add elegance to entertaining*
- *Central Kitchen with walk-in pantry and cooktop island easily serves Dining and Family Rooms, Sun Room and Wood Deck with Garage and Laundry nearby*
- *Spacious Master Bedroom suite features windows on three sides, an ultra Master Bath and a large walk-in closet*
- *Three additional bedrooms share double vanity bath*

Bridge Over Foyer Is A Unique Feature Of This Home

No. 10535

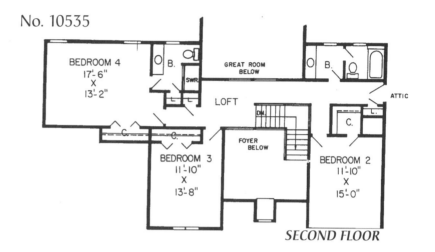

SECOND FLOOR

PLAN INFO:

First Flr.	2,335 sq. ft.
Second Flr.	1,157 sq. ft.
Basement	2,281 sq. ft.
Garage	862 sq. ft.
Sq. Footage	3,492 sq. ft.
Foundation	Basement
Bedrooms	Four
Baths	3(Full), 2(Half)

REFER TO PRICE CODE F

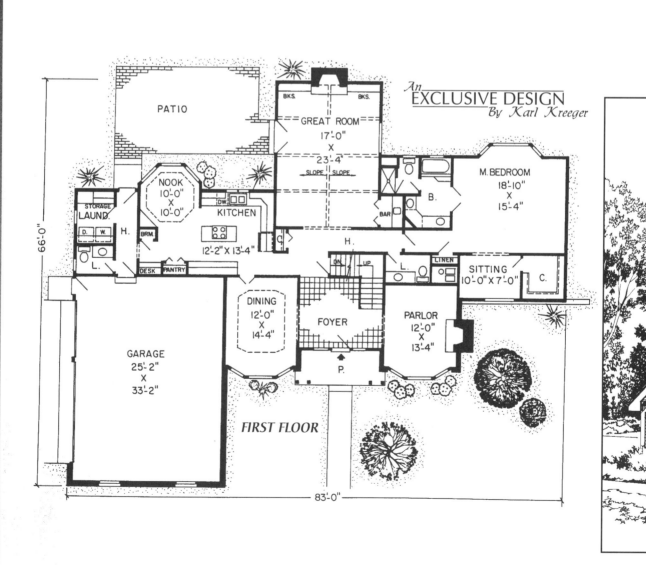

An EXCLUSIVE DESIGN
By Karl Kreeger

FIRST FLOOR

- A dramatic, two-story Foyer opens into a Great Room with a cathedral ceiling and a cozy fireplace framed with built-in bookcases

- Both a formal Parlor, with its own fireplace, and an elegant Dining Room with a decorative ceiling provide a view of the front yard through inviting bay windows

- An octagonal Breakfast Nook adds to the already spacious and well-appointed Kitchen

- A cooktop work island, double sink, built-in pantry, built-in desk and a broom closet are just a few of the amenities awaiting you in the efficient Kitchen

- The first floor Master Bedroom is equipped with a quaint sitting room, private compartmented Bath and a walk-in closet

- Three additional bedrooms share the second floor with a Loft and two full Baths

*I*mpressive Stucco And Stone

PLAN INFO:

First Flr.	1,090 sq. ft.
Second Flr.	1,331 sq. ft.
Basement	1,022 sq. ft.
Garage	562 sq. ft.
Sq. Footage	2,421 sq. ft.
Foundation	Basement or Crawl space
Bedrooms	Four
Baths	2(Full), 1(Half)

*No materials list available

REFER TO PRICE CODE D

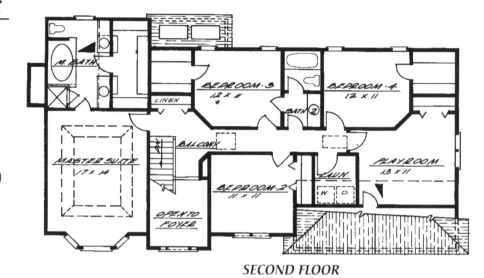

SECOND FLOOR

An EXCLUSIVE DESIGN
By Jannis Vann & Associates, Inc.

No. 93208

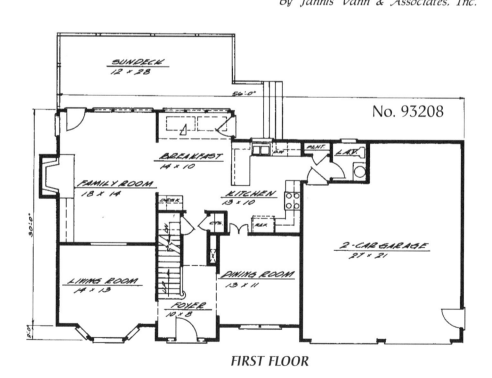

FIRST FLOOR

- *Decorative window over entrance of two-story Foyer provides light and elegance upon entering this home*

- *Formal Living Room with wonderful bay window and Dining Room on opposite side of Foyer offer ease in entertaining*

- *Family Room offers a cozy fireplace with built-in shelves and a wall of windows with access to Sundeck*

- *An efficient Kitchen with built-in pantry and a peninsula counter/snackbar easily serves Breakfast nook and Dining Room*

- *Private Master Suite with lovely bay window topped by a decorative ceiling and pampered by a lavish bath and large walk-in closet*

- *Three additional bedrooms, two with walk-in closets, share a full bath and a Playroom or fifth bedroom*

*D*ynamic *B*rick *A*nd *W*ood *S*iding

PLAN INFO:

First Flr.	*2,250 sq. ft.*
Garage	*543 sq. ft.*
Sq. Footage	*2,250 sq. ft.*
Width	*61'-6"*
Depth	*73'-0"*
Foundation	*Slab or*
	Crawl space
Bedrooms	*Four*
Baths	*2(Full)*

*No materials list available

REFER TO PRICE CODE D

An EXCLUSIVE DESIGN
By Belk Home Designs

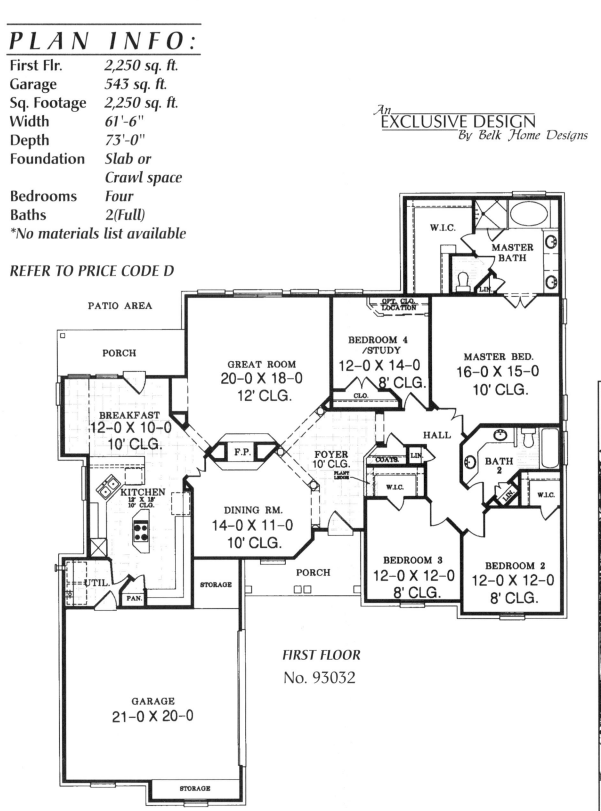

FIRST FLOOR
No. 93032

■ *A pair of graceful arches over Porch leads into tiled Foyer and formal Dining Room and Great Room framed by arched columns.*

■ *The Great Room offers an expansive view of backyard through a wall of windows and warmth with see-through fireplace shared with Dining Room*

■ *A country-size Kitchen with cooktop work island, pantry, Utilities, Breakfast*

area leading to Porch and Patio and adjacent to Garage and Dining Room

■ *French doors lead into Master Bedroom suite with a plush Master Bath with over-sized walk-in closet and shower, double vanity and window whirlpool tub.*

■ *Two additional bedrooms with walk-in closets share a full bath, with another double vanity and a window tub*

Contemporary Two-Story With Secluded Sleeping Area

PLAN INFO:

First Flr.	1,712 sq. ft.
Second Flr.	1,387 sq. ft.
Basement	1,548 sq. ft.
Garage	831 sq. ft.
Sq. Footage	3,099 sq. ft.
Foundation	Basement
Bedrooms	Four
Baths	3 (Full), 1 (Half)

*No materials list available

REFER TO PRICE CODE E

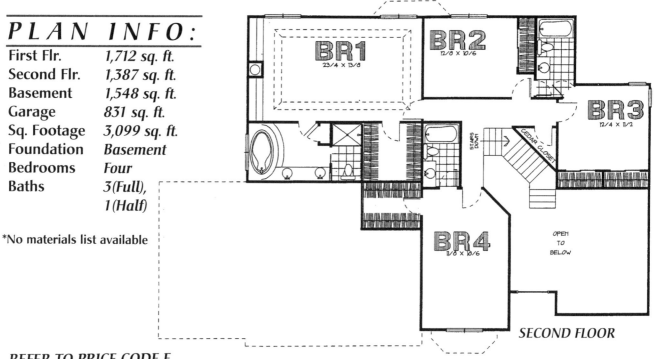

SECOND FLOOR

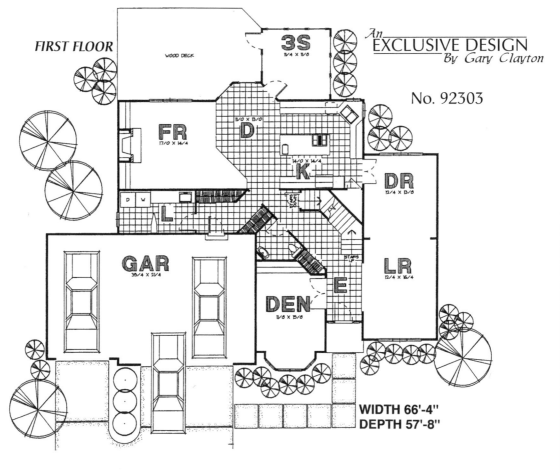

FIRST FLOOR

An EXCLUSIVE DESIGN
By Gary Clayton

No. 92303

WIDTH 66'-4''
DEPTH 57'-8''

- *Beautiful Den with built-in book-shelves located off curved Entry features picturesque bay window*

- *Fireplaced Family Room merges with a sunny Dinette and large Kitchen creating an open airy feeling*

- *Country Kitchen features large center island with vegetable sink and stove top and corner sink*

- *Atrium doors open from Kitchen into formal Dining Room and vaulted Living Room*

- *First-floor Laundry Room conveniently situated off the 3-car Garage doubles as a mudroom*

- *Master suite on upper level has coffered ceilings, massive walk-in closet and luxurious bath with whirlpool tub*

- *Three additional bedrooms sharing a full Bath and Cedar Closet occupy remainder of second level*

- *Three-season porch just off Dinette offers protected outdoor relaxation*

ℛelax On Your Own Private Veranda

PLAN INFO:

First Flr.	*3,051 sq. ft.*
Garage	*646 sq. ft.*
Sq. Footage	*3,051 sq. ft.*
Foundation	*Crawl space*
Bedrooms	*Three*
Baths	*3(Full), 1(Half)*

REFER TO PRICE CODE E

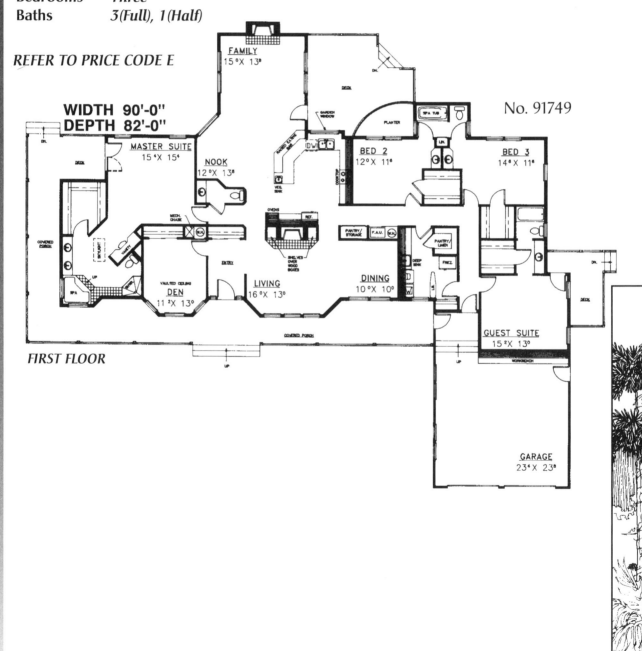

WIDTH 90'-0"
DEPTH 82'-0"

No. 91749

FAMILY
15⁰X 13⁰

MASTER SUITE
15⁴X 15⁴

NOOK
12⁰X 13⁸

BED 2
12⁰X 11⁶

BED 3
14⁶X 11⁶

DEN
11²X 13⁰

LIVING
16⁰X 13⁰

DINING
10⁰X 10⁰

GUEST SUITE
15²X 13⁰

GARAGE
23⁴X 23⁸

FIRST FLOOR

■ *Inspired by warm climates this friendly home features a wrap-around porch accessible from most of the living areas and the Master Suite*

■ *Both the Living Room/Dining Room area and the Family Room feature hearth fireplaces to chase evening chill away*

■ *More than accommodating Guest room has a private Bath*

■ *Skylit Master Suite has an elevated custom spa, double vanity, walk-in closet, and an additional vanity outside of the bathroom*

■ *Each of the three additional bedrooms have walk-in closets and share a full Bath*

$\mathcal{P}$erfect For Large Parties
Or Intimate Gatherings

PLAN INFO:

First Flr.	2,310 sq. ft.
Second Flr.	866 sq. ft.
Garage	679 sq. ft.
Sq. Footage	3,176 sq. ft.
Foundation	Slab
Bedrooms	Three
Baths	3(Full), 1(Half)

REFER TO PRICE CODE E

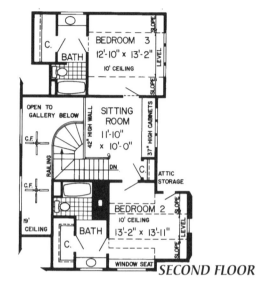

SECOND FLOOR

No. 10663

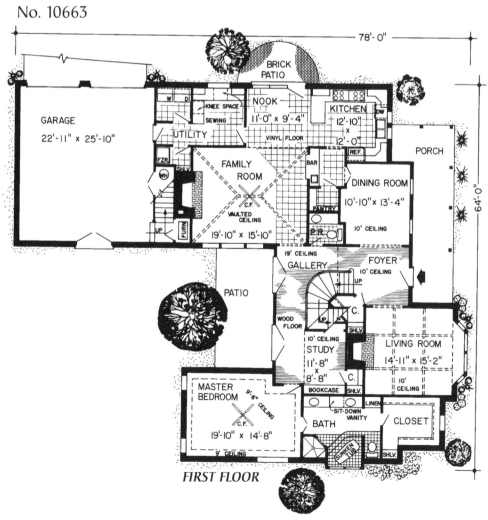

FIRST FLOOR

■ *Greet guests in this fabulous Foyer adorned with an impressive two-story gallery behind a beautiful curving stairway*

■ *Leisurely unwind with family and friends in this Family Room with a vaulted ceiling, large windows, built-in bar, and lots of space*

■ *Entertain guests in the Dining Room for more formal occasions*

■ *Lovely Sitting Room between two second-floor Bedrooms overlooks Gallery below*

■ *Master Bedroom with paddle fan offers cool comfort for a good night's rest*

■ *Lavish Bath in Master Suite features sunken tub to soak away the day's cares*

■ *Two bedrooms on upper floor include individual baths and walk-in closets*

■ *Cheerful Eating Nook has easy approach to efficient Kitchen*

■ *Wood beams on ceiling of Living Room exudes warm welcome*

Colonial Tradition In A Very Neat Layout

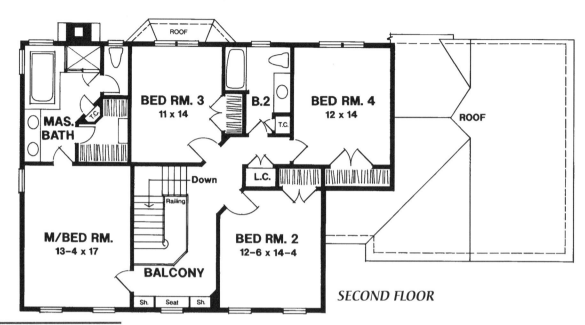

ROOF

MAS. BATH

T.C.

BED RM. 3
11 x 14

B.2

T.C.

BED RM. 4
12 x 14

ROOF

Down

Railing

L.C.

M/BED RM.
13-4 x 17

BED RM. 2
12-6 x 14-4

BALCONY

Sh. Seat Sh.

SECOND FLOOR

PLAN INFO:

First Flr.	1,228 sq. ft.
Second Flr.	1,191 sq. ft.
Basement	1,228 sq. ft.
Garage	528 sq. ft.
Sq. Footage	2,419 sq. ft.
Foundation	Basement
Bedrooms	Four
Baths	2(Full), 1(Half)

*No materials list available

An
EXCLUSIVE DESIGN
By Patrick Morabito, A.I.A. Architect

REFER TO PRICE CODE D

No. 93319

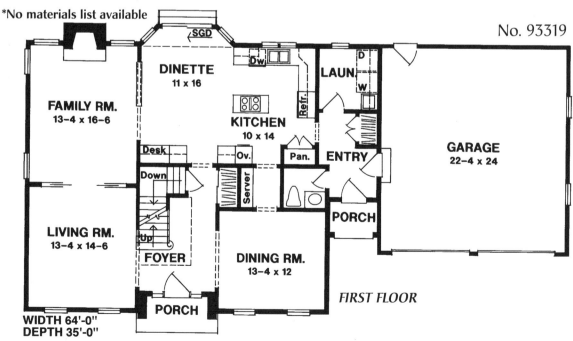

SGD

FAMILY RM.
13-4 x 16-6

DINETTE
11 x 16

Dw

LAUN

D
W

KITCHEN
10 x 14

Refr.

GARAGE
22-4 x 24

Desk

Down

Ov.

Pan.

Server

ENTRY

LIVING RM.
13-4 x 14-6

Up

PORCH

FOYER

DINING RM.
13-4 x 12

PORCH

FIRST FLOOR

WIDTH 64'-0"
DEPTH 35'-0"

- Recessed entrance leads guests into a classic Foyer with a wrap-around stairway, balcony and easy access to all main floor rooms

- Large formal Living Room and Dining Room make entertaining a breeze

- Expansive Kitchen features a cooktop island, built-in pantry, double sink, planning area, and a warm, open Dinette area with alcove sliding doors to the outdoors

- Spacious Family Room, open on all sides, offers convenience and warmth with a hearth fireplace corner

- windows, and sliding doors to the living room and Kitchen area

- Luxurious, front-to-back Master Bedroom Suite with a private, segmented Bath offers a large walk-in closet, double vanity and raised window tub

- Balcony area has a built-in window seat to cuddle up and read a book or just enjoy the view

- Three additional bedrooms, each with ample closet space, share a full hall Bath

Expansive And Elegant Master Suite

PLAN INFO:

First Flr.	1,307 sq. ft.
Second Flr.	1,333 sq. ft.
Bonus	308 sq. ft.
Basement	1,307 sq. ft.
Garage	528 sq. ft.
Sq. Footage	2,640 sq. ft.
Foundation	Bsmt, Slab, Crawl space
Bedrooms	Four
Baths	2(Full), 1(Half)

*No materials list available

REFER TO PRICE CODE E

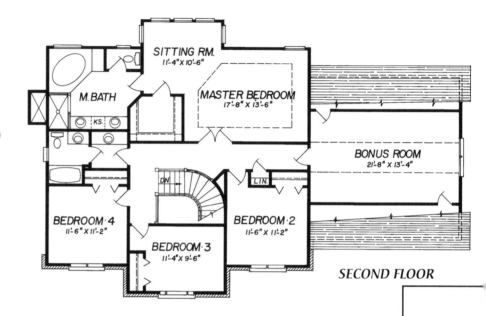

An
EXCLUSIVE DESIGN
By Jannis Vann & Associates, Inc.

No. 93241

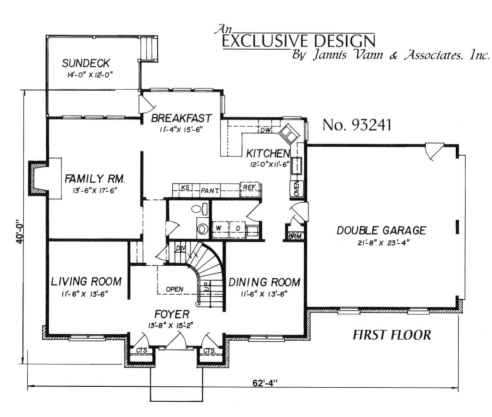

SECOND FLOOR

FIRST FLOOR

■ *A room-sized Foyer features a gracefully curved staircase with formal Living and Dining Rooms on either side for ease in entertaining*

■ *Focal point fireplace and a wall of windows overlooking Sundeck and rear yard compliment Family Room*

■ *An efficient Kitchen with built-in pantry and peninsula counter/snackbar serving Breakfast adjoins laundry, Dining Room and Garage*

■ *Entire rear of second floor devoted to Master Bedroom suite with decorative ceiling, a separate glassed Sitting Room, huge walk-in closet and a lavish Master Bath with a corner garden tub and twin sinks*

■ *Three additional bedrooms with decorative windows share a full bath and a Bonus Room that offers many options*

$\mathcal{D}$ignified Traditional Brick Design

PLAN INFO:

First Flr.	*2,292 sq. ft.*
Garage	*526 sq. ft.*
Sq. Footage	*2,292 sq. ft.*
Foundation	*Slab, Crawl space***
Bedrooms	*Four*
Baths	*2(Full), 1(Half)*

*No materials list available

**Please specify when ordering

An
EXCLUSIVE DESIGN
By Belk Home Designs

WIDTH 80-7

REFER TO PRICE CODE D

No. 93049

DEPTH 50-6

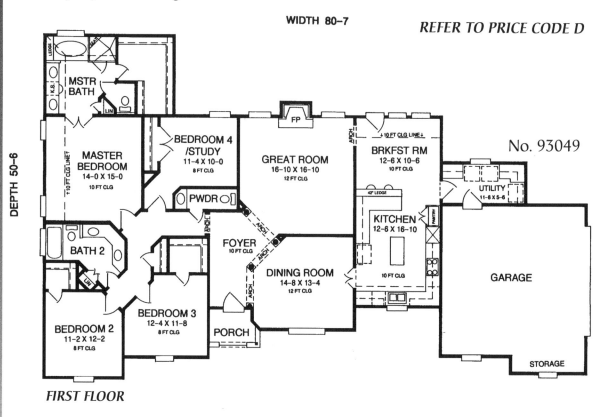

LEDGE

MSTR BATH

MASTER BEDROOM
14-0 X 15-0
10 FT CLG

BEDROOM 4 /STUDY
11-4 X 10-0
8 FT CLG

GREAT ROOM
16-10 X 16-10
12 FT CLG

FP

ARCH

↓10 FT CLG LINE↓

BRKFST RM
12-6 X 10-6
10 FT CLG

UTILITY
11-8 X 5-6

PWDR

FOYER
10 FT CLG

BATH 2

42" LEDGE

KITCHEN
12-6 X 16-10

10 FT CLG

GARAGE

BEDROOM 2
11-2 X 12-2
8 FT CLG

BEDROOM 3
12-4 X 11-8
8 FT CLG

PORCH

DINING ROOM
14-8 X 13-4
12 FT CLG

STORAGE

FIRST FLOOR

■ Covered entrance leads into the open Foyer accented by dramatic columns farming entrance to the elegant Dining Room and the expansive Great Room

■ Convenient floor plan separates living area and sleeping areas all on one level

■ Spacious, gourmet Kitchen made efficient by an abundance of counter and cabinet space, a built-in pantry, work island and snack bar as well as direct access to Dining Room, Utility Room and Breakfast Room

■ Entertaining is a delight in the Great Room with a hearth fireplace framed by windows and adjacent to the kitchen area

■ Lavish Master Bedroom Suite includes an enormous walk-in closet and a ultra Bath with a window tub, extra-large shower and double vanity

■ Three additional bedrooms with huge closets share a full Bath with a double vanity

Unique Balcony Window Seat

PLAN INFO:

First Flr.	*1,536 sq. ft.*
Second Flr.	*1,245 sq. ft.*
Basement	*1,536 sq. ft.*
Garage	*816 sq. ft.*
Sq. Footage	*2,781 sq. ft.*
Foundation	*Basement*
Bedrooms	*Four*
Baths	*2(Full), 1(Half)*

No materials list available

REFER TO PRICE CODE E

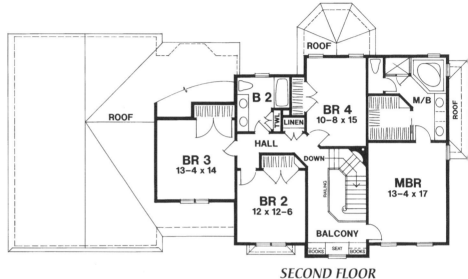

SECOND FLOOR

An
EXCLUSIVE DESIGN
By Patrick Morabito, A.I.A. Architect

No. 93339

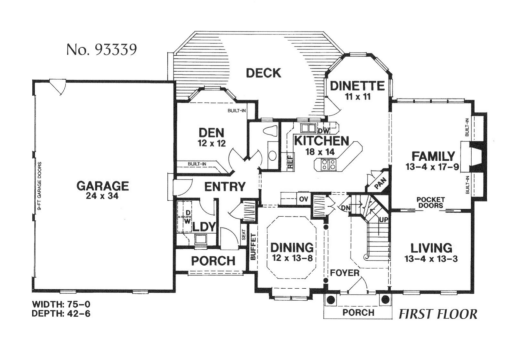

WIDTH: 75–0
DEPTH: 42–6

FIRST FLOOR

- *An arched entry elegantly frames formal front door leading into large Foyer with dramatic staircase*

- *Columns frame formal Dining room highlighted by built-in buffet and decorative window and ceiling*

- *Formal Living room with pocket doors leading to Family room offers flexible living*

- *Family room features large hearth fireplace nestled between built-ins and wall of windows overlooking rear yard*

- *Efficient L-shaped Kitchen with built-in pantry and island cooktop serves glass alcove Dinette area and Deck beyond, Family room, and Dining room*

- *Secluded Den with bay window and built-ins offers many options*

- *Private and spacious Master Bedroom suite features walk-in closet and plush bath with double vanity and corner-window tub*

- *Three additional bedrooms with ample closet space share full double vanity bath*

*U*nique *B*rick *T*reatment
*E*nhances *T*his *F*acade

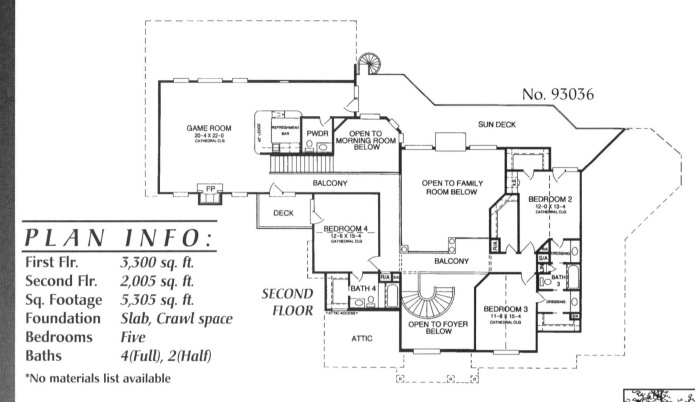

No. 93036

GAME ROOM
20-4 X 22-0
CATHEDRAL CLG

REFRESHMENT BAR

PWDR

OPEN TO MORNING ROOM BELOW

SUN DECK

42" LEDGE

FP

BALCONY

DECK

BEDROOM 4
12-6 X 15-4
CATHEDRAL CLG

OPEN TO FAMILY ROOM BELOW

BALCONY

BEDROOM 2
12-0 X 13-4
CATHEDRAL CLG

DRESSING

S/A

BATH 3

BATH 4

R/A   S/A

BEDROOM 3
11-8 X 15-4
CATHEDRAL CLG

DRESSING

S/A

SECOND FLOOR

ATTIC ACCESS

OPEN TO FOYER BELOW

ATTIC

PLAN INFO:

First Flr.	*3,300 sq. ft.*
Second Flr.	*2,005 sq. ft.*
Sq. Footage	*5,305 sq. ft.*
Foundation	*Slab, Crawl space*
Bedrooms	*Five*
Baths	*4(Full), 2(Half)*

No materials list available

REFER TO PRICE CODE F

An EXCLUSIVE DESIGN
By Belk Home Designs

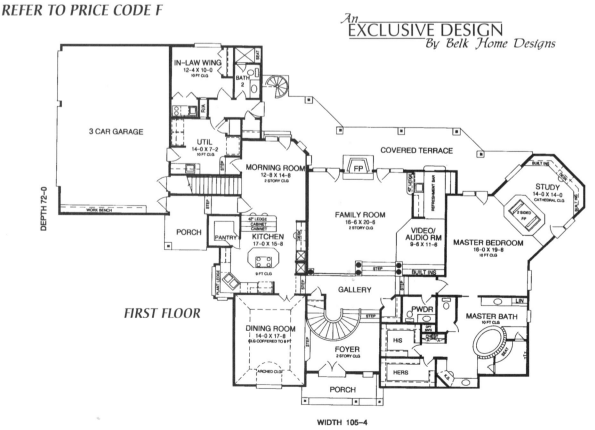

3 CAR GARAGE

IN-LAW WING
12-4 X 10-0
10 FT CLG

BATH 2

SEAT

R/A

UTIL
14-0 X 7-2
10 FT CLG

STEP

WORK BENCH

PORCH

PANTRY

42" LEDGE
CABINET

KITCHEN
17-0 X 15-8

9 FT CLG

PLANT LEDGE

STEP

MORNING ROOM
12-8 X 14-8
2 STORY CLG

FP

COVERED TERRACE

REFRESHMENT BAR

42" LEDGE

FAMILY ROOM
16-6 X 20-6
2 STORY CLG

VIDEO/AUDIO RM
9-6 X 11-6

BUILT INS

STUDY
14-0 X 14-0
CATHEDRAL CLG

2 SIDED FP

BUILT INS

MASTER BEDROOM
16-0 X 19-8
10 FT CLG

DEPTH 72-0

GALLERY

STEP

STEP

BUILT INS

PWDR

LIN

MASTER BATH
10 FT CLG

FIRST FLOOR

DINING ROOM
14-0 X 17-8
CLG COFFERED TO 9 FT

ARCHED CLG

FOYER
2 STORY CLG

HIS

OPT SAFE

CHEST

HERS

SEAT

PORCH

WIDTH 105-4

■ *Two-story Foyer with a dramatic cascading staircase*

■ *Large two-story Family Room opening off the Gallery area includes a video/audio area and a conveniently placed refreshment bar*

■ *Decorative ceiling in the elegant Dining Room adds a sense of style and elegance*

■ *Master Suite with a private Study that is crowned with a cathedral ceiling and separated from the Bedroom by a see-through fireplace*

■ *Master Bath with a centerpiece whirlpool accented by glass blocking is a great retreat after a grueling day*

■ *An In-Law Wing with a Bath and kitchenette affords privacy for its occupants*

■ *Three additional bedrooms, two with deck access, and two full baths on the second floor*

■ *An oversized Game Room with a refreshment bar, powder room and fireplace also on the second floor*

Stucco, Brick & Arched Windows Enhance Facade

PLAN INFO:

First Flr.	1,973 sq. ft.
Second Flr.	1,060 sq. ft.
Garage	531 sq. ft.
Sq. Footage	3,034 sq. ft.
Foundation	Slab, Crawl space
Bedrooms	Five
Baths	2(Full), 1(Half)

*No materials list available

REFER TO PRICE CODE E

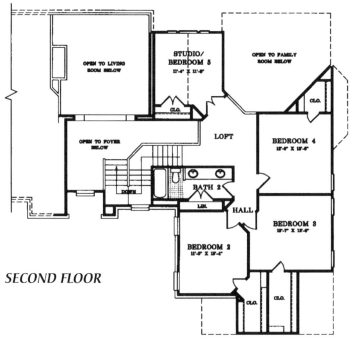

SECOND FLOOR

No. 93041

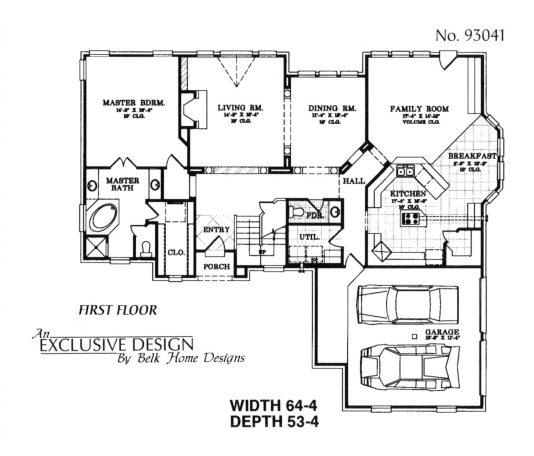

FIRST FLOOR

An EXCLUSIVE DESIGN
By Belk Home Designs

WIDTH 64-4
DEPTH 53-4

■ *A stucco design accented by an impressive arched two-story entry*

■ *All major living areas provide views to the rear grounds, terrific for "on the golf course" location*

■ *Kitchen, Breakfast Room and Family Room are adjacent and open to one another*

■ *An island cook top and double sinks along with an abundance of storage space makes the Kitchen even more convenient*

■ *Fantastic Master Suite has an angled whirlpool tub, separate shower and his-n-her vanities*

■ *The three additional bedrooms are located on the second floor*

English Tudor Country Estate

PLAN INFO:

First Flr.	*1,352 sq. ft.*
Second Flr.	*1,416 sq. ft.*
Basement	*894 sq. ft.*
Garage	*400 sq. ft.*
Sq. Footage	*2,768 sq. ft.*
Foundation	*Basement*
Bedrooms	*Four*
Baths	*2(Full), 1(Half)*

REFER TO PRICE CODE E

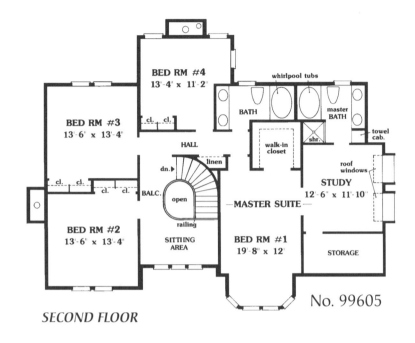

SECOND FLOOR

No. 99605

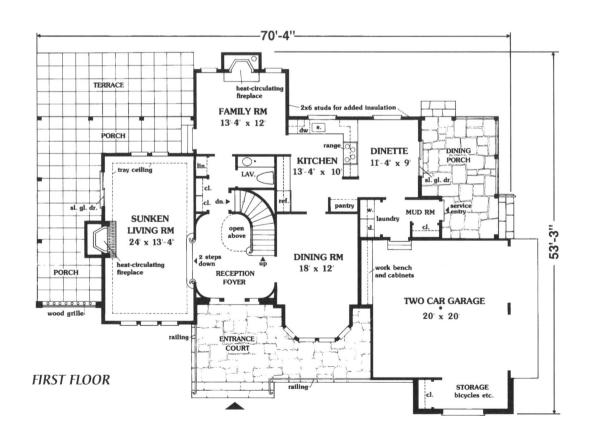

FIRST FLOOR

- *Entrance Court leads into curved Reception Foyer with graceful, curved stairway and steps down to Sunken Living Room*

- *Heat circulating fireplace warms expansive Living Room accented by tray ceiling and sliding glass door to covered Porch and Terrace beyond*

- *Alcove of windows highlights formal Dining Room for elegant entertaining*

- *Efficient Kitchen with pantry and pass-through counter serves Dinette and Dinette, Porch beyond, Family Room and Dining Room*

- *Cozy Family Room with heat circulating fireplace has access to Terrace and rear yard*

- *Service Entry steps from Kitchen through Mud Room*

- *Luxurious Master Bedroom Suite accented by alcove of windows, offers private Study, Storage and double-vanity bath*

- *Three additional bedrooms with double closets share full bath with double vanity*

$\mathcal{B}$uilt To Last A Lifetime

PLAN INFO:

First Flr.	2,579 sq. ft.
Garage	536 sq. ft.
Sq. Footage	2,579 sq. ft.
Foundation	Crawl space
Bedrooms	Three or Four
Baths	3(Full), 1(Half)

*No materials list available

REFER TO PRICE CODE D

No. 93708

57'6"

73'2"

M. Bath

clos.

Garage
24'0" x 22'4"

Mstr. Bdrm.
16'10" x 15'4"
10'h. tray ceil.

Porch

Breakfast
12'10" x 11'6"

Utility

Ktchn.
13'8"x13'0"

Bedroom
13'8" x 11'10"

Great Rm.
19'10"x16'4"
11'h. tray ceil.

Gallery

dome

Foyer

Dining Room
16'8" x 12'4"
10'6" ceil.

Bedroom
13'0"x11'10"
vault ceil.

Bdrm. 4 /
Study
14'2"x11'4"
vault ceil.

Porch

FIRST FLOOR

- *Porch entry into elegant, domed Foyer, Study, Dining Room and Great Room*

- *Expansive Great Room defined from Gallery by pillars with focal point fireplace topped by decorative ceiling*

- *Formal Dining Room accented by pillars and large, decorative window*

- *Central Kitchen with built-in pantry, work island and peninsula counter/snackbar serves glass*

- *Breakfast alcove and Dining Room*

- *Secluded Master Bedroom suite with tray ceiling, huge walk-in closet features double door to plush Master Bath with garden tub and direct access outdoors*

- *Two additional bedrooms with ample closet space share double-vanity bath*

- *Private Study/Bedroom with full bath offers many options*

Floor To Ceiling Window Treatment Enhances Design

Study
11 x 14-8

M. Bath

L.C.

DN.

M.Bedroom
14 x 20-6

OPEN TO BELOW

SECOND FLOOR

Deck

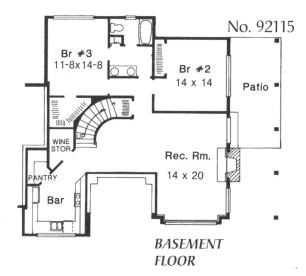

No. 92115

Br #3
11-8x14-8

Br #2
14 x 14

Patio

WINE STOR

UP

PANTRY

Rec. Rm.
14 x 20

Bar

BASEMENT FLOOR

PLAN INFO:

First Flr.	1,587 sq. ft.
Second Flr.	905 sq. ft.
Basement	1,289 sq. ft.
Garage	1,020 sq. ft.
Sq. Footage	3,781 sq. ft.
Foundation	Basement
Bedrooms	Three
Baths	3(Full), 1(Half)

REFER TO PRICE CODE F

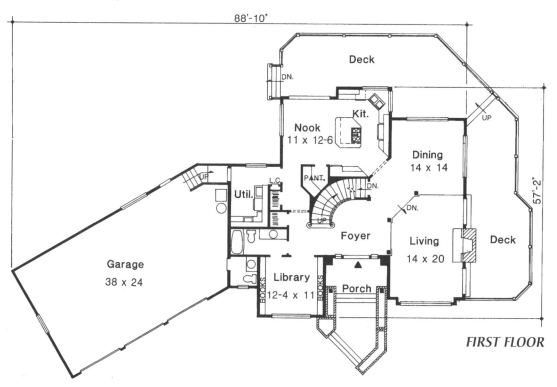

88'-10"

Deck

DN.

Kit.

Nook
11 x 12-6

Dining
14 x 14

UP

UP

Util.

L.C.

PANT.

DN.

57'-2"

UP

Foyer

DN.

Living
14 x 20

Deck

Garage
38 x 24

BOOKS

Library
12-4 x 11

BOOKS

Porch

FIRST FLOOR

- Unique front porch with elegant brick angled wall makes for a grand entrance to the gracious Foyer

- Recreation Room affords efficient uniqueness of full Kitchen, Bar, and Wine Storage, and exit to a spacious patio

- Curved staircase from another era in Foyer combines with open concept allowing for ease in entertaining

- Kitchen with island surrounded by cabinets features a Pantry and opens to the sunny Nook which steps onto a wrap-around bi-level Deck

- Book-shelved Library has interesting window treatment and extends to Bath

- Master Bedroom features a fireplace, double windows and a sliding glass door leading to a private deck

- Three-car angled Garage steps up to enter roomy Utility Area with separate linen closet

Impressive Two-Story Entrance

PLAN INFO:

First Flr.   1,210 sq. ft.
Second Flr.   1,039 sq. ft.
Lower Flr.   464 sq. ft.
Sq. Footage   2,713 sq. ft.
Foundation   Basement
Bedrooms   Three
Baths   3 (Full), 1 (Half)
No materials list available

REFER TO PRICE CODE E

No. 93707

SECOND FLOOR

- Bedroom 12'8" x 12'2"
- clos.
- M. Bath
- util.
- clos.
- Bedroom 12'2" x 11'4"
- Open To Foyer Below
- Master Bedroom 18'0" x 15'6"

LOWER FLOOR

- Recreation Room 17'9" x 16'2"
- Garage 30'1" x 21'9" 9'6" Ceiling
- Mud Rm.

FIRST FLOOR

- Deck 40'10"
- Family Room 17'10" x 16'4"
- Breakfast 11'8" x 10'6"
- Kitchen 17'4" x 11'2"
- Parlor 12'4" x 12'2"
- dn
- Foyer 12'0" x 10'8"
- Dining Room 13'4" x 12'2"
- 35'10"

■ Room-size, two-story Foyer highlighted by dramatic staircase leads to formal Parlor and Dining Room

■ Spacious Master Bedroom suite features two walk-in closets, two vanities and whirlpool, corner window tub

■ Huge, but efficient Kitchen with ample counter and storage space, built-in pantry and cooktop/snackbar island serves Breakfast area, Deck, Family Room and Dining Room

■ Two additional bedrooms with ample closet space share double-vanity bath and Utility room

■ Lower level offers Recreation Room with access to rear yard under Deck, Mud Room and two-car Garage

*I*ntricate *Details Highlight A*
Spectacular Design

No. 92504

PLAN INFO:

First Flr.	2,553 sq. ft.
Second Flr.	1,260 sq. ft.
Garage	714 sq. ft.
Sq. Footage	3,813 sq. ft.
Foundation	Slab, Crawl space
Bedrooms	Four
Baths	3(Full), 1(Half)

REFER TO PRICE CODE F

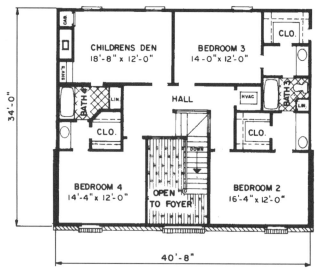

SECOND FLOOR

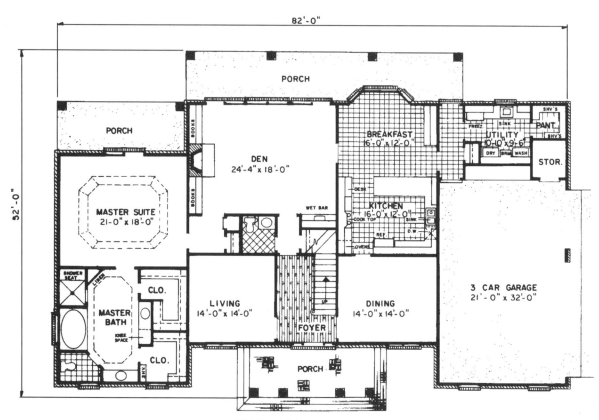

FIRST FLOOR

- *An intricately detailed entrance leads into a magnificent two-story Foyer*

- *Formal Living Room and Dining Room, located on each side of Foyer, feature large decorative windows*

- *Amenities abound in the efficient Kitchen equipped with a peninsula counter and Breakfast Area*

- *Beyond the Foyer, the large Den equipped with a fireplace, built-in shelves and wetbar provides a* spacious relaxing atmosphere for informal gatherings

- *Decorative ceilings add more elegance to the grand Master Suite and the Master Bath which includes two walk-in closets, two vanities, an oversized shower and window tub*

- *Three additional bedrooms located on the second floor offer walk-in closets, adjacent full baths and a terrific Children's Den*

$\mathcal{K}$eystone Pediments And Curved Glass

PLAN INFO:

First Flr.	2,115 sq. ft.
Second Flr.	914 sq. ft.
Basement	2,115 sq. ft.
Garage	448 sq. ft.
Sq. Footage	3,029 sq. ft.
Foundation	Basement, Slab
Bedrooms	Four
Baths	3(Full), 1(Half)

*No materials list available

REFER TO PRICE CODE E

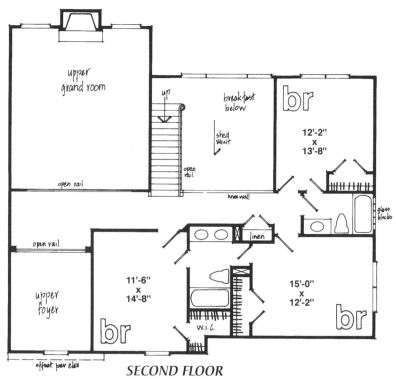

SECOND FLOOR

An
EXCLUSIVE DESIGN
By Garrell Associates Inc.

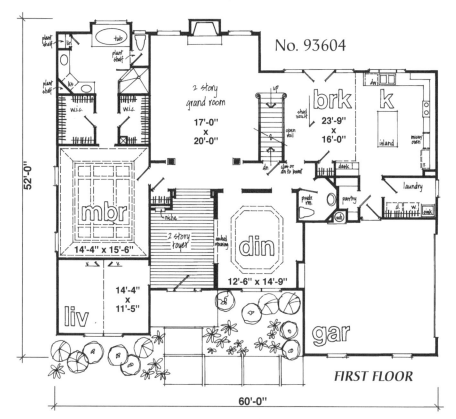

No. 93604

FIRST FLOOR

■ *A dramatic entrance into two-story Foyer and Grand Room beyond with hearth fireplace as focal point between decorative windows*

■ *Decorative ceilings in Living and Dining Rooms invite entertaining*

■ *A spacious, but efficient Kitchen offers walk-in pantry, work island, built-in desk, adjacent to Laundry area and Garage, and a Breakfast area with*

shed vault ceiling and double doors to backyard

■ *Tray ceiling tops private Master Bedroom suite with double walk-in closets, double vanity, atrium tub and many plant shelves*

■ *Three additional second floor bedrooms share two full baths and an hallway overlooking first floor*

Brick-Pillared Front Entrance Catches The Eye

PLAN INFO:

First Flr.	2,746 sq. ft.
Second Flr.	1,984 sq. ft.
Bonus Rm.	420 sq. ft.
Sq. Footage	4,730 sq. ft.
Foundation	Crawl space
Bedrooms	Four
Baths	Four

REFER TO PRICE CODE F

No. 91338

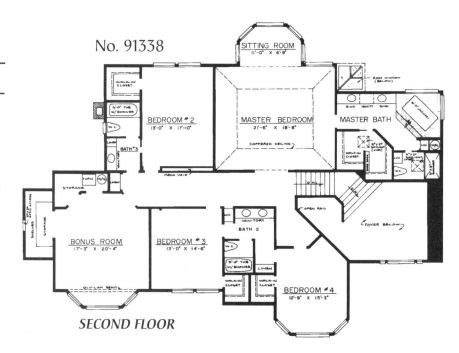

SITTING ROOM
11'-0" X 6'-9"

WALK-IN CLOSET

6'-0" TUB w/ SHOWER

W.C.

BEDROOM #2
13'-0" X 17'-10"

BATH #3

MASTER BEDROOM
21'-6" X 18'-8"
COFFERED CEILING

MECH. VOID

FURN.

STORAGE

STEP ATTIC ACCESS

SHELVES

STORAGE

BONUS ROOM
17'-3" X 20'-4"

GLU-LAM BEAMS

BEDROOM #3
13'-0" X 14'-6"

W.C.

WALK-IN CLOSET

5'-0" TUB w/ SHOWER

LINEN

WALK-IN CLOSET

MASTER BATH

ROSE WINDOW (BELOW)

SINK VANITY SINK

6'-0" JACUZZI

WALK-IN CLOSET

SKYLIGHT (ABOVE)

W.C.

VANITORY

BATH 2

DN.

OPEN RAIL

FOYER BELOW

BEDROOM #4
12'-9" X 15'-3"

SECOND FLOOR

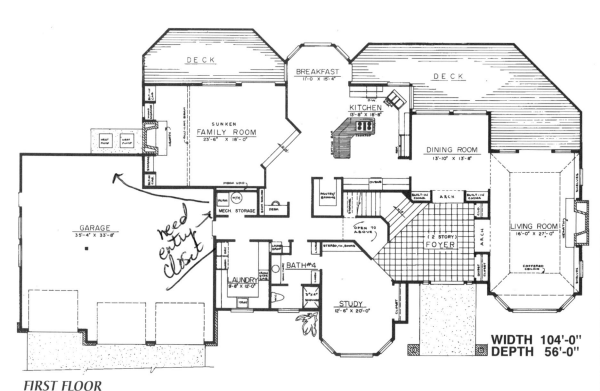

DECK

BREAKFAST
11'-0 X 15'-4"

DECK

KITCHEN
13'-8" X 18'-6"

HEAT PUMP   HEAT PUMP

HEARTH

SUNKEN FAMILY ROOM
23'-6" X 18'-0"

GLU-LAM BEAM

MECH. VOID

FURN. W/H

MECH. STORAGE   DESK

DINING ROOM
13'-10" X 13'-8"

OVENS

PANTRY BROOM

BUILT-IN CHINA   ARCH   BUILT-IN CHINA

CLO.

ARCH

SHELVES

LIVING ROOM
16'-0" X 27'-0"
COFFERED CEILING

GARAGE
35'-4" X 33'-8"

need entry closet

LAUNDRY
9'-8" X 12'-0"

BATH #4

STEREO, TV, BOOKS

OPEN TO ABOVE

(2 STORY) FOYER

CLOSET

CLOSET

STUDY
12'-6" X 20'-0"

WIDTH 104'-0"
DEPTH 56'-0"

FIRST FLOOR

-254-

■ *An arched, two-story entrance leads to a formal Living Room that is crowned by a coffered ceiling, flooded by natural light through the great front window and enhanced by a large fireplace*

■ *Elegant Dining Room has direct access to either the Kitchen or the formal Living Room*

■ *An island cooktop with an eating bar, walk-in pantry, and a sunny Breakfast area makes this gourmet Kitchen a fantasy come true*

■ *Spacious, sunken Family Room offers a large hearth fireplace, built-in*

cabinets and connecting outdoor deck to provide a great place for informal gatherings

■ *Master Bedroom suite features a coffered ceiling, adjacent Sitting area, and private Bath that includes a double walk-in closet, garden tub, double vanity and a separate shower*

■ *Three additional bedrooms, each with a walk-in closet and adjacent full bath, will accommodate children of any age*

■ *Great Bonus room will handle a variety of future needs*

Accent On Curved Staircase
& Staggered Rooflines

No. 10537

PLAN INFO:

First Flr.	3,282 sq. ft.
Second Flr.	956 sq. ft.
Basement	3,235 sq. ft.
Garage	936 sq. ft.
Sq. Footage	4,238 sq. ft.
Foundation	Basement
Bedrooms	Four
Baths	4(Full), 1(Half)

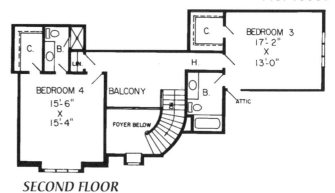

SECOND FLOOR

REFER TO PRICE CODE F

An EXCLUSIVE DESIGN
By Karl Kreeger

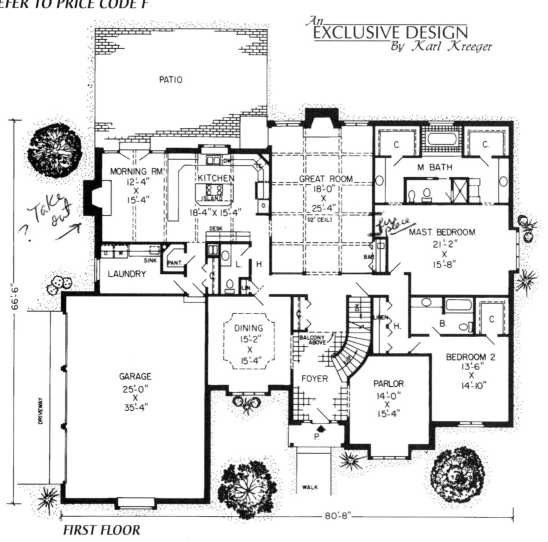

FIRST FLOOR

- *Overlook the impressive tiled Foyer with gracefully curving staircase from the Balcony on the second floor*

- *Enter the spacious Great Room featuring wood ceiling beams, bar, and welcoming fireplace*

- *Generous Laundry Room leads to 3-car Garage*

- *Expansive Kitchen includes lots of counter space, cook center island, pantry, and desk*

- *Formal Dining Room with interesting ceiling lies just steps away from Kitchen*

- *Large fireplace and entry onto patio for year round enjoyment complement unique Morning Room*

- *Luxurious Master Bedroom boasts his-n-her basins and roomy walk-in closets*

- *Three additional bedrooms each have walk-in closets and personal Baths*

Victorian Touches Grace The Exterior Of This Exciting Home

No. 91724

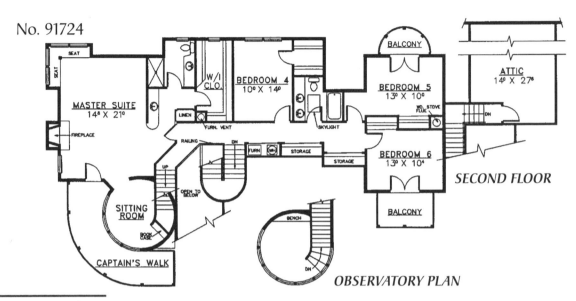

SECOND FLOOR

OBSERVATORY PLAN

PLAN INFO:

First Flr.	3,031 sq. ft.
Second Flr.	1,578 sq. ft.
Garage	514 sq. ft.
Sq. Footage	4,609 sq. ft.
Foundation	Crawl space
Bedrooms	Six
Baths	Four

REFER TO PRICE CODE F

WIDTH 101'-0"
DEPTH 56'-0"

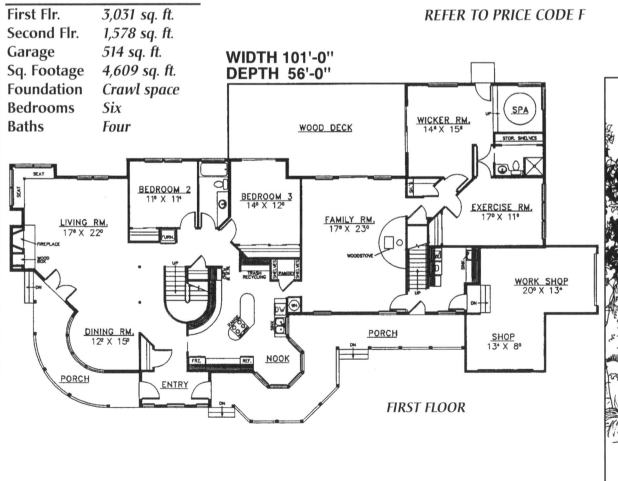

FIRST FLOOR

- *Richly embellished covered porches sweep across majority of front while turrets and gables adorn every turn*

- *Unique to this home, Kitchen and Entryway have vaulted ceilings*

- *Octagon-shaped eating Nook brightens any mealtime with windows at ground level, another row above, and ceiling stretching to window-lined turret overhead*

- *Huge Kitchen features range and oven*

- *located in work island, lots of counter space, and trash recycling center*

- *Circular Sitting room partially surrounded by captain's walk balcony leads up to observatory on higher level*

- *Two upstairs bedrooms feature private balconies while a third includes step-in closet*

- *Large Workshop supplies room for conversion to Garage if desired*

*T*hree *F*ireplaces *A*dd Coziness & Warmth

PLAN INFO:

First Flr.	2,849 sq. ft.
Second Flr.	1,086 sq. ft.
Garage	721 sq. ft.
Sq. Footage	3,935 sq. ft.
Foundation	Slab
Bedrooms	Five
Baths	4(Full), 1(Half)

REFER TO PRICE CODE F

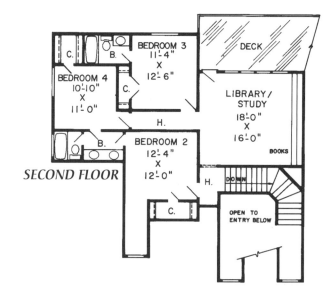

SECOND FLOOR

BEDROOM 3
11'-4"
X
12'-6"

DECK

BEDROOM 4
10'-10"
X
11'-0"

LIBRARY/
STUDY
18'-0"
X
16'-0"

BOOKS

BEDROOM 2
12'-4"
X
12'-0"

DOWN

OPEN TO
ENTRY BELOW

No. 10670

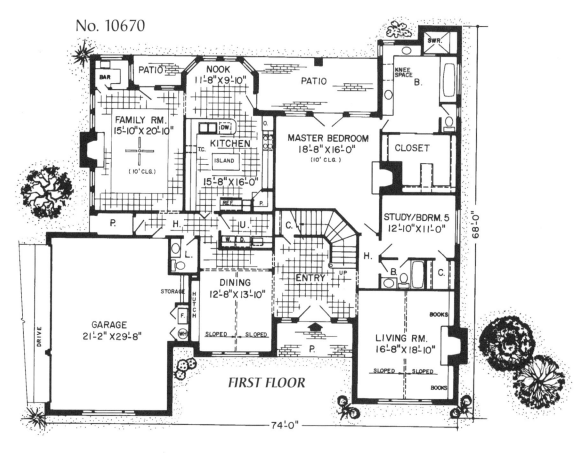

BAR

PATIO

NOOK
11'-8"X9'-10"

PATIO

KNEE
SPACE

B.

FAMILY RM.
15'-10"X 20'-10"

(10' CLG.)

KITCHEN
ISLAND
DW

MASTER BEDROOM
18'-8"X16'-0"
(10' CLG.)

CLOSET

15'-8"X16'-0"

REF

STUDY/BDRM. 5
12'-10"X11'-0"

STORAGE

GARAGE
21'-2" X29'-8"

DRIVE

HUTCH

F.

WH

DINING
12'-8"X 13'-10"

SLOPED   SLOPED

ENTRY

UP

W D

L.

B.

C.

LIVING RM.
16'-8"X18'-10"

SLOPED   SLOPED

BOOKS

BOOKS

FIRST FLOOR

68'-0"

74'-0"

- *Vaulted ceiling, gently curving staircase and high, arched windows in entry create airy celebration of light and space*

- *Formal Dining Room with built-in hutch and Living Room with appealing ceiling lines frame impressive Entry*

- *Large island Kitchen opens into a cheery Eating Nook*

- *Oversized pantry outside Kitchen lends extra room for day-to-day necessities*

- *Family Room includes fireplace, paddle fan, built-in, room-size wetbar, and direct access to backyard patio*

- *Superb Master Bedroom warmed by its own fireplace has French doors leading to personal patio*

- *Three additional bedrooms on second level with walk-in closets assure ample storage space*

- *Enjoy sunny afternoons on deck off Library on second floor*

_H_earth _R_oom _H_ighlights _T_his _P_lan

No. 10527

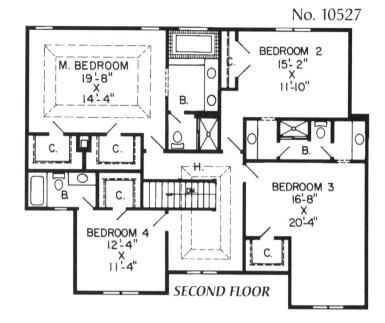

SECOND FLOOR

PLAN INFO:

First Flr.	_1,697 sq. ft._
Second Flr.	_1,624 sq. ft._
Basement	_1,697 sq. ft._
Garage	_586 sq. ft._
Sq. Footage	_3321 sq. ft._
Foundation	_Basement_
Bedrooms	_Four_
Baths	_3(Full), 1(Half)_

REFER TO PRICE CODE F

_An_
EXCLUSIVE DESIGN
By Karl Kreeger

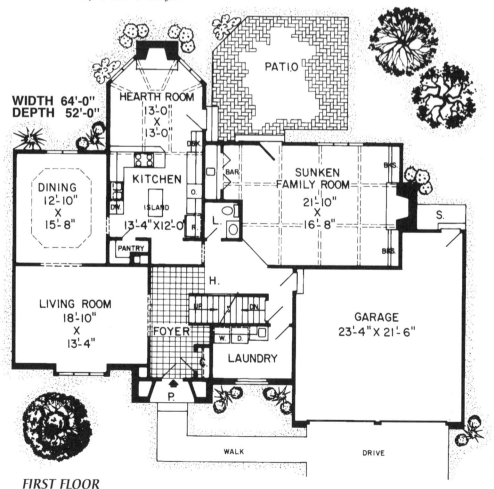

WIDTH 64'-0"
DEPTH 52'-0"

FIRST FLOOR

- Unusual ceiling adds distinctive beauty to unique Hearth Room
- Spacious Kitchen features plenty of counter space with central work island
- Step down to the sunken Family Room for refreshments at the built-in bar
- Fireplace in Family Room flanked by bookcases invites informal relaxation
- Sizable Dining Room lends itself for formal entertaining

- Fireplace in Hearth Room surrounded by windows for warm cozy atmosphere
- Master Bedroom sports his-n-her walk-in closets plus private Bath
- Bedrooms two and three share a Bath but have individual basins
- Bedroom four has a personal Bath and ample closet space

Traditional Splendor With Modern Accents

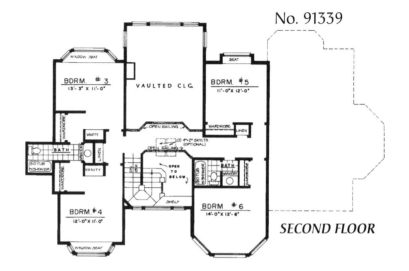

No. 91339

PLAN INFO:

First Flr.	*2,498 sq. ft.*
Second Flr.	*1,190 sq. ft.*
Basement	*1,464 sq. ft.*
Garage	*3-car*
Sq. Footage	*3,688 sq. ft.*
Foundation	*Basement*
Bedrooms	*Six*
Baths	*4(Full), 1(Half)*

*No materials list available

SECOND FLOOR

REFER TO PRICE CODE F

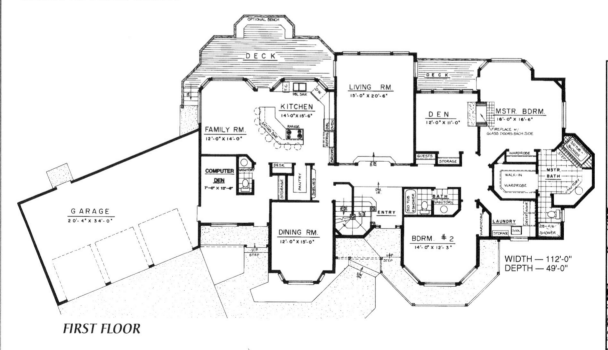

FIRST FLOOR

WIDTH — 112'-0"
DEPTH — 49'-0"

- Gourmet Kitchen with elegant eating bar comfortably seats seven people

- Enjoy family barbeques on backyard deck with optional bench and convenient access to Kitchen and Family Room

- Dining Room on other side of room-sized pantry in close proximity of Kitchen for ease in formal entertaining

- Overlook impressive Foyer on one side and vaulted Living Room from opposite side of skylit balcony

- Six bedrooms and 4-1/2 baths accommodates large families

- Bayed sitting area in Master Bedroom provides ideal quiet spot for avid readers

- Master Bath features plenty of storage space with huge walk-in closet and separate wardrobe

- Daylight basement to rear of home designed for two guest rooms, multi-purpose area and full bath

Colonial Classic Is Convenient & Spacious

- *Clapboard siding, twin chimneys, a central entry and shuttered, multi-paned windows present a Colonial face to the neighborhood*

- *An open Foyer leads to a formal Parlor with a hearth fireplace and an expansive Family Room with decorative beams, built-in bar and large hearth fireplace*

- *His-n-her walk-in closets, a decorative ceiling and skylights in the segmented Master Bath highlight the Master Suite*

- *Three additional bedrooms, two with walk-in closets, share a full hall bath with a double vanity*

An
EXCLUSIVE DESIGN
By Karl Kreeger

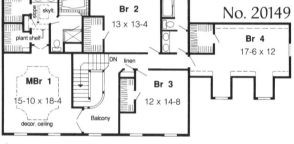

No. 20149

SECOND FLOOR

FIRST FLOOR

PLAN INFO:

First Flr.	1,508 sq. ft.
Second Flr.	1,722 sq. ft.
Basement	1,494 sq. ft.
Garage	599 sq. ft.
Sq. Footage	3,230 sq. ft.
Foundation	Basement
Bedrooms	Four
Baths	2(Full), 1(Half)

REFER TO PRICE CODE F

Ignoring Copyright Laws Can Be A $1,000,000 Mistake

Recent changes in the US copyright laws allow for statutory penalties of up to **$100,000** per incident for copyright infringement involving any of the copyrighted plans found in this publication. The law can be confusing. So, for your own protection, take the time to understand what you can and cannot do when it comes to home plans.

——— *What You Cannot Do* ———

You Cannot Duplicate Home Plans

Purchasing a set of blueprints and making additional sets by reproducing the original is *illegal*. If you need multiple sets of a particular home plan, then you must purchase them.

You Cannot Copy Any Part of a Home Plan to Create Another

Creating your own plan by copying even part of a home design found in this publication is called "creating a derivative work" and is *illegal* unless you have permission to do so.

You Cannot Build a Home Without a License

You must have specific permission or license to build a home from a copyrighted design, even if the finished home has been changed from the original plan. It is *illegal* to build one of the homes found in this publication without a license.

What Garlinghouse Offers

Home Plan Blueprint Package

By purchasing a single or multiple set package of blueprints from Garlinghouse, you not only receive the physical blueprint documents necessary for construction, but you are also granted a license to build one, and only one, home. You can also make any changes to our design that you wish, as long as these changes are made directly on the blueprints purchased from Garlinghouse and no additional copies are made.

Home Plan Vellums

By purchasing vellums for one of our home plans, you receive the same construction drawings found in the blueprints, but printed on vellum paper. Vellums can be erased and are perfect for making design changes. They are also semi-transparent making them easy to duplicate. But most importantly, the purchase of home plan vellums comes with a broader license that allows you to make changes to the design (ie, create a hand drawn or CAD derivative work), to make an unlimited number of copies of the plan, and to build up to three homes from the plan.

License To Build Additional Homes

With the purchase of a blueprint package or vellums you automatically receive a license to build one home or three homes, respectively. If you want to build more homes than you are licensed to build through your purchase of a plan, then additional licenses may be purchased at reasonable costs from Garlinghouse. Inquire for more information.

Everything You Need to M
You pay only a fraction of the original cost

You've Picked Your Dream Home!

You can already see it standing on your lot... you can see yourselves in your new home... enjoying family, entertaining guests, celebrating holidays. All that remains ahead are the details. That's where we can help. Whether you plan to build-it-yourself, be your own contractor, or hand your plans over to an outside contractor, your Garlinghouse blueprints provide the perfect beginning for putting yourself in your dream home right away.

We even make it simple for you to make professional design modifications. We can also provide a materials list for greater economy.

My grandfather, L.F. Garlinghouse, started a tradition of quality when he founded this company in 1907. For over 85 years, homeowners and builders have relied on us for accurate, complete, professional blueprints. Our plans help you get results fast... and save money, too! These pages will give you all the information you need to order. So get started now... I know you'll love your new Garlinghouse home!

Sincerely,

TYPICAL WALL SECTIONS

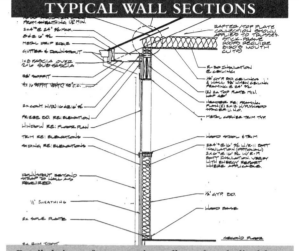

Detailed views of your exterior walls, as though sliced from top to bottom. These drawings clarify exterior wall construction insulation, flooring, and roofing details. Depending on your specific geography and climate, your home will be built with either 2x4 or 2x6 exterior walls. Most professional contractors can easily adapt plans for either requirement.

KITCHEN & BATH CABINET DETAILS

These plans or, in some cases, elevations show the specific details and placement of the cabinets in your kitchen and bathrooms as applicable. Customizing these areas is simpler beginning with these details. Kitchen and bath cabinet details are available for most plans featured in our collection.

EXTERIOR ELEVATIONS

Exact scale views of the front, rear and both sides of your home, showing exterior materials, details, and all necessary measurements.

DETAILED FLOOR PLANS

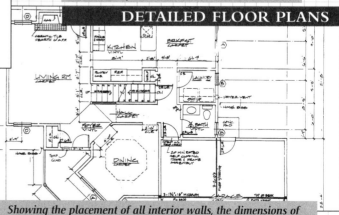

Showing the placement of all interior walls, the dimensions of rooms, doors, windows, stairways, and other details.

ake Your Dream Come True!

for home designs by respected professionals.

FIREPLACE DETAILS

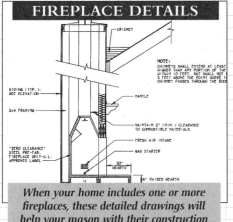

When your home includes one or more fireplaces, these detailed drawings will help your mason with their construction and appearance. It is easy to review details with professionals when you have the plans for reference.

TYPICAL CROSS SECTION

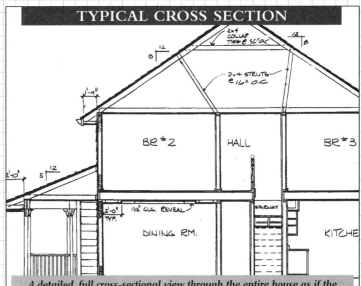

A detailed, full cross-sectional view through the entire house as if the house was cut from top to bottom. This elevation allows a contractor to better understand the interconnections of the construction components.

FOUNDATION PLAN

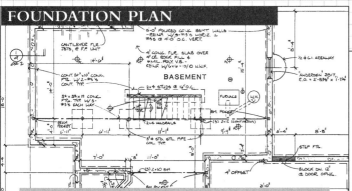

With footings and all load-bearing points applicable to your home, including all necessary notation and dimensions. The type of foundation supplied varies from home to home. Local conditions and practices will determine whether a basement, crawlspace or a slab is best for you. Your professional contractor can easily make the necessary adaption.

SCHEMATIC ELECTRICAL LAYOUTS

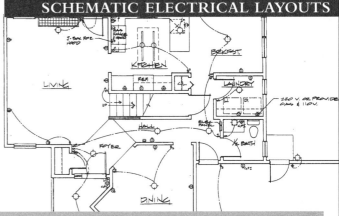

The suggested locations for all of your switches, outlets and fixtures are indicated on these drawings. They are practical as they are, but they are also a solid taking-off point for any personal adaptions.

ROOF PLAN

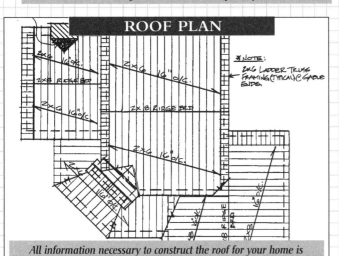

All information necessary to construct the roof for your home is included. Many blueprints contain framing plans showing all of the roof elements, so you'll know how these details look and fit together.

STAIR DETAILS

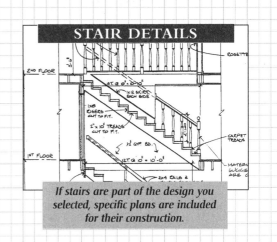

If stairs are part of the design you selected, specific plans are included for their construction.

GARLINGHOUSE OPTIONS & EXTRAS
MAKE THE DREAM TRULY YOURS.

Reversed Plans Can Make Your Dream Home Just Right!

"That's our dream home... if only the garage were on the other side!"

You could have exactly the home you want by flipping it end-for-end. Check it out by holding your dream home page of this book up to a mirror. Then simply order your plans "reversed". We'll send you one full set of mirror-image plans (with the writing backwards) as a master guide for you and your builder.

The remaining sets of your order will come as shown in this book so the dimensions and specifications are easily read on the job site... but they will be specially stamped "REVERSED" so there is no construction confusion.

We can only send reversed plans with multiple-set orders. But, there is no extra charge for this service.

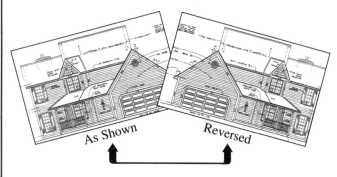

As Shown   Reversed

Modifying Your Garlinghouse Home Plan

Easy modifications to your dream home such as minor non-structural changes and simple material substitutions, can be made between you and your builder and marked directly on your blueprints. However, if you are considering making major changes to your design, we strongly recommend that you purchase our reproducible vellums and use the services of a professional designer or architect. For additional information call us at 1-860-343-5977.

Our Reproducible Vellums Make Modifications Easier

With a vellum copy of our plans, a design professional can alter the drawings just the way you want, then you can print as many copies of the modified plans as you need. And, since you have already started with our complete detailed plans, the cost of those expensive professional services will be significantly less. Refer to the price schedule for vellum costs. Call for vellum availability for plan numbers 90,000 and above.

Reproducible vellum copies of our home plans are only sold under the terms of a license agreement that you will receive with your order. Should you not agree to the terms, then the vellums may be returned unopened for a full refund.

Yours FREE With Your Order

FREE
SPECIFICATIONS AND CONTRACT FORM
provides the perfect way for you and your builder to agree on the exact materials to use in building and finishing your home before you start construction. A must for homeowner's peace of mind.

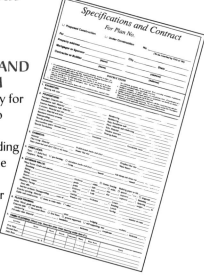

Remember To Order Your Materials List

It'll help you save money. Available at a modest additional charge, the Materials List gives the quantity, dimensions, and specifications for the major materials needed to build your home. You will get faster, more accurate bids from your contractors and building suppliers – and avoid paying for unused materials and waste. Materials Lists are available for all home plans except as otherwise indicated, but can only be ordered with a set of home plans. Due to differences in regional requirements and homeowner or builder preferences... electrical, plumbing and heating/air conditioning equipment specifications are not designed specifically for each plan. However, non plan specific detailed typical prints of residential electrical, plumbing and construction guidelines can be provided. Please see next page for additional information.

Questions?

Call our customer service number at 1-860-343-5977.

How Many Sets Of Plans Will You Need?

The Standard 8-Set Construction Package

Our experience shows that you'll speed every step of construction and avoid costly building errors by ordering enough sets to go around. Each tradesperson wants a set — the general contractor and all subcontractors; foundation, electrical, plumbing, heating/air conditioning, drywall, finish carpenters, and cabinet shop. Don't forget your lending institution, building department and, of course, a set for yourself.

The Minimum 5-Set Construction Package

If you're comfortable with arduous follow-up, this package can save you a few dollars by giving you the option of passing down plan sets as work progresses. You might have enough copies to go around if work goes exactly as scheduled and no plans are lost or damaged. But for only $50 more, the 8-set package eliminates these worries.

The Single-Set Decision-Maker Package

We offer this set so you can study the blueprints to plan your dream home in detail. But remember... one set is never enough to build your home... and they're copyrighted.

New Plan Details For The Home Builder

Because local codes and requirements vary greatly, we recommend that you obtain drawings and bids from licensed contractors to do your mechanical plans. However, if you want to know more about techniques — and deal more confidently with subcontractors — we offer these remarkably useful detail sheets. Each is an excellent tool that will enhance your understanding of these technical subjects.

Residential Construction Details

Eight sheets that cover the essentials of stick-built residential home construction. Details foundation options - poured concrete basement, concrete block, or monolithic concrete slab. Shows all aspects of floor, wall, and roof framing. Provides details for roof dormers, eaves, and skylights. Conforms to requirements of Uniform Building code or BOCA code. Includes a quick index.

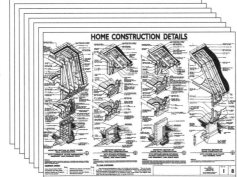

$14.95 per set

Residential Plumbing Details

Nine sheets packed with information detailing pipe connection methods, fittings, and sizes. Shows sump-pump and water softener hookups, and septic system construction. Conforms to requirements of National Plumbing Code. Color coded with a glossary of terms and quick index.

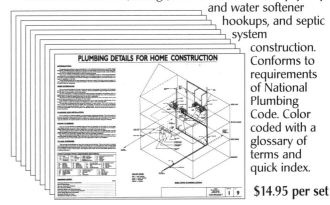

$14.95 per set

Residential Electrical Details

Nine sheets that cover all aspects of residential wiring, from simple switch wiring to the complexities of three-phase and service entrance connection. Explains service load calculations and distribution panel wiring. Shows you how to create a floor-plan wiring diagram. Conforms to requirements of National Electrical Code. Color coded with a glossary of terms and a quick index.

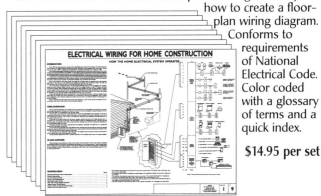

$14.95 per set

Important Shipping Information

Your order is processed immediately. Allow 10 working days from our receipt of your order for normal ground delivery. Save time with your credit card and our "800" number. Our delivery service must have a street address or Rural Route Box number — never a post office box. Use a work address if no one is home during the day.

Orders being shipped to Alaska, Hawaii, APO, FPO or Post Office Boxes must go via First Class Mail. Please include the proper postage.

Only Certified bank checks and money orders are accepted and must be payable in U.S. currency. For speed, we ship international orders Air Parcel Post. Please refer to the chart for the correct shipping cost.

An important note:

All plans are drawn to conform to one or more of the industry's major national building standards. However, due to the variety of local building regulations, your plan may need to be modified to comply with local requirements — snow loads, energy loads, seismic zones, etc. Do check them fully and consult your local building officials.

A few states require that all building plans used be drawn by an architect registered in that state. While having your plans reviewed and stamped by such an architect may be prudent, laws requiring non-conforming plans like ours to be completely redrawn forces you to unnecessarily pay very large fees. If your state has such a law, we strongly recommend you contact your state representative to protest.

Please submit all Canadian plan orders to:
Garlinghouse Company
20 Cedar Street North, Kitchener, Ontario N2H 2W8
Canadian Customers Only: 1-800-561-4169/Fax #: 1-519-743-1282
Customer Service #: 1-519-743-4169

ORDER TOLL FREE— 1-800-235-5700
Monday-Friday 8:00 a.m. to 5:00 p.m. Eastern Time
or FAX your Credit Card order to 1-860-343-5984
All foreign residents call 1-860-343-5977

Please have ready: **1. Your credit card number 2. The plan number 3. The order code number** ⇨ **H6LX4**

GARLINGHOUSE BLUEPRINT PRICE CODE SCHEDULE: *Additional sets with original order $25*

PRICE CODE	A	B	C	D	E	F	G	H
8 SETS OF SAME PLAN	$330	$350	$375	$400	$430	$470	$510	$555
5 SETS OF SAME PLAN	$280	$300	$325	$350	$380	$420	$460	$505
1 SINGLE SET OF PLANS	$210	$230	$255	$280	$310	$350	$390	$435
VELLUMS	$420	$440	$465	$490	$520	$560	$600	$645
MATERIALS LIST	$25	$25	$30	$30	$35	$40	$40	$45

DOMESTIC SHIPPING*	1-2 Sets	3+ Sets
UPS/RPS Ground Service	$6.50	$8.50
First Class Mail	$8.00	$11.00
2-Day Express	$16.00	$20.00
Overnight Express	$26.00	$30.00

INTERNATIONAL SHIPPING	1-2 Sets	3+ Sets
Canada	**$11.00**	**$15.50**
All Other Nations	$40.00	$52.00

Plan Numbers 90,000 & Above For Domestic Shipping —
Standard Express 3-5 Days -- $20.00

Canadian Orders and Shipping: To our friends in Canada, we have a plan design affiliate in Kitchener, Ontario. This relationship will help you avoid the delays and charges associated with shipments from the United States. Moreover, our affiliate is familiar with the building requirements in your community and country. We prefer payments in U.S. Currency. If you, however, are sending Canadian funds please add 40% to the prices of the plans and shipping fees.

GARLINGHOUSE — *Blueprint Order Form* — Order Code No. **H6LX4**

Send your check, money order or credit card information to:
(No C.O.D.'s Please)
Please Submit all <u>United States</u> & <u>Other Nations</u> plan orders to:
Garlinghouse Company
P.O. Box 1717
Middletown, CT 06457

Please Submit all <u>Canadian</u> plan orders to:
Garlinghouse Company
20 Cedar Street North
Kitchener, Ontario N2H 2W8

Plan No.
☐ As Shown   ☐ Reversed *(mult. set pkgs. only)*

	Each	Amount
8 set pkg.		$
5 set pkg.		$
1 set pkg. (no reverses)		$
_____ (qty.) Add'l. sets @		$
Vellums		$
Materials List (with plan order only)		$
Residential Builder Plans		
_____ set(s) Construction	@ $14.95	$
_____ set(s) Plumbing	@ $14.95	$
_____ set(s) Electrical	@ $14.95	$
Shipping		$
Subtotal		$
Sales Tax (CT residents add 6% sales tax, KS residents add 6.15% sales tax) (Not required for other states)		$
Total Amount Enclosed		**$**

Prices guaranteed until 1-15-97
Payment must be made in U.S. funds
Foreign Mail Orders: Certified bank checks in U.S. funds only

Bill To: (address must be as it appears on credit card statement)

Name _____

Address _____

City/State _____ Zip _____

Daytime Phone (_____) _____

Ship To (if different from Bill to):

Name _____

Address _____

City/State _____ Zip _____

Credit Card Information
Charge To: ☐ Visa   ☐ Mastercard

Card # | | | | | | | | | | | | | |

Signature _____ Exp. _____ / _____